D1681222

Additional Praise for *Overcoming Debt, Achieving Financial Freedom: 8 Pillars to Build Wealth*

"Cindy Zuniga-Sanchez has such a gift for teaching and her straightforward guidance makes it easy for anyone pursuing financial freedom to start (or keep going)! This book is a great companion to get you through the bumps along the road so you can reach financial freedom with ease and confidence."

—JEN HEMPHILL,
AFC®, host of *Her Dinero Matters* podcast

"Too much personal finance advice is unclear, irrelevant, and outmoded. Thank the money gods for giving us Cindy Zuniga-Sanchez, who shares her personal success story in support of an even grander mission: to materially change the lives of hardworking people who've long been left out of these important conversations about building wealth."

—AMANDA HOLDEN,
Founder, Invested Development

"In *Overcoming Debt, Achieving Financial Freedom,* Cindy Zuniga-Sanchez confronts the reality of a changing American Dream—one that isn't defined by a specific salary, job title or milestone, but by the flexibility, autonomy and options to spend our time, money, and energy in whatever ways align with our own personal priorities. With empathy, understanding, and a clear step-by-step action plan, Cindy empowers readers to overcome common barriers, like student loans and credit card debt, to achieve that financial freedom on their own terms."

—STEFANIE O'CONNELL RODRIGUEZ,
Host, REAL SIMPLE Magazine's *Money Confidential* podcast

"I'm a first gen Latina, and last Christmas my cousin asked me 'Do you know Cindy from Zero-Based Budget? She's a huge inspiration to me, as a Latina lawyer.' Cindy has written a book that my cousin and so many other Latinas need and want; it's a toolkit and representation all in one."

—KARA PEREZ,
Founder, Bravely Go

"Cindy's powerful story and uniquely accessible way of talking about finance makes her the perfect teacher for anyone looking to transform their relationship with money, especially coming from being in debt. This book is practical, easy to understand, and takes the reader through the full process of building a healthy relationship to money without ever feeling overwhelming. I love Cindy's work!"

—CHELSEA FAGAN,
Founder & CEO, The Financial Diet

OVERCOMING DEBT, ACHIEVING FINANCIAL FREEDOM

OVERCOMING DEBT, ACHIEVING FINANCIAL FREEDOM

8 PILLARS TO BUILD WEALTH

CINDY ZUNIGA-SANCHEZ

WILEY

Published by John Wiley & Sons, Inc., Hoboken, New Jersey.
Published simultaneously in Canada.

For general information on our other products and services or for technical support, please contact our Customer Care Department within the United States at (800) 762-2974, outside the United States at (317) 572-3993 or fax (317) 572-4002.

Wiley also publishes its books in a variety of electronic formats. Some content that appears in print may not be available in electronic formats. For more information about Wiley products, visit our web site at www.wiley.com.

Library of Congress Cataloging-in-Publication Data is Available:

ISBN 9781119902324 (Hardback)
ISBN 9781119902331 (ePDF)
ISBN 9781119902348 (ePub)

Cover Design: Wiley
Cover Image: © MJgraphics/Shutterstock
Author Photo: Jenessy Krystne Photography

SKY10036142_092122

This book is dedicated to my parents, Mercedes and Arnold Zuniga.

Thank you, Mom and Dad, for everything.

Este libro está dedicado a mis padres, Mercedes y Arnold Zuniga.

Gracias mami y papi por todo.

Contents

Contents

Preface

In 2015, I graduated law school with honors and a job offer at a top national law firm. As the daughter of immigrants, from a low-income community in the Bronx, these accomplishments were reflective of my commitment to honor my parents' sacrifices and goal of achieving the American Dream. These milestones also surely held the key to financial success and security, right? Not necessarily.

My fancy law degree and new job could not mask my deep financial insecurities. I had $215,000 of debt, which consisted of $13,000 in credit card debt and $202,000 in student loans. I had little to no confidence in how I was managing my money. I didn't understand why my credit card balance continued to increase despite my timely payments. I was unaware that most of my payments to my student loans were going to the tens of thousands of dollars in accrued interest rather than the loans' principal. I didn't know how to save for life's big expenses like a wedding or a down payment on a home . . . and don't even get me started on how clueless I was about investing.

Conversations about money, specifically debt, were *uncommon* and *uncomfortable* to have with family and friends, so I turned to books, podcasts, and the internet. My quest to become financially literate exposed me to a new world full of knowledge, strategies, guidance, and support that I desperately craved. I learned how to create a plan to pay off my six-figure debt, which included targeted monthly payment amounts and even a goal debt-free date that I wrote in bold lettering in my planner. I also learned how to budget, save an emergency fund, increase my net worth, improve my credit score, and open my first investment account.

This newfound world also revealed a new term: *financial freedom*. People in the personal finance community used it to describe a goal they were striving for in their money journeys. Everyone had their own interpretation. Some used it to refer to having enough money to absorb financial emergencies; for some it meant being able to comfortably afford their lifestyle; and for others it meant having enough money to quit their jobs and pursue their personal passions. When I first stumbled upon the term, I interpreted it as being debt-free and having a specific dollar amount in the bank that would then—and only then—provide me with the financial security I desired. But my definition has since evolved.

Financial freedom is more than a fixed number or specific milestone. Financial freedom is when you no longer perceive money as a constant burden; rather, you perceive it as a tool that you control. It means having an intentional plan that allows you to work toward your money goals while unapologetically spending on what you value. It means stability that does not anxiously await the next paycheck. It means the flexibility to say yes to opportunities that will enrich your life and no to those that will not serve it.

Financial freedom is about confidently having the financial foundation to live your best life. For most of us, this involves learning a new language and topics that school or our upbringing may not have exposed us to. It involves incorporating newfound knowledge into our everyday lives and *sharing* that knowledge while *encouraging* conversations about money with our loved ones. Financial freedom takes time, patience, and—as this book will demonstrate—it requires a plan.

■ ■ ■

When I sat down to write this book, I asked myself: What do you wish you knew about money when you started your financial freedom journey? What topics do you wish you had learned in school? What information has transformed your finances? What has helped you go from having six figures of debt to a six-figure net worth?

■ ■ ■

In the first few chapters of this book, I share my personal money story. I discuss the money lessons I learned as a first-generation daughter of immigrants that have shaped my relationship with money, the financial hurdles I overcame in pursuit of the American Dream, and the why and how of conquering $215,000 of debt.

The core of this book is dedicated to the financial pillars that have been instrumental to my personal finances. Everything from conducting a financial audit, creating a plan to best manage your money, spending according to your values, saving for life's emergencies and significant expenses, creating a realistic plan to crush your debt, improving your credit score and becoming credit card savvy, growing your investment portfolio, and exploring ways to increase your income. These chapters are also full of examples to help you understand how these pillars are applied in practice.

The book wraps up with a financial roadmap summarizing these pillars and contains helpful checklists and templates so that you can get to work and start implementing them.

My hope is that this book will serve as your friendly guide to financial freedom. You can read it straight through from beginning to end or jump ahead to a chapter that resonates with you. You are not required to complete each pillar before moving on to the next. In fact, our personal finance journeys often require that we simultaneously balance various money goals—we might be saving an emergency fund while creating a debt repayment plan while improving our credit score. As you read through this book, I encourage you to highlight new terms and take notes. After you've read it, keep it as a resource that you can reference throughout your financial freedom journey.

I hope you're excited! Let's dive in.

Acknowledgments

To my husband and life partner, John, for your endless love and support. Thank you for listening to my ideas, volunteering to read drafts, offering suggestions, and for being a source of comfort and calm through this book-writing journey. Thank you for always believing in me and encouraging me. I could not have done this without you.

To my parents, Mercedes and Arnold, for your unconditional love. Thank you for all the sacrifices you made to ensure that I receive the best education possible. Mom, thank you for teaching me to always lead with love and kindness. Dad, thank you for the strong work ethic you have instilled in me. I could not have asked for better parents.

To my sisters, Rosemary and Susan, for being the best sisters and cheerleaders I could ask for. Our daily texts comfort me, encourage me, make me laugh, and serve as an overall sounding board for basically every life decision that I make. I am blessed to have you both as the role models that have helped shape me into the woman I am today.

To my brothers-in-law, Freddy and Tom, for enthusiastically supporting my pursuits. Thank you for celebrating the milestones with me, listening, and being a great source of humor and wisdom.

To my nephew and niece, Miles and Mya, for bringing so much joy to our family. Being your tía is one of the greatest honors of my life. You both have added to my "why" for financial freedom.

To my best friends, Matilde, Yovanna, and Ariel, for exemplifying the meaning of friendship. Thank you for being there for me since high school—through the ups and downs, through the major and small moments. Thank you for always supporting my endeavors—no matter how far-fetched they may be.

To my family, friends, teachers, professors, and mentors, thank you for your encouraging messages of support throughout this journey. Thank you for always being willing to share links, engage with my content, and provide feedback so that I could make my platform the best it can be.

To the Wiley publishing team, specifically Sheck, Carla, Susan, and Sam, for believing in my vision for this book and helping make it a reality.

To the personal finance community for all your support these past few years. A special thank you to my friends and interviewees Brittany, Carmen, Cinneah, Delyanne, Jannese, Marc, Melissa, Nika, Soledad, and Yanely for sharing your stories and words of wisdom.

Finally, to my ZBB Fam, thank you. Thank you for rooting for me as I was tackling my mountain of debt, celebrating with me when I became debt-free, and for allowing me to continue to share my journey. Your support has allowed me to promote financial literacy in ways that I never thought possible, including through writing and publishing this book.

With love and endless gratitude,
Cindy

About the Author

Cindy Zuniga-Sanchez, Esq., is a money coach, speaker, and the founder of Zero-Based Budget Coaching LLC. After graduating law school in 2015 with $215,000 of debt, Cindy documented her debt payoff journey on social media, while sharing the personal finance knowledge that she was learning in a simple and relatable way. She has spoken to thousands and coached hundreds on budgeting, saving, debt payoff, investing, credit, building generational wealth, and more. She is committed to helping millennial women, particularly women of color, create a realistic money plan to achieve financial freedom.

Cindy has been featured in national publications including *Forbes, Business Insider, Kiplinger, CNBC, CNET, NextAdvisor, Real Simple, HipLatina, Remezcla,* and *Refinery 29,* and has appeared on national and local television, including *Good Morning America, The Rachael Ray Show, Pix11 News,* and *Telemundo.* She has partnered with the White House's National Economic Council to raise awareness on the American Rescue Plan and the Emergency Rental Assistance Program.

Cindy practiced law as a commercial litigation attorney at an Am Law 100 firm before diving into full-time entrepreneurship. She is a graduate of Stony Brook University and obtained her Juris Doctor degree from the Benjamin N. Cardozo School of Law. She was born, raised, and currently resides in the Bronx, New York, with her husband.

You can find her on Instagram @zerobasedbudget and at www.zerobased budget.com.

Part 1

My Money Story

Chapter 1

Money Lessons from the Bronx

I have a "typical" daughter of immigrants story. My parents immigrated to the United States in the early 1970s in pursuit of the American Dream, better financial opportunities, and an overall better future.

My father was born and raised in Honduras and immigrated when he was 25. He had accepted a job with a shipping company that provided supplies overseas during the Vietnam War. His company flew him from Honduras to New York, where he then departed for nine months at sea. Upon his return, he settled in New York City. Despite not speaking any English and lacking the financial resources to survive in a city like New York, my dad knew he had hit the jackpot when he was presented with the opportunity to apply for a work visa and extend his stay in the United States.

My mother was born and raised in Ecuador and immigrated when she was 18. My grandfather, who was separated from my grandmother and had legal status in the United States, had offered to sponsor my mother's visa application. My mom accepted on the condition that she would remain in the United States for only two years. Her objective was clear—get a job, earn enough money to send back to my grandmother and my mom's younger siblings in Ecuador, and return to Ecuador within two years. That was her plan . . . until she met my father.

My parents met at a mutual friend's party in the Bronx. She was 19 and he was 26. Their courtship lasted just a few months before they decided to get married. My parents, with little more than a mattress and clothes to fill two suitcases, moved into a one-bedroom apartment in the East Bronx. It is the place they still call home today.

Two years into their marriage, my oldest sister, Rosemary, was born. Six years later, my middle sister, Susan, was born. Seven years after Susan was born, I made my entrance and the Zuniga family was complete. The five of us lived in the same one-bedroom apartment that my parents had moved into on their wedding day. My sisters and I shared the bedroom (bunk bed life until I left for college), while my parents divided the living room to create a small second bedroom for themselves.

It would take me decades to realize that, for most of my life, my family's household income hovered around the federal poverty line for a family of five. Although I have always been mindful of money, I was protected from much of the economic hardships that immigrant households endure because my parents did all they could to ensure that my sisters and I never lacked the necessities. What we lacked in material possessions and "personal space" (I wouldn't understand this concept until I moved into my own studio apartment during law school), we made up for with love. My home had everything I needed. Like my father says, our home was *humilde, pero lleno de amor* (humble, but full of love).

As I reflect on my childhood, I think about the many money lessons I learned from my parents and community. The money lessons we learn are unique to us and our personal circumstances. They are heavily impacted by our environment—be it one that fosters a healthy and positive relationship with money, one that is riddled with scarcity, trauma, and struggle, or something in between.

It took me time to fully appreciate how these childhood money lessons impacted my relationship with money as an adult. Here are some of the notable ones.

Money Lesson #1: Early Exposure to Money Can Serve as a Financial Literacy Building Block

As a child, I was not exposed to personal finance topics like budgeting, the emergency fund, credit, or investing, but my parents taught me about the importance of banking and proper credit card use. The latter took me time to fully internalize, but more on that later.

My parents got me involved with banking at an early age. One of my earliest memories is going to Emigrant Savings Bank, our neighborhood bank, with my mom to open my first savings account. I was about five years old, and I could vividly remember our trips to the old bank with its impressive architecture, high ceilings, and golden fixtures. My mom taught me how to complete the deposit and withdrawal slips, which involved memorized account numbers and neat penmanship. She also taught me how to interact with the bank teller when it was time to deposit the $5 or $10 that I received after a birthday or special event. My parents quickly took notice of my curiosity and interest in money. They frequently involved me in matters regarding their own banking, particularly when they needed me to serve as a translator.

When I got to high school, I closed my childhood savings account, and opened an account at the local Chase Bank, where my father banked. My father told me that, because I would soon start my first job, I needed a place that would safeguard my money and allow me to both save money and deposit my paychecks. Together we opened a savings and checking account—accounts that I have to this day.

In addition to banking, my parents emphasized using credit cards properly—that is, do not use them to fund a lifestyle that you cannot afford. My dad had a Macy's credit card that he would use when we visited our local Macy's or the flagship store in Herald Square. He always paid his card's balance by the end of the month, oftentimes by making a cash payment at the register. My dad informed me that although his card gave him rewards and access to cardholder discounts, the perks were only worth it if he paid off his card in full. Otherwise, he would be subject to paying high interest to the credit card company. His lesson was simple: do not use a credit card unless you have the cash to immediately pay it off.

I wish I could say that my father's healthy credit card habits instantly rubbed off on me. They didn't. Like many, I swiped my credit cards to purchase things that I couldn't afford during much of my early and mid-twenties. But my father's foundational lesson of using credit cards responsibly eventually resurfaced. Now that I can fully appreciate my father's advice, I not only strive to emulate his good habits, but I also teach them.

Despite their limited English, lack of financial resources, and lack of knowledge on certain personal finance topics, my parents did what they could with the knowledge they had. Even limited financial literacy can help establish the foundation for healthy money habits. And—regardless of where we are in our money journey—learning how to manage what we currently have impacts how we will manage what we receive in the future.

Money Lesson #2: Incorporate Gratitude into Your Financial Freedom Journey

Children of immigrants raised in a low-income household learn to go without certain American staples. For me, that included a microwave, dishwasher, washer and dryer, and those trendy snacks that were heavily marketed on television—my fellow 1990s kids know what I mean. But let's discuss the one that mattered most to me: cable television. Not having cable meant being excluded from playground conversations centered on the latest episode of *Rugrats* or *Hey Arnold*. For this reason, my favorite weekend destination as a kid was our neighborhood laundromat. The laundromat had a television and cable box that sat on top of a vending machine.

I loved my Saturday laundry day routine—help Mom load the washer, ask the laundromat owner to put on Nickelodeon or the Disney Channel, sit back, and enjoy.

Missing out on something like cable television seems trivial, particularly given the lack of access to basic resources, like adequate shelter, food, and transportation, that many immigrant families experience. But growing up without the little luxuries that those around me seemingly had has impacted my perspective on money and what money can buy.

It's tempting to take lifestyle improvements—no matter how grand or small—for granted. Making progress in our careers and financial circumstances might mean access to updated electronics, higher-quality household items, and perhaps even a larger home. My personal lifestyle improvements have included updated appliances and electronics, carefree trips down the snack aisle, cable television and streaming services, and global travel. These are luxuries that my 10-year-old self could never have imagined, but that I know she would be proud of and grateful for.

My childhood memories of living in a low-income household have fostered an immense sense of gratitude that I regularly reflect upon in my wealth-building journey. These memories have consistently kept me grounded, no matter the new financial milestone that I reach.

Money Lesson #3: There Are Seasons for Hustle

Side hustles are all the rage in the personal finance community. These forms of supplemental income help accelerate your financial goals such as paying off debt, building savings, and increasing investments. But the personal finance community didn't introduce me to side hustles; my parents did.

Growing up, side hustles were as important to my household as my parents' full-time jobs. These additional sources of income allowed my parents to cover my Catholic school education, pay for my school uniforms, and financially provide for our family back in Ecuador and Honduras. My parents took on all sorts of side hustles—everything from photography, selling ready-to-eat foods like *ceviche* (a staple Ecuadorian dish) or *cuajada* (a popular Honduran cheese), and selling toys to offering childcare services to neighbors and friends. My parents were creative in their pursuits to provide for their family.

Hustle is often synonymous with *sacrifice*. This intense focus, necessary for survival, was a way of life for my parents and neighbors. It was ever present in the Puerto Rican bodega owner, the Dominican hair salon stylists, the Jamaican restaurant workers, and the single mothers in my community who worked multiple jobs to provide for their children. That deep-rooted determination and focus that I saw around me drove me to pursue higher education, land a job at a reputable national law firm, and pay off my six-figure student loan debt, all of which involved a great deal of sacrifice.

Your financial freedom journey may require short-term sacrifice for long-term gains. Paying off lingering credit card debt, building an emergency fund for the first time, and/or funding a retirement investment account require careful planning. These goals may call for picking up a side hustle (or two). But it is critical to acknowledge that there are seasons for hustle and sacrifice. Long-term hustle is not sustainable and can lead to burnout and resenting your journey. Rest is necessary.

Although my parents and neighbors may not have had the luxury of seeking respite from the hustle, one way that I honor their sacrifice is by being intentional. I have learned to embrace the seasonality of hustle by creating written plans. These plans allow for "targeted hustle seasons" and contain a clear purpose, defined goals, deadlines, and the systems to support the habits needed to accomplish my goals. Part 2 of this book details how you can create these plans for the various money goals that you are pursuing.

Money Lesson #4: Give Generously

Of all the money lessons from my childhood, the most important has been to give generously, no matter how little or how much you have.

Being raised in a Catholic home meant going to church every Sunday. One way that my mom expected me to actively participate in weekly Mass (Catholic church service) was to contribute to the *ofrenda* (offering). Prior to Mass, my mom would give me two quarters to drop into the collection basket. She taught me that even though our gifts were small, they helped contribute to the larger work of our church, including distributing free meals and facilitating access to social services for members of our community.

Outside of church, my parents made giving part of our everyday lives. This looked like preparing an extra serving of dinner for an elderly neighbor or stopping by the bodega before school to buy a coffee and buttered roll for the homeless man who patiently waited for a generous passerby. It also looked like helping local Bronx organizations prepare donation boxes for victims of Hurricane Mitch, one of the deadliest Atlantic hurricanes, which claimed the lives of over 7,000 Hondurans.[1]

Regardless of circumstance, my parents always found a way to be generous. Their example is the reason "giving" is the first line item in my budget. This category includes planned amounts that I give to church, charities, my parents, and the occasional GoFundMe campaign. There is a stark

7

Money Lessons from the Bronx

contrast between what I was able to give while I tackled six-figure debt and what I can give now that I am debt-free. But I have learned that giving is less about the amount that you give and more about making an intentional effort to give what you can.

Money Lesson #5: Always Keep Your "Why" in Mind

When I reflect on what has underscored my financial freedom journey—what gave me the motivation to go from six-figure debt to a six-figure net worth—I credit it to my "why."

Your "why" is your reason for pursuing financial freedom. This could be your family, your desire to travel the world, buy a dream home or car, give more generously to your community, or achieve financial independence so that you can quit your day job. Establishing your "why" will keep you motivated and give you the momentum that you need to achieve your money goals.

My "why" has always been my parents. My goal isn't to repay my parents because no amount of money could repay them for what they have sacrificed for my sisters and me. Rather, my goal is to have the financial resources to make their retirement years comfortable—taking them on a trip, upgrading their appliances, covering household bills, or lending a helping hand to family abroad that may need financial assistance.

Beyond my parents, my "why" includes thinking about the next generation. Generational wealth is about laying the building blocks for the financial success of future generations. It starts with getting your own finances in order—building an emergency fund, paying off debt, funding your retirement account, growing your wealth. It then may also involve setting up savings and investment accounts for the children in your lives, the way I have done for my nephew and niece. More on this in Chapter 10.

To find your "why," answer these questions: Why do you want to achieve financial success? What motivates you to learn about money? What does financial freedom mean to you? What could you accomplish if you achieved financial freedom? Who would you help? What would you buy? Where would you go?

■ ■ ■

Money isn't just about the numbers; it's inherently emotional. And it may take us years to realize how much our upbringing has impacted our relationship with money. But this introspection at the outset will reveal what we truly value and what will keep us motivated as we embark on the journey to financial freedom.

Chapter 2

Financial Hurdles in Pursuit of the American Dream

In a 2009 national back-to-school address to students, President Barack Obama said, "no matter what you want to do with your life—I guarantee that you'll need an education to do it."[1] My parents would take the President's advice a step further and say that an education is the key to achieving the American Dream.

Like many immigrant parents, mine made our schooling their priority. They worked hard to ensure that I received a quality education, actively participated in parent-teacher conferences, and attended all my awards ceremonies. The rhetoric of education being the way out of poverty surrounded me through elementary school, high school, and college. This is reasonable, given the ample research demonstrating the significance of higher education in promoting economic mobility.[2]

However, what is less discussed are the financial hurdles intertwined with higher education—particularly for those from low-income backgrounds aspiring to break into the middle class.[3] These hurdles are even more pronounced for first-generation students who are often the first in their families to attend college—everything from deciphering complicated financial aid forms, to understanding the options for financing your degree (e.g., loans, grants, scholarships), to figuring out how to cover costs beyond tuition (e.g., fees, books, cost of living expenses), to managing student debt after graduation. Achieving the American Dream to honor my parents' sacrifice inevitably meant confronting and overcoming these challenges, often at a price.

Deciphering Financial Aid Forms

I attended Cardinal Spellman High School in the Bronx. Spellman is a Catholic school known for its Advanced Placement courses, impressive college acceptance and graduation rates, and notable alumni like Supreme Court Justice Sonia Sotomayor. The school also comes with a hefty price tag.

My parents couldn't afford private high school tuition for my older sisters. But when the time came for me to attend high school, my parents and sisters collectively came up with the tuition money for my dream school. I witnessed firsthand the tremendous sacrifice that my family made so that I could receive the best education. I knew that the greatest way to thank them would be to continue my work as a straight-A student and receive funding for college.

In my junior year of high school, I started wondering about how I would pay for college. I sought advice from guidance counselors and teachers, and read countless books on college, career, and funding options. I learned that the first step would be to complete the Free Application for Federal Student Aid (FAFSA). Submitting the FAFSA form is a necessary step to qualify for federal grants, work-study programs, and loans. Part of the FAFSA data that colleges use in determining federal aid eligibility and award amount is the Expected Family Contribution (EFC). The EFC evaluates your family's income, assets, and benefits.[4] My family's EFC was 0, which meant that my family was unable to contribute to my college education and that I would be a strong candidate for need-based aid, including federal and state grants.

During my senior year, I eagerly awaited the arrival of thick, large envelopes from the colleges I had applied to. Thick envelopes generally meant an acceptance; thin envelopes generally meant a rejection. (This was before colleges sent their decisions via email.) My college acceptance letters came with a congratulatory and welcome packet, which included a detailed breakdown of the cost of attendance and the financial aid packages they were offering.

I had applied to dozens of universities and was accepted by many of my top choices. Unfortunately, the financial aid packages for most of the private universities were scant and proposed that I take on tens, if not hundreds, of thousands of dollars in loans. At the time, I had my mind set on attending medical school. Medical school meant at least 10 years of higher education, which meant *lots* of debt. I decided that it would be best to minimize the debt that I took on at the undergraduate level, so I focused on schools that offered me the best financial aid packages and those with lower tuition rates.

I ultimately chose Stony Brook University, a public university that is part of the State University of New York (SUNY) system. Stony Brook has a reputable medical school and is known for its STEM coursework. The deciding factor was Stony Brook's generous financial aid package.

A combination of academic scholarships and need-based federal and state grants would essentially cover my entire cost of attendance—including room *and* board!

I had reached my ambitious goal of getting into a great university that would have little to no economic burden on my family. But I would soon discover that the economic burdens in college do not end with covering the cost of your degree. These burdens often extend into other areas, including the work experience that many graduate schools and entry-level jobs expect from college graduates. I'm talking about internships—specifically, the unpaid kind.

Navigating Unpaid Work

In the fall semester of my second year at Stony Brook, I realized that pursuing medical school was not the route for me. I changed my major from biology to a dual major in business and political science. Because I had developed a great interest in law and government, my career counselor recommended that I intern to build on the work experience on my resume. I saw an internship opening for the local office of then-Senator Hillary Clinton. The issue was that, like most public interest internships, it was unpaid. An internship during the academic year would mean that I would have to juggle my on-campus job, full-time course load, and internship. Nonetheless, I applied and was accepted.

Shortly after I started my internship, President Obama announced that he would be appointing Senator Clinton to the position of Secretary of State. Much of my work therefore focused on assisting the Senator in her transition, which was a unique experience that gave me my first bit of exposure to the federal government. The internship also opened the door for my next opportunity—an internship in the office of Senator Charles Schumer. In the spring of 2009, I transferred to Senator Schumer's office, where I would eventually work as a regional, casework, and legislative intern in his Long Island, New York City, and Washington, DC offices. It was the DC internship, however, that would not only change the trajectory of my career, but would also demonstrate the lengths that my family would go to for my academic and professional success.

In the spring semester of my third year at Stony Brook, I was presented with the opportunity to complete a summer internship in Senator Schumer's DC office. As a legislative intern on Capitol Hill, I would manage constituent matters, perform research, write memos, attend hearings, lead tours of the Capitol building, and more. It was the opportunity of a lifetime. But, in addition to not being paid for my work, I would have to cover the costs of housing, transportation, and food for the summer in a new city.

Although I knew there was no way that my parents could afford to send me to DC, I shared the opportunity with them. They insisted that I accept and promised that they would figure out how to cover the costs. And figure it out they did. My mother withdrew money from her small savings account so that I could cover my housing deposit. She also applied for a credit card for me to use to cover my expenses over the summer. My sister generously took on the responsibility of paying off that credit card. Once we established our game plan on how we would handle the expenses, I enthusiastically accepted the internship offer. I held my parents' *bendiciones* (blessings) close to my heart, packed my bags, and headed to DC.

When I got to DC, I was fascinated by the national landmarks, museums, and impressive credentials of my fellow "Hillterns" (the nickname for the undergrad interns who packed Capitol Hill in the summers). Many of them hailed from the nation's top universities like Yale, Harvard, and Stanford. They were also very . . . privileged.

My DC internship was the first time that I felt extremely out of place—socioeconomically, ethnically, and racially. Many of my fellow interns lived in the Georgetown summer intern housing, which cost thousands,[5] while others stayed in their parents' second home in DC. I, on the other hand, had found a small room in an apartment that I shared with others in Alexandria, Virginia. My rent was $500/monthly, or $1,000 for the summer. Every day I commuted nearly an hour by shuttle bus and train to the Hart Senate Office Building. I packed my lunch and took advantage of every free food event that I could find (luckily, there were many!). On weekends, I took advantage of the free Smithsonian museums and libraries, and attractions in DC.

Despite the stark contrast between my financial circumstances and that of those around me, I made the most of my internship experience. That summer, I met elected officials, including then-Senator Joe Biden, attended an event with (and was selected to ask a question to) my role model, Justice Sonia Sotomayor, attended interesting and sometimes heated legislative hearings, and witnessed the work that went into the Dodd-Frank Wall Street Reform and Consumer Protection Act: federal legislation in response to the 2007–2009 financial crisis. My summer internship as a Hilltern in Washington, DC served as a natural stepping stone for the next phase of my career—law school.

Applying to and Funding Law School

My DC internship solidified my career path. I was set on applying to law school and becoming the first lawyer in my family. After I got back from my summer internship, I started focusing on the law school application process. The first step would be to take the Law School Admission Test (LSAT). Prospective law school candidates typically take courses to prepare for this standardized exam, which meant another financial hurdle to overcome.

The LSAT prep course offered on my school's campus was over $1,000. I paid for the course with my credit card and picked up extra shifts at my on-campus job to pay off my debt. In addition to the LSAT prep course, I paid for the exam itself and had to figure out how I would pay for my law school application fees—which ranged $50–$75 *per school*! Thankfully, a friend encouraged me to apply for the Law School Admission Council (LSAC) fee waiver, which subsidized most of my application fees. These "inside" pieces of knowledge—much of which I was able to find through blogs and forums—helped me get through the law school application process.

Law school is expensive—extremely expensive. The average tuition for most of the law schools I was applying to at the time was $50,000. As of the time of this writing, the tuition for those same schools is averaging $70,000. That is a $20,000 increase in just 10 years![6]

I devoted myself to the information on the Federal Student Aid website, law school websites, and blogs that discussed funding law school. Unfortunately, they all led me to the same conclusion: I needed to take out loans— *lots* of loans. To minimize my debt, I applied for as many scholarships as I could. Unfortunately, scholarships at the graduate and professional degree level were scant.

In the winter of my last year at Stony Brook University, the law school acceptance and financial aid letters started coming in. I was very fortunate to receive a few partial and even a couple of full-tuition scholarship offers. When evaluating my offers, I looked at the school's ranking (the legal community is unfortunately consumed with prestige and pedigree),[7] career prospects, location, and, of course, cost.

I decided on the Benjamin N. Cardozo School of Law. Cardozo offered me a half-tuition scholarship of $25,000. I would cover the other half of tuition ($25,000) through loans. I also needed to take out a loan to cover my school fees, books, and cost of living expenses like housing, transportation, and food. Cardozo estimated these additional expenses would run students roughly $25,000 annually.[8] With this in mind, my school loans were as follows:

Category	Debt*
Undergraduate debt	$10,000
Law school year 1	$50,000 ($25,000 for tuition + $25,000 living expenses)
Law school year 2	$50,000 ($25,000 for tuition + $25,000 living expenses)
Law school year 3	$50,000 ($25,000 for tuition + $25,000 living expenses)
TOTAL	**$160,000**

*These are approximate amounts that represent the principal only (i.e., the amount that I borrowed); they do not reflect the interest that I ultimately paid on my loans.

Becoming a lawyer would be the ultimate way to honor my family's collective sacrifice. Law school held the key to making the American Dream a reality. And I was ready to become the first lawyer in my family no matter the cost.

Managing Money during Law School

In my quest to figure out how to manage my money during law school, I stumbled upon a few blog posts that would help me structure my finances for the following three years. And, although it would take me years to feel comfortable with budgeting and overall money management, this initial setup worked surprisingly well.

My first step was to open a checking and savings account with a new bank. This bank held the money from my loan disbursements that I would use to cover my law school expenses. After covering my law school tuition and fees, a little over $12,000 was deposited each semester into my new savings account ($24,000 annually). Every month I would transfer $2,000 into my checking account to cover my monthly living expenses. This way, I could make the $24,000 that was meant to cover the 10-month academic year (August–May) stretch to cover the entire year, including summers.

Living off $24,000 annually in New York City was a challenge. But I knew how to stretch a dollar. I was fortunate to secure a studio apartment in a fourth-floor walk-up in Harlem for $1,150, which made what is typically most people's largest expense more manageable. When I went grocery shopping, I always went in with a list and a plan. I followed popular meal prep bloggers who documented their health journeys and shared their grocery lists. I knew how to select cuts of meat, shop for in-season produce, and shop the bulk section for grains and snacks. My mom's voice telling me to *apagar la luz* (turn off the light) when it was not in use came to mind when monitoring my gas and electric use. I limited my transportation costs to my monthly MetroCard, which took me to school, the Trader Joe's on the Upper West Side, weekly visits to my parents' place, and anywhere that a New Yorker needed to be. One expense that I was not willing to cut, and which served as a necessary distraction during law school, was cable television. No surprise there.

Not all costs were as manageable. One thing that I had not prepared for, but which was inevitable each semester, was the cost of books. A new case book easily costs between $200 and $300. If I took four courses in one semester, that meant over $1,000 in books per semester. At the start of each semester, I scoured the used books section on Amazon, monitored bulletin posts from students who were selling their used books, and relied on the generosity of students and groups, including my school's Minority Law Student Alliance (MLSA). In addition to higher than average book expenses, attempts to keep up with my classmates led to thousands in credit card charges that would take me years to pay off. But more on that in later chapters.

Discovering My Path

I originally applied to law school because I aspired to one day run for office. At the time, the U.S. Senate had never had a Latina Senator. I had my heart set on becoming the first.[9] After my first year of law school, I took on a legal internship in the New York State Attorney General's office, which put me at the intersection of law and public policy. And, although I had a positive experience at my first legal internship, law school was exposing me to career options that I had never considered.

Many of my law school classmates were buzzing about securing summer associate positions at "Big Law" firms. *Big Law* is a term used to describe prestigious law firms in the United States that are synonymous with the "Am Law 100," which is "*The American Lawyer*'s annual ranking of the 100 highest-grossing law firms in the country."[10] These law firms customarily recruit students on campus for paid summer internship positions at their firms. The real prize, however, comes at the end of the summer. Depending on performance and the needs of the firm, summer associates receive an offer to join the firm as a full-time associate, with first-year associates earning, at that time, a base salary of $160,000.[11]

Prior to law school, I had never heard of Big Law; nor had I ever considered a career in the private sector. I started researching Big Law firms and was exposed to their wide range of practice areas—everything from litigation to intellectual property to real estate and advertising—recognizable big-name clients, and impressive caseloads. My interest was piqued. And how could I ignore the fact that the starting salary was more money than I could have ever dreamed of.

But Big Law jobs were notoriously competitive. These prestigious law firms held high expectations for summer associate candidates. They looked at school prestige, stellar academic performance, and exceptional interpersonal skills that would be assessed throughout a series of interviews. Nonetheless, I was determined to get the best grades I could so that I could secure a Big Law summer associate position. I spent many late nights in school (often taking the train back home after 11 p.m.), made regular visits to my academic advisor, and memorized my professors' office hours schedule. My hard work paid off. I finished my first year of law school with impressive grades and secured a spot as a staff editor on the *Cardozo Law Review*, my school's student-run scholarly journal that invited students with academic distinction as members.

After an intense bout of on-campus interviews, I received an offer from Venable LLP, an Am Law 100 firm with offices nationwide, including Washington, DC, Maryland, California, and, of course, New York. As a summer associate at Venable, I worked on matters in both federal and state courts and was exposed to various practice groups, including real estate, labor and employment, and commercial litigation. I also worked on *pro bono* matters representing refugees seeking asylum. After an unforgettable summer experience, Venable offered me a full-time position in its New York commercial litigation group.

In June 2015, I graduated from Cardozo Law School in the top 10% of my class, with *magna cum laude* honors. A few months later, after taking the bar exam, I started my legal career in Venable's New York office as a full-time associate. I had done it. The American Dream. The goal I set out to honor my parents' sacrifice . . . realized.

I was eager to transition out of my student lifestyle and into my career, which I knew would provide me with the professional experience and financial opportunities I had always dreamed of. But my financial woes would not dissipate simply because I had landed a coveted job at a prestigious law firm. I would soon have to confront my loans that had been—unbeknownst to me—growing and accumulating interest as I sat in my law school classroom. By the time I graduated law school, the original $150,000 in loans that I took out to fund my three-year degree had already accumulated thousands in interest. That debt would eventually accrue *tens of thousands* in interest.

Chapter 3

The Journey to Financial Freedom

My "Aha" Moment

It was January 2017, and I was going through our mail. One of the envelopes had "IMPORTANT TAX DOCUMENT" stamped on the front. It was the 1098-E Student Loan Interest Statement, a tax form specifying the interest that I had paid toward my student loans in the previous year.[1] After reviewing the form and frantically logging into my student loan accounts, I came to an unnerving realization.

After graduating law school, I had a six-month grace period until my loan repayment kicked in. Prior to expiration of the grace period, I had to select a repayment plan. I went with the "standard" option because it seemed to be the most straightforward. If I dutifully made my payments, I would pay off my loans in 10 years. Satisfied with the prospect of becoming debt-free by age 36, I signed up for the standard repayment plan. The plan came with a $2,000 monthly payment. Yes, you read that correctly. My student loan payment was nearly double my rent. In my first year of repayment (2016), I paid $24,000 toward my student loans (12 months × $2,000 monthly payment = $24,000 total paid in 2016).

That day, in January 2017, as I reviewed my 2016 Student Loan Interest Statement forms and saw how much of my student loan payments went to the principal versus the interest, I came to the harsh realization that of the $24,000 that I had paid toward my student loans in 2016, only $4,000 had gone toward the principal; $20,000 went to the interest. Less than 17% of the total amount I had paid in that first year of repayment went to the original debt that I had taken on.

I knew that interest had accumulated on my loans but, to be honest, I had never paid attention to the amount. I had never done the math on how much I would ultimately repay, nor did I understand much about principal or interest—let alone capitalized interest. Despite my law degree, the perceived prestige of being an attorney, and all the fancy accolades,

I had graduated law school with little financial literacy. I never learned how to create a budget, where to save an emergency fund, how to build my credit score, or how to manage my student loans. As far as real-world money smarts, I was no better off than I had been when I had graduated high school.

My whole life, I had fought to overcome the deck that had been stacked against me as the daughter of immigrants from a low-income community in the Bronx. I thought that formal education alone would lead to success and wealth. But my formal schooling had neglected to teach me the very thing I needed as I reviewed those tax forms—financial literacy.[2] An overwhelming sense of dread took over. If only a tiny portion of my monthly payment was tackling my six-figure student loans, how was I ever going to get out of debt?

Rather than wallow in despair, I used that moment as fuel. That day I committed to learning everything I could about money. I had to get rid of the massive debt boulder on my shoulders and wanted to do so as quickly as possible. And I wouldn't stop there. In the short months to follow, I would learn about budgeting, saving, credit, credit cards, and even investing. I prepared myself to, once again, become a student.

Seeking Financial Literacy

"How do I get out of debt?" I typed into the Google search bar.

After my "aha" moment, I was ready to start my financial literacy journey, but I did not know where to start. No one around me was having open and candid conversations about money, let alone debt. I knew that for the time being, I was on my own.

The top Google hits led me to personal finance educators and authors like Suze Orman, Dave Ramsey, and David Bach. I listened to their podcasts, read their books, and watched their interviews on debt and money management. But I longed for more. I yearned to learn from people who looked like me or who had a similar life experience to mine—millennial women, people of color, children of immigrants. After some research, I found exactly what I was looking for.

Shortly into my journey, I discovered Bola Sokunbi, founder of Clever Girl Finance; Jamila Souffrant, founder of Journey To Launch; and Yanely Espinal, founder of MissBeHelpful. These women used their first-hand experiences as immigrants or as first-generation children of immigrants, knowledge, personal anecdotes, and even humor to teach others about money. I learned how to track my spending and stick to a budget, save for an emergency fund, avoid lifestyle inflation, increase my credit score, and create a debt payoff plan. Importantly, I learned from women who had faced similar financial challenges as I had and who I could relate to. They served to show that I too could one day become financially stable and achieve financial success.

Creating My Debt-Free Plan

I got to work. I first had to understand my current money inflow and out-flow. Specifically, I asked myself these questions:

- How much money was I bringing in?
- How was I spending my money?
- How did I feel about how I was spending my money? (This was a tough one!)
- What percentage of my money was going toward my financial goals?

Then, I gathered information on my debt. I started with the basic information like loan balance, interest, and minimum monthly payment. Finally, and per the advice of the financial educators I was following, I plugged my numbers into debt repayment calculators to determine how I could potentially shorten my debt repayment time frame. These calculators showed me the dramatic impact that additional payments could have on both lowering the interest (and, in turn, total debt) I would repay and shortening my repayment timeline.

After understanding my income and expenses, debt numbers, and experimenting with debt repayment calculators, I came up with a three-step plan:

1. Create a budget
2. Maximize the gap between my income and expenses
3. Refinance my student loans

Creating a Budget

Every piece of financial advice that I read, heard, or saw pointed me to one tool: the budget. Regardless of the money goal, I needed to have a budget. As we dive into in Chapter 5, a budget is an intentional money plan. It gives you the opportunity to decide how much of your income will go toward saving, investing, debt, expenses, and any other financial goals you may have.

Up until that point, although I was aware of my regular fixed monthly expenses and could estimate my variable expenses, I did not have a written budget. I decided to give the "zero-based budget" a try. The zero-based budget is a budgeting method where you give every dollar that you bring in (e.g., work income, commissions, bonuses, side hustle money) a specific purpose.[3]

I downloaded a simple and free zero-based budget template. I customized the template by inserting my monthly net income, debt payments, and expenses. I reviewed my credit and debit card statements to ensure that I was capturing all my numbers. That was an eye opener. Inserting my numbers into my budget gave me a clear picture of how I was managing my money. It also revealed areas of overspending and unnecessary expenses that I knew I could cut back on.

Maximizing the Gap between My Income and Expenses

My next step was to increase the gap between my income and expenses so that I could direct as much as possible to my debt. To support this goal, I had to avoid something that tempts many, particularly a recent law grad who just landed a well-paying job: lifestyle inflation. Lifestyle inflation occurs when you increase your spending, typically as your income increases. Things you once viewed as luxuries suddenly become necessities, prompting you to spend more than you used to when you had a lower income.

For example, say you live off $3,000 a month and feel like you're living paycheck to paycheck. You receive a better-paying job, resulting in an additional $1,000 monthly net pay. Rather than directing that additional money to a financial goal, you allow your spending to increase. You spend on fancy dinners, shopping, and new tech gadgets. You're back to that paycheck-to-paycheck cycle. Sound familiar?

Let me be clear: lifestyle inflation is not necessarily a bad thing. As we progress in our careers, it is natural to desire material possessions and experiences, especially things that we could not once afford. But the key is to be *intentional* with how we spend. Like many, I too desired to live in a nice home, travel the world, and indulge in fine dining. But avoiding lifestyle inflation meant balancing my wants with my long-term goals.

The average American household spends about 63% of their money on the "big three" expenses: housing, food, and transportation.[4] I therefore focused on these big three expenses in my budget rather than obsessing over small expenses. I kept my rent costs low by extending the lease for my law school studio apartment. I later split the rent for a one-bedroom apartment with my then-boyfriend (now husband) in Harlem, which featured more affordable rents than other parts of Manhattan. I kept my food costs under control by sticking to a strict monthly grocery and dining out budget. I continued the meal planning and prep habits I had developed in law school. Rather than spending $15 daily on lunch near my office, I brought my lunch from home. I limited my transportation spending to my MetroCard and gave myself a modest budget for cabs and rideshares. Opting out of owning a car meant that not only did I save on a monthly car note or lease, but I also avoided expenses like insurance, gas, garage, tolls, and car maintenance (which would add up to hundreds of dollars).

My lifestyle was more akin to that of a law student than an attorney working at a Big Law firm. Because I had opted for an aggressive debt pay-off strategy, I knew that these short-term sacrifices would be worth it.

Refinancing My Student Loans

My third big step in my debt payoff plan was to refinance my student loans.

My original plan put me on track to pay off my student loans in 10 years. But after running the numbers, I realized that that would result in paying approximately *$80,000 in interest alone*. I had to find a way to lower that amount. Refinancing was the best solution for me.

Refinancing my student loans meant that I would have an agreement with a new lender featuring new repayment terms. The main benefits to refinancing my student loans were lowering my interest rate and shortening my repayment time frame.

In addition to my monthly minimum payment, I regularly made additional payments to my new, refinanced loan. I also directed most of my annual bonuses and tax refunds to my debt. Refinancing ultimately saved me *tens of thousands in interest* and cut my debt repayment term by nearly half! More on the pros and cons of refinancing in Chapter 8.

Sharing the Knowledge

About a year after starting my financial literacy journey, I created an anonymous account on Instagram with the handle @zerobasedbudget. I used the page to document my debt-free journey. Every month I shared updates on my debt payments and decreasing debt balance. At the same time, I started sharing money tips on my personal Instagram page for family and friends to see. At first, I felt awkward sharing this type of information and was unsure whether anyone would be interested. But to my surprise, family members, friends from high school, and even my law school colleagues messaged me with great interest, asking for more.

I decided to make @zerobasedbudget a public account with the dual purpose of sharing money tips and my debt payoff story. I sought to normalize conversations about money through leading by example. I shared financial tidbits, articles, and my personal finances, including my journey to tackle over $200,000 of debt. Importantly, I shared this from the perspective of a first-generation Latina. The information that I shared was not one-dimensional. It included candid conversations on privilege, generational wealth, providing financial support to loved ones, social justice issues, and yes, even politics.

Eventually, I started receiving texts from friends asking for help with their finances. Some sought help on creating a budget, others needed tips for saving for big-ticket items like a home down payment and travel, and most expressed feeling overwhelmed with their debt. I offered free budget coaching services to family and friends and started sharing this experience with my social media community. The demand was instant. I received dozens of messages requesting coaching services.

I launched Zero-Based Budget Coaching LLC in early 2019. My mission was to offer low-cost money coaching services while promoting financial literacy, diversity, and transparency. I coached hundreds—mainly millennial women—on creating a realistic money plan to achieve financial freedom. My clients spanned all parts of the income spectrum and had a wide range of financial goals: from the recent college graduate with an entry-level job who wanted to move out of their parents' home, to the single mom who wanted to save an emergency fund while tackling credit card debt, to the couple who wanted to save for a wedding and honeymoon, to the first-generation law graduate who—like I had once been—was overwhelmed with their six-figure debt and was looking for support and guidance. My personal journey has allowed me to connect and empathize with my clients' needs and goals and helped me become a better coach.

Debt-Free Living

In December 2019, I became 100% debt-free. I paid off $215,000 of debt—$13,000 in credit card debt and $202,000 in student loans (including interest)—in exactly 48 months. I celebrated this financial milestone with my family, friends, coaching clients, and the tens of thousands who were now part of my social media community, which I lovingly refer to as my "ZBB Fam."

After becoming debt-free, I reassessed my budget. Freeing myself of my monthly debt payment, which was my largest expense, gave me the room to increase my spending on things I valued, like travel and dining out. And, thanks to the foundation that I had established while I was paying off debt, I did so in a thoughtful and intentional manner.

I replaced my debt-free goals with investing goals. I maxed out my retirement investing account contributions through my employer. I also regularly invested in nonretirement brokerage accounts. Consistent investing contributions, compound interest, and significant market gains (particularly in 2020 and 2021) grew my net worth to over $250,000.

Careful financial planning has also allowed me to help those around me. I have increased my financial support to my parents and family abroad. I have also increased my giving to churches, charities, and social justice organizations. I have put generational wealth into practice by opening investment accounts for my nephew and niece.

In the short time since launching my business, I have expanded my reach through speaking engagements, national and local media, educational digital content, and brand partnerships. My passion for and mission to make financial literacy accessible to my community has deepened and opened doors that I never could have imagined.

■ ■ ■

That moment in January 2017 when I received those student loan interest forms and frantically attempted to figure out what I was doing with my money served as the catalyst I needed to get on the road to financial freedom. That moment has led me to you.

In the pages that follow, you will learn about the tools that this Latina, daughter of immigrants, from a low-income neighborhood in the Bronx, used to go from having six figures of debt to a multiple six-figure net worth. These tools are financial pillars that, regardless of your background, I hope will serve you on your financial freedom journey.

Part 2

Eight Wealth-Building Pillars

Chapter 4

Take Inventory of Your Numbers

$\mathbf{A}$ugust 2018 was the first time that I sat down to calculate my net worth. I had been on a debt-free journey for over two years but was too scared to confront the number that would reveal my financial picture *as a whole*. I knew my net worth was in the negative, so I resorted to ignoring the number rather than facing it. I was more comfortable running a Google search for "what's [insert celebrity here]'s net worth?" than calculating my own.

But early that month I had publicly launched my social media account @zerobasedbudget. I had done so to: (i) document my debt-free journey and (ii) simplify personal finance information for my community. I knew that if I was going to share my journey with others, including my loved ones, I had to understand my complete financial picture.

Net Worth

To quote Drake's 2018 hit, "In My Feelings," "What's your net-net-net worth?"

Your net worth is a calculation that measures your liabilities (what you owe) against your assets (what you own). It is an excellent way to measure your financial progress because it provides a complete picture of your financial situation. Regardless of your age, how much you own or owe, or even your income, your net worth is the most important number to track on your financial freedom journey.

"What gets measured gets managed."[1]

Calculate Your Net Worth

Calculating your net worth involves a straightforward formula:

$$\text{Assets}\,(\text{what you own}) - \text{Liabilities}\,(\text{what you owe}) = \text{Net Worth}$$

Assets = What You Own

Assets are resources with economic value. Think of assets as money or something you can easily convert to cash (i.e., by selling it). For example, assets can include:

- Cash
- Savings accounts
- Checking accounts
- House
- Car
- Retirement investment accounts—for example, money invested in 401(k), 403(b), individual retirement accounts (IRAs), or Roth IRAs
- Nonretirement investments—for example, money invested in stocks, bonds, index funds, exchange-traded funds (ETFs), or cryptocurrencies
- Goods—for example, phones, computers, cameras, handbags, artwork, jewelry

What you choose to include in your net worth calculation is up to you. Keep in mind that, depending on what you choose to include as an asset, the value of certain items such as technology, furniture, or even a car may change when accounting for depreciation (an asset's decrease in value over time).

Let's Get Personal

These are the assets that I include in my personal net worth calculation:

- Cash
  Although I do not use cash for most purchases, I try to keep a small amount on hand.
- Money in my savings and checking accounts
  I currently have one checking account and three savings accounts.
- Money in my retirement investment accounts
  I used to have a 401(k) through my old employer but have since rolled over that money into an IRA[2].
- Money in my nonretirement investment accounts
  I have two accounts with robo-advisors and one self-directed account.

Overcoming Debt, Achieving Financial Freedom

Could I include my small luxury handbag collection in my net worth calculation? Of course, especially because my collection's resale value is at or higher than the amount that I originally paid for the bags. I could also include my wedding rings and the art hanging on our living room walls. But for simplicity's sake, I only include financial accounts in my net worth.

Liabilities = What You Owe

Liabilities are any form of debt. For example, liabilities can include:

- Credit card balance
- Student loan
- Personal loan
- Car loan
- Mortgage
- Medical debt

Confronting your debt, especially your total debt balance, is overwhelming and stressful. It is a daunting task that many of us will be doing for the first time upon reading this book. But it is necessary. Without fully understanding how much debt we have, we are unable to create an honest money plan to overcome it.

A coaching client once shared that she had completely avoided her student loans since graduating college. At the time of our meeting, she had not logged into her student loan account in over a year. After a password reset, helping her navigate the updated website, and deciphering terminology, we gathered the necessary information to calculate her net worth (and create her debt repayment plan, which you too will learn how to do).

TIP: Review your credit report to ensure that you are capturing all your debts.[3]
Your credit report will show the debts that are under your name. You can access your credit report for free at annualcreditreport.com.

Because I am currently debt-free and do not own a home or car (I am grateful for New York City's public transportation system), I do not have any liabilities. However, if my husband and I choose to purchase a home in the future, we would include our mortgage as a liability in our net worth calculation.

Net Worth Examples

Example: Francesca's Net Worth

Francesca has $5,000 in her savings account and $1,000 in her checking account. She also has $1,000 in cash.

Francesca recently graduated law school and has a $200,000 balance on her student loans. She also has $5,000 of credit card debt.

What is Francesca's net worth?

First, calculate Francesca's total assets and liabilities:

Assets		Liabilities	
Category	**Amount**	**Category**	**Amount**
Savings account	$5,000	Law school debt	$200,000
Checking account	$1,000	Credit card	$5,000
Cash	$1,000		
Total Assets	**$7,000**	**Total Liabilities**	**$205,000**

Next, plug in her numbers into the net worth formula:

$$\$7,000 \ (\text{assets}) - \$205,000 \ (\text{liabilities}) = -\$198,000$$

Francesca's net worth is − $198,000.

Example: Wanda's Net Worth

Wanda has a car worth $15,000, with a $10,000 car note. She has $20,000 in a savings account and $5,000 in her checking account. She also has $20,000 in her 401(k) retirement account with her employer.

Wanda has a $20,000 student loan and two credit cards, one with a $1,000 balance and the other with a $3,000 balance.

What is Wanda's net worth?

Assets		Liabilities	
Category	**Amount**	**Category**	**Amount**
Car	$15,000	Car note	$10,000
Savings account	$20,000	Student loan	$20,000
Checking account	$5,000	Credit card 1	$1,000
401K retirement account	$20,000	Credit card 2	$3,000
Total Assets	**$60,000**	**Total Liabilities**	**$34,000**

$$\$60,000 \ (\text{assets}) - \$34,000 \ (\text{liabilities}) = \$26,000$$

Wanda's net worth is + $26,000.

Your Net Worth ≠ Your Self Worth

If you are anything like me, you are likely dreading calculating your net worth or you have already done so and are filled with a sense of gloom. But remember that your net worth does not represent your value as a person. It is simply an objective dollar amount that we can all improve.

Let's Get Personal

When I first calculated my net worth in August 2018, I learned that it was over –$100,000. *Negative!* I was deep in the red. I had less than $0. I had been aggressively paying off my debt for over two and a half years and was still more than $100,000 away from having a $0 net worth. Ouch.

In that moment, my anxiety was compounded by the fact that I alone had to get myself out of the red. But I found comfort and calm by reflecting on my parents' perseverance. When my parents first immigrated to

(continued)

(continued)

the United States, they had little familial support, no possessions, and no command of the English language. Despite their bleak circumstances, they knew there was only up from their current situation. Achieving the American Dream would take them decades—but they would eventually get there. So, channeling my parents' energy, I focused on getting to $0.

If your net worth is in the negative, strive for $0. If your net worth is in the negative hundreds of thousands (I'm looking at you, with the six-figure student loans), break up what seems like an impossible goal into smaller chunks. Focus on getting to –$100,000, and then –$80,000, and then $–50,000, until you get to $0. Yes, it can be exhausting, but setting clear milestones (and taking time to celebrate those victories) will keep you motivated.

If your net worth is in the positive, congratulations! Set a big goal and then break that amount into smaller milestone chunks. For example, if your big net worth goal is $1,000,000, break up that amount into smaller chunks—for example, $50,000 in five years, $100,000 in 10 years, and so on.

Track It

Tracking your net worth will give you the best indication of your financial progress. I recommend doing so at least once a month. It is also a good idea to take note of *why* your net worth decreased or increased in a given month.

If your net worth increased, celebrate the win, and take note of the reasons why. For example, perhaps you saved, invested, or paid off debt. If your net worth decreased, recognize that some reasons—such as decreases in the stock market—are out of your control. However, if the decrease was due to incurring additional debt (e.g., credit card debt), acknowledge that fact and account for how you will address it in your budget for the following month.

Track It with a Spreadsheet

There are many free and paid options for net worth trackers, but you do not need anything fancy. For a simple solution, copy the template in Chapter 12 into your favorite spreadsheet software and create 12 tabs for the corresponding months of the year.

Update your numbers once a month, preferably the same time each month (e.g., on the first of each month or the last Sunday of each month). I promise you will be surprised by how much progress you can make with your net worth in one or even five years' time!

Track It with an App

An alternative to manually tracking your net worth is to use a net worth–tracking app. Here are a few options:

- **Personal Capital:** This is my personal favorite. This free app automatically syncs to your financial accounts, including your bank and investment accounts, credit cards, mortgage, and loans. It updates your net worth based on your account balances. You can also manually upload information on other assets or liabilities such as your car, jewelry, art, or information on the money that your cousin owes you (or vice versa).

- **You Need a Budget (YNAB):** YNAB is a budget app that keeps track of your spending. It generates a net worth report based on your linked accounts. A downside of it is that, as of the time of this writing, the app requires you to manually input information on investment accounts. I recommend this app for net worth tracking if you are also going to regularly use it for your budgeting needs.

- **Mint:** This is a popular, simple, and free app that has been around for years. The app connects to your financial accounts and pulls in your transactions, which allows you to create customized budgets and analyze your spending. The app has reports in its "trends" section where you can see your net worth over a desired time period.

Your Net Worth ≠ Your Income

Someone once said, "it's not about how much you earn, rather what you do with what you earn." I am not suggesting that we diminish the role that income has on building wealth because it is certainly significant. However, to assume, for example, that those in traditionally high-earning professions (e.g., doctors, lawyers, investment bankers, celebrities, or professional athletes) have an impressive net worth simply by virtue of their occupation is inaccurate.

When I was a junior attorney, I went to dinner with a few colleagues. One of them had invited a friend (we'll call him Todd) to join us. As the night progressed, we got to talking about law school and our debt. (I know what you're thinking: seriously, Cindy? Yes, seriously.) Todd shared that he had over $300,000 of debt—not uncommon for lawyers. However, he had graduated law school a few years before me and earned well over $200,000 annually (salaries for most large law firms are public knowledge), so his revelation surprised me.

Compare Todd to a former coaching client, "Ana." Ana was a teacher at an elementary school in the Bronx. Ana had attended City University of New York (CUNY), a public university in New York City, and had graduated debt-free. Ana's salary was about one third that of Todd's, but she had over $50,000 in savings and was working toward purchasing her first home.

Income alone is simply insufficient to determine someone's net worth. The lesson here is to focus on your own net worth progress and avoid assumptions about the net worth of others based on their apparent lifestyle, profession, or even age.

Average Net Worth of American Households by Age

Now that you understand why it is important to calculate your net worth and how to track it, if you are anything like me, you might be curious on how your net worth compares to that of those in your age range.

In 2020, the Federal Reserve analyzed data on consumer finances, including income, net worth, debt, and credit use.[6] The collected data on median and average net worth in 2019 was as follows:[7]

Age	Median Net Worth	Average Net Worth
Less than 35	$13,900	$76,300
35–44	$91,300	$436,200
45–54	$168,600	$833,200
55–64	$212,500	$1,175,900
65–74	$266,400	$1,217,700
75+	$254,800	$977,600

I have always enjoyed reviewing these types of data to have a general rule of thumb in mind. But to end the conversation with this chart would be disingenuous. Although net worth ultimately depends on an individual's unique circumstances, external factors also play a role.

A closer look at the Federal Reserve's data reveals the significant disparities in household net worth across racial groups:[8]

Race or Ethnicity of Respondent	Median Net Worth	Average Net Worth
White non-Hispanic	$188,200	$983,400
Black or African American non-Hispanic	$24,100	$142,500
Hispanic or Latino	$36,200	$165,500
Other or multiple race	$74,500	$657,200

White families have the highest level of wealth across racial groups, with a median wealth of $188,200. Compare this to the median wealth of Black families at $24,100 or Hispanic families at $36,200.[9]

That the median net worth for White families is eight times higher than that of the typical Black family and five times that of the typical Hispanic family is attributed to many factors, including intergenerational transfers of wealth, homeownership opportunities, savings, access to banking services, access to tax-advantaged accounts, including college and retirement accounts, and investment opportunities.[10] Intergenerational transfers of wealth—inheritances, monetary gifts (e.g., down payment for a home, wedding gifts)—"account for more of the racial wealth gap than any other demographic or socioeconomic indicator."[11]

I could dedicate an entire book to this topic, but I'll leave you with this: wealth building is not only critical to our individual journeys, it is key to creating generational wealth. As encouraging or discouraging as our current net worth number may seem, we must acknowledge it. Once we are armed with this knowledge, we can create a sound plan to change the trajectory of our financial futures—and that of those to come.

Gather Your Four Core Monthly Numbers

In addition to net worth, a set of four numbers is critical to our financial planning. Before gathering these numbers, here are some tips:

- **Time:** Set aside sufficient time for this exercise. Depending on your situation, this process can take anywhere from one to a few hours.
- **Kindness:** Confronting your monthly cash flow is often one of the biggest roadblocks to starting your financial freedom journey. This process often exposes the control (or lack thereof) that we have over

our day-to-day finances. Regardless of where you fall on the spectrum, be kind to yourself and remember that we are here to learn and improve.

- **Patience:** Deciphering your paycheck's numerous deductions or making sense of your recent credit card statement can be frustrating, but it is an important step in creating your money plan.

- **Tools:** Grab a pen, paper, notebook, highlighter, calculator, and/or laptop.

Ready? Let's get to it.

Step 1: Calculate Your Monthly Income

Gross income: This is based on your gross annual salary (if you are a salaried employee) or your revenue (if you are self-employed). Your gross income is the amount you receive before any taxes or deductions are taken from your pay.

Net income: This is your take-home pay. Your net income is what you receive after taxes and other deductions are taken from your pay. If you are self-employed, this may be the amount that you draw from your business after setting money aside for taxes. For most salaried employees, this is the direct deposit that hits your checking account on payday.

To obtain your gross and net income, gather the following:

- **Compensation documents:** Documents with information on your gross pay (e.g., offer or compensation letters).

- **Paycheck:** Pull your paychecks for the past two months. This will help you observe any changes in your pay across pay cycles.

TIP: Take this time to review your paycheck for any taxes, payments, and other deductions that are taken from your pay. You would be surprised by how many of my coaching clients have never taken the time to review what gets taken from their pay!

Paycheck Guide

Here is a quick guide for understanding the various taxes and deductions you may see on your paycheck.

- **Income taxes:** These taxes are based on your income.
  - *Federal taxes:* Unless you qualify for specific exemptions, most people pay taxes on their income to the federal government.
  - *State taxes:* States also have the right to impose a tax on income, but not all do.
    - o As of this writing, the following states do not tax income: Alaska, Florida, Nevada, New Hampshire, South Dakota, Tennessee, Texas, Washington, and Wyoming.[12]
  - *Local, municipal taxes:* Local governments may also impose their own tax.
    - o For example, I live in the Bronx, New York, and pay (i) federal taxes, (ii) New York State taxes, and (iii) New York City taxes.
- **Payroll taxes:** The Federal Insurance Contributions Act (FICA) tax is a mandatory payroll tax that is based on a percentage withheld from wages. FICA includes:
  - *Social Security tax:* This money goes to the Social Security Trust Fund, which provides payment to those who are retired, disabled, or are children of deceased workers.
  - *Medicare tax:* This money goes to the Hospital Insurance Trust Fund, which funds Medicare Part A and administration of the Medicare Program.
    - o Medicare is the health insurance program for those 65 and older.
  - *Medicare surtax:* This is an additional tax imposed on those at high income levels.
    - o In 2022, the threshold amount for those filing single is $200,000; for those married filing jointly, it is $250,000.[13]
- ***Other:*** Your state or city may also impose additional taxes.
  - For example, I pay into New York State Family Leave Insurance. The maximum contribution is 0.511% of an employee's pay.[14]

The current tax rate for Social Security is 12.4% total (6.2% for the employer and 6.2% for the employee). This means that the employer pays 6.2% of an employee's income to Social Security and the employee pays the other 6.2%. The current rate for Medicare is 2.9% total (1.45% for the employer and 1.45% for the employee). Similarly, the employer and employee split the obligation.[15]

However, those who are self-employed are obligated to cover *both* the "employer" and "employee" portions of these taxes. The self-employment tax rate is 15.3% total and consists of 12.4% for social security and 2.9% for Medicare.[16]

How to Estimate Your New Pay before Starting a New Job or Receiving a Pay Increase

If you are starting a new job or have received a promotion at work and want to estimate what your pay will be, use a paycheck calculator. I like the free paycheck calculators at SmartAsset.com. You can insert your filing status (single or married), zip code, and any pre-tax or post-tax deductions that you may have.

Example: Glenn's New Pay Glenn was recently offered a new job in New York City with a gross annual salary of $80,000. He would like to know how much to expect as his *net pay* so that he can start planning his monthly budget. Glenn will be paid on a semi-monthly basis—on the 1st and 15th of every month.

His gross paycheck will be $3,333:

$80,000 annual gross salary ÷ 24 paychecks (2 per month) = $3,333 gross paycheck

He uses a paycheck calculator, which provides the following estimates:

Paycheck Estimate for $80,000 Salary in New York City[17]

Taxes	**24.19%**	**$806**
Federal income tax	15.60%	$520
State income tax	5.05%	$168
Local income tax	3.54%	$118
FICA and State Taxes	**7.80%**	**$260**
Social Security	6.20%	$207
Medicare	1.45%	$48
State disability	.04%	$1
State family leave insurance	.11%	$4
Pre-Tax Deductions	**0%**	**$0**
Post-Tax Deductions	**0%**	**$0**
Take-Home Salary	**68.02%**	$2,267

Glenn estimates that his *net* take-home pay will be about $2,267. Although this is only an estimate (he does not yet know how much will be deducted from his pay for health insurance or retirement), he can use this number as a starting point for his budget.

Step 2: Calculate Your Monthly Expenses

In two minutes or less, can you recall how much you spent on groceries last month? How about dining out? Entertainment? What about clothing?

Most people can easily recall their *fixed expenses*—expenses that generally remain consistent, such as rent—but *variable expenses*—those that vary, such as dining out—are tough to recall on a whim.

Review Your Credit and Bank Statements

To determine your monthly expenses, review your credit card and bank statements for the past three months. I know this sounds like a lot but stick with me. When I first started coaching clients, I originally asked them to provide me the amounts for their expenses without consulting the actual source of their spending. Their numbers were usually wildly inaccurate. This is because we tend to underestimate how much we actually spend, particularly on our variable and discretionary expenses.

To have a complete understanding of your spending, go through your paper receipts (if you are a cash user), and credit and debit statements with a highlighter (or different colored pens) and categorize your expenses. You do not need precise categories, but I recommend using at least the following:

- Groceries
- Dining out
- Transportation (e.g., car payment, gas, tolls, parking)
- Household bills (e.g., rent, utilities)
- Personal spending (e.g., entertainment, clothing, beauty)
- Subscriptions

After you have categorized your expenses, add them to obtain a grand total for each category and for each month.

TIP: *This is a great time to review your subscriptions. Subscription-based services have become increasingly popular, and our spending shows it.*[18] *Cancel subscriptions that you no longer value or that you forgot you signed up for!*

Take the Average

Once you have the amounts for your corresponding categories for the past three months, calculate the average amount.

For example:

Category	Month 1	Month 2	Month 3	Average
Groceries	$420	$360	$450	$410
Personal spending	$250	$340	$410	$333

Since our expenses, especially our variable expenses, tend to fluctuate month to month, use the *average* amount when creating your budget (which we discuss in the next chapter).

Step 3: Calculate Your Monthly Savings and Investments

You should have the total balances in your savings and/or investments accounts from when you calculated your assets for your net worth calculation. For this step, write the *monthly* amount that you contribute to these accounts. If you do not have a specific amount that you save or invest each month, review your past three months of contributions and take the average.

When I started my journey, my honest response to this step would be "I don't know" or "$0." I was not saving with intention, and I certainly was not investing. If your answer is similar to what mine was, that is okay. We will discuss saving and investing in detail, including how to incorporate these goals in your money plan.

Step 4: Calculate Your Monthly Debt Payments

Like the previous step, you should have already logged into your debt accounts to determine your total debt balances for your net worth calculation. Now, write down your *monthly* payments for each of your debts.

For example:

Category	Monthly payment
Car note	$300
Credit card 1	$150
Credit card 2	$50
Student loan 1	$300
Student loan 2	$100
Medical debt	$50

Now that you have a solid understanding of your numbers—your net worth and four core monthly figures: (i) income, (ii) expenses, (iii) savings/investments, and (iv) debt—let's get to budgeting!

MEET MELISSA JEAN-BAPTISTE

Melissa Jean-Baptiste is a first-generation Haitian American. She was a full-time educator in New York City public high schools for 11 years, where she tackled and paid off $102,000 in student loans on a teacher's salary. As the creator of the award-winning Millennial in Debt web series, she has pivoted into personal finance coaching and brand consulting. This "Beyoncé of Personal Finance" helps millennials build generational wealth and gain financial freedom in a shame-free digital environment. She can be found at millennialindebt.com and millennialindebt on all social platforms.

Q. You have grown your net worth to over $400,000—most of which you built as a New York City high school teacher. Please tell us how you did this!

A. In 2013, I had a negative net worth, despite not even knowing what a net worth was! At 25 years old, I made my first attempt to purchase a home. It was an unsuccessful endeavor that was both eye-opening and life-changing.

It revealed three things: (i) what the term *debt-to-income ratio* meant, (ii) that my student loan balance was ballooning, and (iii) my net worth. These three things pushed me into super drive as I turned all my attention to paying off my student loans. With each passing year, I paid off one loan in its entirety and watched both my net worth and confidence with money increase. The more debt I got rid of, the more income I was able to use to invest in my 403(b) retirement account, and into savings.

While I was paying off debt, I continued to contribute to my 403(b), increased my savings, and opened an individual brokerage account. I wanted my money working for me in as many ways as possible. In 2018, after making my final loan payment I was also approved for a mortgage for my first home.

After I purchased my home, I continued to invest (on a teacher's salary!) in my 403(b), individual brokerage account, and a Roth IRA. My diversified assets thrived for two main reasons. First, I could contribute

(continued)

(*continued*)

more often because I no longer had student loan debt as a large liability. Second, because I started investing at 22 in my 403(b) retirement account, the time in the market has been tremendously advantageous to my portfolio.

Q. What do you believe has had the greatest impact on growing your net worth?

A. I think what has had the greatest impact on growing my net worth was seeing that negative net worth back in 2013 and realizing just how much of a hindrance my student loans were on so many aspects of my personal finance journey. I wanted to move out of my parents' home, I wanted to buy a home of my own, and I knew that would be next to impossible with a negative net worth.

I started tackling my debt instead of running from it. As my liabilities decreased, my assets increased and pushed my net worth further and further into the positive. Once I finally hit a positive net worth, it really felt like the sky was the limit.

Q. What advice would you give to someone who has a negative net worth and is discouraged by their number?

A. There's so much hype on the internet about having a six-figure net worth. And, of course, it is exciting and worth celebrating. However, it is important to remember that your net worth does not define who you are. Our value and worth as people in society are not tied to a number.

Use your net worth as a tool to help guide your personal finance journey. If it is in the negative, that is okay. It is your starting point, and you can use that as a marker for the pivotal moments in your journey to financial freedom. Your action plan will be based on the steps you find necessary to help you achieve your money goals, and those plans don't have to look like anyone else's. They are yours!

Q. What is generational wealth and why is it so important?

A. In its most basic form, generational wealth is the financial concept of passing down or leaving behind financial security to your beneficiaries. However, I like to think that the generational wealth I am building will have a larger reach to impact future generations as well. This level of generational wealth will provide resources and opportunities for my family for generations to come.

Q. What does *financial freedom* mean to you?

A. *Financial freedom* to me is having the opportunity to live the life I want without being overly fearful or stressed about how my decisions will impact my financial security.

Chapter 5

Choose the Best Budget for You

I lived off $24,000 per year in New York City during law school. Although I did not have an actual written budget, I did something that I call "budgeting lite," which looked as follows:

- Rent: $1,150
- Utilities: $50
- Cable: $100
- Food: $250
- Transportation: $120

I simply listed my main bills and expenses. Because I was more focused on survival, I did not have an actual *plan* for my money. I did not have any clear financial goals nor was I consistently tracking my spending.

From my coaching experience, I have found that this "bill listing" method is what many people call their "budget." This is straightforward and simple to create. It is also a great place to start if you have never budgeted. However, simply listing certain expenses often fails to accurately account for your discretionary and irregular expenses, fails to create a plan for any remaining or extra income that you may receive, and often overlooks financial goals such as saving, investing, and debt payoff.

What Is a Budget?

What comes to mind when you think of the word *budget?* Perhaps you think of the following:

- Restrictive, limiting
- Boring
- Time-consuming

But a budget does not have to be any of those things.

A budget analyzes your income and expenses over a period of time, and allows you to plan for your financial goals. The key word to focus on is *plan*. Instead of wondering where your money went, you are going to tell it exactly where to go. A budget gives you permission to spend on what you value, while getting you closer to your financial goals.

A budget is the foundation for financial freedom.

> **TIP:** *If you do not like the word* budget, *swap it for* money plan. *Call it your money plan!*

Why You Need a Budget

Every year my former law firm hosted a meeting for its associate attorneys. We would join a firmwide video conference from our respective offices across the country to hear from our firm's chairperson or other executive. During the conference, they would deliver a report on the firm's finances. One of the parts that I looked forward to the most (aside from compensation and bonus talk) was the budget breakdown. The annual firm budget allocated funds for various expenses, including compensation, business development, marketing, and overhead. It was refreshing to hear in detail the plans for the firm's revenue and how these expenses would contribute to the firm's growth.

If successful businesses have budgets, why shouldn't you?

If a successful business like my former law firm, your current employer, or perhaps even your own business, has a budget, why shouldn't you have your own? Are your personal finances worth less than those of a multimillion-dollar business? I say no.

When thinking about the money you earned last year, or the tax refund you received last spring, or even that quarterly or annual bonus that you worked so hard for, have you ever thought: "I have no clue where that money went?"

I once had a coaching client who earned over $70,000 a year. She lived at home with her parents, did not have any children, and her bills were relatively low. We started our session by taking an inventory of her numbers, as described in Chapter 4. I vividly remember her expression as she interrupted me to say, "All of that money and I have nothing to show for it." She was ashamed of her lack of savings and investments despite a stable income and no housing expenses.

I explained to her that the underlying issue was that she did not have a plan for her income. Without a clear plan for the money that you earn, you will be left wondering where it all went. I assured her that this is very common, but that it is important to acknowledge our shortcomings so that we can create a plan to move forward.

Once you have a budget established, you will be able to:

- Improve your money management
- Increase savings
- Increase investments
- Efficiently pay off your debt

Types of Budgets

The 50/30/20 Budget: For Those Who Like Rules of Thumb

The 50/30/20 budget is also known as the "proportional" budget because you divide your monthly income into categories based on percentages. This budget was popularized by U.S. Senator Elizabeth Warren[1] and provides that your monthly income be allocated according to the following percentage guidelines:

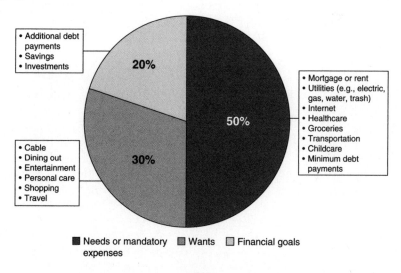

Choose the Best Budget for You

- Needs or mandatory expenses = 50%
  - Mortgage or rent
  - Utilities (e.g., electric, gas, water, trash)
  - Internet
  - Healthcare
  - Groceries
  - Transportation
  - Childcare
  - Minimum debt payments
- Wants = 30%
  - Cable
  - Dining out
  - Entertainment
  - Personal care
  - Shopping
  - Travel
- Financial goals = 20%
  - Additional debt payments
  - Savings
  - Investments

Example: Carolyn's 50/30/20 Budget

Carolyn recently started a new job and earns a gross annual salary of $55,000. Her health insurance premium and retirement contributions are both deducted from her pay pre-tax. Her monthly net income, or take-home pay, is approximately $3,000.

Carolyn likes the 50/30/20 budget's straightforward guidelines and budgets as follows:

Monthly Net Income	$3,000
Needs (50%)	**$1,500**
Rent	$750
Utilities	$50

Monthly Net Income	$3,000
Transportation	$150
Groceries	$250
Cell phone[2]	$50
Credit card minimum payment	$50
Student loan minimum payment	$200
Wants (30%)	**$900**
Personal/fun/entertainment	$300
Dining out	$300
Clothing	$100
Fitness classes	$200
Financial goals (20%)	**$600**
Credit card additional payment	$200
Student loan additional payment	$100
Savings	$300

Pros

- For those looking for guidelines or rules of thumb, this budget might be the one for you!
- Because it is percentage driven, the math is straightforward and simple to apply.
- You have the flexibility of spending 30% on your wants, while also having the assurance that you are allocating 20% of your money to your goals.

Cons

- The recommended percentages may not be realistic for your situation.
  - If you live in an area with a high cost of living, your rent alone may take up a considerable portion of your budget, with your needs exceeding the 50% recommendation.[3]

    Consider Carolyn's preceding budget. Her $750 for rent may not be realistic in an area with a high cost of living, unless she lives with a roommate (or two).
- The 50/30/20 budget places a greater emphasis on wants (30%) than financial goals (20%), which may not align with your plan.

My Tips for a Successful 50/30/20 Budget

- **Honestly distinguish between needs and wants:** A simple way to determine if something is a need or a want is to ask yourself whether you would need to cover that expense in the event of a job loss. For example, groceries would certainly fall under "needs," while dining out would generally fall under "wants."

- **Prioritize your financial goals:** Although you should certainly make room in your budget for wants, I recommend allocating a larger percentage to your financial goals.

  - The early years of your financial freedom journey are critical to laying the foundation for success. If I had allocated a larger percentage of my budget to my wants rather than to my debt payoff, savings, and investing goals early in my journey, I would not have made the progress I have been able to make.

- **Adjust as needed:** The "50/30/20" guideline is a great way to create a structure for your finances, but adjust the percentages to suit your circumstances—for example, 60/20/20, 50/15/35, and so on.

The Zero-Based Budget: For Those Who Like Details

The zero-based, or zero-sum, budget is a budgeting method where you give every dollar that you bring in a specific purpose. All your income is specifically allocated to savings, investments, expenses, and/or debt payments.

The goal is that when you subtract your monthly "spending" (the money that gets directed to your savings, investments, expenses, and debt payments) from your monthly income (the money that you bring in), you are left with zero.

Monthly income – Monthly spending (savings, investments, expenses, and debt payments) = $0

Example: Amira's Zero-Based Budget

Amira has a monthly net income of $4,000. Because she is implementing a zero-based budget, she must give every dollar that she brings in (i.e., all $4,000) a specific purpose. She budgets as follows:

Monthly Net Income	$4,000
Savings/Investments	**$800**
Savings	$500
Investments	$300
Expenses	**$2,500**
Rent	$1,200
Utilities	$100
Cell phone	$100
Transportation	$200
Groceries	$300
Dining out	$250
Personal/fun/entertainment	$100
Clothing	$100
Fitness	$100
Miscellaneous	$50
Debt	**$700**
Credit card	$100
Student loan	$300
Additional debt payment	$300
Monthly income – monthly spending (savings, investments, expenses, and debt) =	**$0**

$4,000 (net income) – $4,000 (savings and investments [$800], expenses [$2,500], and debt [$700]) = $0

Pros

- This budget allows you to make room for your various financial goals, such as saving for an emergency fund or paying off debt, while covering your expenses (e.g., rent and utilities) and enjoying your daily coffee or yoga class.

- Because of the level of detail involved in allocating every dollar to a specific category, this budget allows you to regain control over your money and spending. The days of wondering where our money went are long behind us!

- Because there are no recommended percentages, you can modify the categories and the amounts allocated to align with your individual circumstances and goals.

51

Choose the Best Budget for You

Cons

- This budget requires effort and can be time consuming. It requires you to carefully plan for and track what you are spending so that the budget can balance out, or "zero" out, at the end of the month.
- If you fail to account for irregular expenses, your tightly created budget may not leave much room to cover those expenses.
- It takes time to get used to. The process of zero-based budgeting does not come intuitively to most people. So, if you choose this method, give it at least a few months to get used to.

My Tips for a Successful Zero-Based Budget

- **Be honest with how much to budget for a category:** Do not underestimate your numbers. Doing so will put you at risk of going over budget. Instead, refer to your numbers from Chapter 4 and use the average numbers that you calculated for your past three months of spending as a baseline when creating your budget.
- **Keep a buffer in your bank account:** Because the zero-based budget allocates all your income to specific categories, keeping a buffer in your checking account can protect against overdraft. I recommend keeping anywhere from $500 to $1,000 in your account as a buffer.
- **Always have a "miscellaneous" category:** Something always comes up, so be prepared for the unexpected. Include a miscellaneous category in your budget. I recommend budgeting at least $50 per person in your household whom you financially support—for example, if you are single, budget $50; if you financially support a sibling or child, budget $100.

Let's Get Personal

I have followed a zero-based budget for over five years. To say that I first found budgeting to be a challenge is an understatement. In those early days, the buffer in my checking account kept me from going into overdraft territory. Zero-based budgeting is now second nature to me, but I still like to keep a $1,000 buffer in my checking account.

Reverse Budget: For Those Who Do Not Like to Budget

This may come as a surprise, but not everyone likes to budget. Shocking, I know! If you cannot be bothered with budgeting, do not want to maintain a meticulous spreadsheet, or get dizzy at the thought of tracking every single dollar you spend, I've got you covered. However, to make this method work, we need to do some prep work. Stick with me.

The reverse budget, also known as the "pay yourself first" budget, prioritizes your financial goals. You *first* direct money to your saving, investing, and debt payoff goals, and *then* spend the rest. With this budgeting strategy, instead of making your expenses the focus of your budget, your financial goals become the star of the show.

How to Create a Reverse Budget

Step 1: Assess your monthly cash flow In Chapter 4, you calculated your four core monthly numbers: income, savings/investments, expenses, and debt. If you have not already completed this step, set aside time to review your monthly spending. Doing this will show you whether you need to trim expenses or whether you need to take on an additional income opportunity.

Importantly, this step will show you how much you can realistically direct toward your financial goals while covering your necessary and discretionary expenses.

Step 2: List your financial goals and determine how much you will pay yourself After you have reviewed your monthly cash flow, ask yourself: "What are my money goals?" Perhaps you are working on building an emergency fund, saving for a trip to Costa Rica, or paying off a credit card that you have had for years. Write down your goals with the corresponding amounts that you will direct to these goals monthly.

Add up these amounts. This is the amount you will prioritize every month.

Step 3: **Create a system for your reverse budget** Now that you have identified the amount that you will pay yourself, set up a workflow across your financial accounts to ensure that you stick to your plan.

For example, if you have decided that you will *save $400 monthly* and will send an *additional $100 payment to your credit card debt*, you could do the following:

(i) Set an *automatic* transfer from your biweekly paycheck direct deposit to your savings account for $200 per paycheck ($200 × 2 = $400), and

(ii) Set an *automatic* additional payment of $50 per paycheck ($50 × 2 = $100) to your credit card.

Step 4: Spend the rest Because you have already covered your financial goals, you are now free to spend the rest. You do not need to create specific budget categories or track every dollar that you spend because your financial goals are already covered.

However, to ensure success with this step, I have a few recommendations.

Example: Khalil's Reverse Budget

Khalil earns a monthly net income of $4,000. He has never been much of a budgeter and cringes at the thought of tracking every single dollar he spends. He tries to save what is left over at the end of the month but has found that he is making little progress with his goals. He wants to have better control of his money and decides to implement the reverse budget or "pay yourself first" method.

Step 1: When reviewing his monthly cash flow, Khalil finds that he is overspending on areas like dining out and shopping on Amazon. He is confident that he can reduce this spending by at least 25%.

Step 2: Khalil wants to pay off his credit card balance that has been lingering since college. He also wants to build his emergency fund.

He would like to direct $1,000 each month toward these goals: $400 to his credit card and $600 to his emergency fund.

Step 3: Khalil is paid on the 1st and 15th of every month. He sets up an automatic transfer of $300 per paycheck from his employer to his savings account. This way, he will never even see the money in his checking account! He also sets up an automatic payment of $400 from his checking account to his credit card every 15th of the month.

Monthly income	$4,000
Financial goal #1: emergency fund	$600 (auto transfer of $300 per paycheck)
Financial goal #2: credit card debt	$400 (auto payment of $400 monthly)
Remaining for expenses	**$3,000**

Step 4: Because Khalil has taken care of his financial goals, the remaining $3,000 in his checking account is for him to spend. However, because Khalil has had issues with shopping in the past, he decides to open a **second checking account**.

His *primary checking account* will be for his fixed expenses and bills (rent, utilities, etc.) and the *second checking account* will be for his discretionary spending. This separation will allow Khalil to "spend the rest" with much more ease and confidence.

Pros

- This method prioritizes saving, investing, and other financial goals. Because you are putting yourself first, you can be confident that you are making consistent progress toward your goals.
- You do not need to categorize your various expenditures or carefully track your spending.

Cons

- Because you are free to spend what is remaining, this method may not be ideal for those who have had issues with controlling their spending habits. Even though you are free to spend the rest, you must ensure that you are adequately covering your bills.
- If you are too ambitious and direct too much money to paying yourself first, you could risk overdraft if an unplanned expense comes up and you do not have sufficient funds to cover that expense.

My Tips for a Successful Reverse Budget

- **Automate your "pay yourself first" goals:** To ensure that you are honoring your financial goals, automate the process! As discussed earlier, creating systems at the outset will ensure that you are setting yourself up for success.
  - Take the time to coordinate with your employer's payroll department so that your designated amount goes to, for example, your savings account.
  - If your employer does not offer this option or if you do not work for an employer, set this up yourself with your banks—for example, an automatic transfer every 5th of the month from your checking account to your investment account.
- **Multiple checking accounts:** Have at least two checking accounts— one for your "bill pay" (e.g., rent, utilities, cell phone, debt payments) and another for your "discretionary spending" (e.g., entertainment, dining out, personal).
  - This will give you flexibility with your spending, while creating boundaries so that you do not put your financial obligations at risk.

These are just a few ways that you can budget your money. Find the method that works best for you and your lifestyle. If you are undecided on which will work best, try them each for a month—don't be afraid to experiment!

MEET CARMEN PEREZ

Carmen manages MakeRealCents.com, a personal finance platform dedicated to helping people achieve financial independence and avoid some of her early money mistakes. In 2016, Carmen was sued after defaulting on her student loan. Since then, she has completely transformed her finances and paid off approximately $57,000 of debt in two and a half years. Carmen is currently the CEO of Much, a banking platform for Millennials and Gen-Z.

Q. You paid off $57,000 of debt in less than three years. Tell us about the role that budgeting played in your debt-free journey.

A. Budgeting gave me a sense of control in a situation where I felt helpless. It's scary when you're getting sued for $30,000, and you have less than $3,000 saved. I didn't have a choice but to figure out my finances and get my act together.

    I turned to budgeting and failed many times before getting it down to a science. Once I got good at it, I felt like I had a plan for my money and at least knew where it was all going instead of wondering where it all went, as I had in the past. Once I saw it all on paper, even though I was fighting my way through a mountain of debt, it gave me a sense of peace. It showed me that paying it off was possible, though it might take some time.

Q. Do you still budget now that you are debt-free? What does that look like?

A. I still budget now that I am debt-free. I use the same habits that got me out of $57,000 of debt and apply them to saving money and investing. My budget, aside from adding a line item for our dogs, has remained largely unchanged, but now allows for more fun spending than before. Instead of having a line item for "extra payments toward debt," it says, "extra for savings/investing." Even though I can't always put money toward that line item because I am a new business owner, I still maintain a budget to help keep me organized and honest.

Q. What advice do you have for someone who is struggling with budgeting?

A. Budgeting is not intuitive and generally isn't something you're going to get right on the first try. There are different budgeting frameworks out there for a reason. Different styles for different folks. It takes some trial and error to figure out which one will work best for you.

I encourage you to try them all until you find your secret sauce. You may also have to make modifications and experiment, which is okay! Keep trying, because it's magic for your money when you find something that clicks.

Q. You created a banking platform! Tell us about it and why you decided to create it.

A. We are in the platform's early stages and currently offer an automated zero-based budget for users. We do all the heavy lifting, so you don't have to figure out how to budget. We do that for you based on how you currently spend your money. We will eventually be rolling out checking, savings, and other tools on the platform to help members live their best financial lives.

Q. What does *financial freedom* mean to you?

A. *Financial freedom* to me means more options and less stress. It looks like being able to take financial risks without the fear of losing it all. It means more opportunities to do the things that align with my values and less stress about having to stay at a job that doesn't serve me just to pay the bills.

Budgeting Challenges

When You Are in the Red

After taking inventory of your numbers and creating your budget, you might find that your expenses exceed your income—that is, you are operating in the red.

First, I want to assure you that this is more common than you may think. When I coached clients, I often found that many who were in the red were not even aware that their monthly expenses exceeded their monthly income. This awareness is an important first step in taking corrective measures.

Second, there are two ways to address this:

- Decrease expenses
- Increase income

The solution ultimately comes down to math—you must increase the gap between your income and expenses. To do so, you need to trim your expenses or increase your income. These are much easier said than done, so consider the following suggestions.

Decrease Expenses

As you take inventory of your numbers, identify any expenses that you can cut back on.

The two most common expense categories that I have found to challenge clients are dining out and personal spending/shopping. I never recommend that my clients completely remove these categories from their budgets, because deprivation gets us nowhere. Instead, I recommend that they trim as appropriate and reevaluate.

For example, if you are currently spending $400/month on dining out, cutting this category completely from your budget or allocating a low amount will not set you up for success. Instead, try trimming the category by $50 or $100. At the end of the month, reassess whether your new dining out budget of $350 or $300 is doable.

As you review your expense categories, ask yourself the following:

- Am I overspending in this category?
- Is this a necessary expense?
- Do I value this expense?
- Can I decrease the amount I am spending in this category by $20, $50, $100?

Let's Get Personal

When I started budgeting, I looked for ways to trim my expenses. I reviewed the various charges on my cell phone bill and realized that I was being charged for unnecessary features. With one call to my provider, I reduced my bill by about $30, resulting in annual savings of $360.

I also found myself with more monthly subscriptions than I could count. I had apps on my phone that I no longer used but was being charged for. I unsubscribed from subscriptions that were no longer serving me and simplified my monthly subscriptions to the few that I use on a frequent basis.

Here are just some ways that past clients have reduced their expenses:

- **Rent:** negotiate with landlord by using positive renter history as leverage; move in with a roommate
- **Utilities:** carefully review bill and dispute any unnecessary charges
- **Cable/internet:** downsize package; negotiate a lower rate; cut the cord and opt for a streaming service
- **Cell phone:** call provider and ask if there are any promotions available to their loyal customers and/or identify competitor pricing as leverage during negotiation
- **Groceries:** meal plan/prep; follow budget-friendly cooking inspiration (my personal favorite is Budget Bytes (budgetbytes.com))
- **Dining out:** focus on quality rather than convenience—for example, spend on brunch with a friend but save on takeout by meal prepping or having quick go-to recipes that you can easily make at home
- **Entertainment:** take advantage of free or low-cost events; use websites such as Groupon

Small changes—$30 here, $40 there—can have a significant impact on increasing the gap between your income and expenses.

Increase Income

There is only so much that we can cut back on when it comes to our expenses. Therefore, increasing income is often the most practical way to get out of the red. Ask yourself these questions:

- When was the last time I negotiated my pay or asked for a promotion at work?
- Is it time for me to look for another, higher paying, job?
- Given my current skill set, is there a side hustle that I can take on to supplement my income?

I am a big proponent of looking for ways to increase your income and encourage everyone—regardless of where you are in your journey—to explore ways to do so whether within your current job or elsewhere. We dive into ways to increase your income in Chapter 11.

Budgeting on an Inconsistent Income

Freelancers, independent contractors, or commission-based workers may experience challenges when budgeting because of the unpredictable nature of their income. If this is you, I suggest basing your budget off the *lowest reasonable income* that you can expect in any given month.

If your actual pay for a month is on the low end, then you can rest assured that your income will at least cover your basic expenses.

If your actual pay is on the higher end, then you can direct that extra income toward your financial goals—for example, savings, investments, or additional debt payments.

This conservative approach of budgeting based on the lowest reasonable income will protect you from going over budget.

Example: Jolene's Budget as a Freelancer

Jolene is a freelance graphic artist. Her typical pay is anywhere from $3,000 in a slow month to $5,000 in a busy month.

She opts for the zero-based budget and budgets using $3,000 (the pay she can expect in a slow month) as her base income.

Monthly Budget with Lowest Reasonable Income

Monthly Net Income	$3,000
Savings/Investments	**$800**
Savings	$50
Investments	$0
Taxes	$750
Expenses	**$1,900**
Rent	$1,000
Utilities	$70
Cell phone	$80
Transportation	$250
Groceries	$300
Dining out	$100

Monthly Budget with Lowest Reasonable Income

Monthly Net Income	**$3,000**
Personal/fun/entertainment	$50
Miscellaneous	$50
Debt	**$300**
Credit card	$50
Student loan	$250
Additional debt payment	$0
Monthly income – monthly spending (savings, investments, expenses, and debt) =	**$0**

By budgeting using her lowest reasonable income, Jolene is confident that she can cover her basic expenses and debt payments, even in a slow month.

If the following month turns out to be a higher-income month, Jolene can adjust her budget. She can direct the extra income above her lowest reasonable number to her financial goals and/or other budget categories.

> *TIP: If you are a freelancer or entrepreneur, don't forget to account for taxes! A general rule of thumb is to set aside 25–30% of your income for taxes.[4] I recommend creating a "taxes sinking fund" in your budget. We cover sinking funds in detail in Chapter 7.*

Budgeting for Family

When I was in law school, I was having a conversation with a friend. As we waited for our next class to start, she received a phone notification and shared her relief that her parents had just deposited money in her checking account. She explained that her parents gave her a monthly allowance for food and other incidentals. I masked my jealousy by replying, "Yay, that's so great!"

After I turned 18, and especially after I had graduated college, I never expected my parents to financially support me. To the contrary, financially providing for them has been one of my main motivations throughout my academic and professional career. I am not alone in this. For many children of immigrants or children from low-income backgrounds, our families—both at home and abroad—often rely on us for financial support. It is an honor to provide for our loved ones but, if we are not careful, their reliance or expectation can be a burden on our own goals.

When clients ask how to balance their financial goals with familial obligations, my response is to "put it in the budget." Yes, include "family" or any other "giving" you do as categories in your budget. Make this a part of your money plan. For example, if you help your parents with their electric bill every month, put "parents' electric bill—$100" in your budget.

I once had a client who shared that her mother frequently asked her for money and that these requests made it difficult for my client to make any progress on her financial goals. I first assured her that this is a very common issue that I see in our communities. I next recommended a candid conversation with her mother to establish healthy boundaries. Although these conversations are difficult to have, they are necessary to prevent disagreements or any future resentment with our loved ones.

Consider something like the following:

[Mom/Dad/Grandma/Grandpa], I want to share that I am learning more about personal finance and how to improve my money management. I have created a budget that allows me to cover my expenses, save for my future, and help you. I am happy to help with [blank] expense(s), and wanted to ask what you think is a good amount that I can give you monthly to cover [blank] expense(s)?

They will likely hesitate or not give you a concrete answer. But you can be proactive and respond by explaining what you can cover and suggesting a dollar amount that you can give. For example:

I can cover the electric bill, which is about $100/month. I can give you $100 every first Friday of the month. How does that sound?

By doing this, you will create healthy boundaries for both parties. The discomfort they may experience when asking you for money will lessen and you can have the confidence that the financial assistance you are providing is part of your overall money plan.

How to Stick to Your Budget

The process of budgeting is twofold: *creating* a money plan and *sticking* to that plan. You can create the most attractive budget on the most sophisticated software or in the prettiest notebook with color-coded categories, but it is useless if you are not sticking to it.

Sticking to a budget is not intuitive because our brains do not function the way a calculator does. It is difficult to recall what you spent a few days ago, let alone a few weeks ago. And although you do not need to track every single dollar that you spend (though you certainly could), there are habits that you can incorporate to stick to your budget.

Track Your Spending

Regardless of the budgeting method you choose, track your spending for at least a few months to understand your spending habits. Doing this exercise, especially early into your financial freedom journey, will make you more mindful about your spending moving forward.

Pen and Paper or Spreadsheet

Whether you keep it traditional with pen and paper or opt for a spreadsheet, track the following: (i) how much you spend, (ii) on what, and (iii) when.

Example: Jennifer's Spending Tracker

At the start of the new year, Jennifer purchased a small notebook to track her spending. She created a simple spending tracker, which she checks in with once a day. If she skips a day, for whatever reason, she carves out a few extra minutes the following day to stay on track.

January Spending Tracker

Date	Expense	Amount	Category
January 2	Trader Joe's	$84.90	Groceries
January 5	Amazon	$40.23	Household items
January 6	Electric bill	$120.00	Utilities
January 7	Target	$68.99	Clothing

If you are looking for premade Excel templates or printables, I recommend supporting small business owners on Etsy that offer budget templates and spending trackers, often at a low and reasonable cost. You can also copy the spending tracker template in Chapter 12 into your notebook or software of choice!

Budgeting Apps

Track your budget and spending with a budget app. Here are some popular options:

- **Mint:** This is a free and straightforward app that syncs to your financial accounts. It organizes your spending into budget categories. You can personalize and create limits for your categories.
- **Personal Capital:** Like Mint, Personal Capital is free and syncs to your financial accounts. Its budgeting feature allows users to review their transactions for various categories. It also keeps a record of past spending so that users can easily compare their current data to past months.
- **Every Dollar:** This is a zero-based budget app. There is a free and simple version (which I have used for several years) that allows you to manually track your spending. If you prefer to automatically sync your transactions to the app, there is an upgraded version available at a fee.
- **You Need a Budget (YNAB):** Like Every Dollar, YNAB is a zero-based budget app. This is ideal for the hands-on budgeter. The app provides users with various reports, including spending trends. Although I have not personally used it, it is well rated in the personal finance community. As of this writing, the app has a $14.99 monthly fee and is free to college students for a year.

30-Day Spending Challenge

Try a 30-day spending challenge! For 30 days, record everything you spend. At the end of the challenge, treat yourself to something fun like brunch at your favorite restaurant.

Let's Get Personal

I started tracking my spending during my debt-free journey because I needed accountability on how I was spending my money. Although it took some getting used to, I became more mindful about my spending habits and started having a better outlook on my purchasing decisions.

I took a few minutes each day to track my spending—usually on my commute or as soon as I got home. I would ask myself: "What did I spend money on today? How much did it cost?" Rather than leaving this task for the end of the week and risking forgetting about my various purchases, I did it every day. This only took a few minutes because I never had more than a handful of transactions to record on any given day. This made the spending tracking habit much easier to build.

Think of it this way:

If you have two minutes for social media, you have two minutes for your financial future.

Mic drop. Track your spending—at least through a 30-day spending challenge! You've got this.

Date Your Money

Regardless of your budgeting style, set a monthly budget date and put it in your calendar. You can schedule this date with yourself, your partner, and/ or other family members. Grab a snack, a fun beverage, put on some music, and carve out at least one hour at the end of each month to (i) review your budget for the month and (ii) plan for the next month.

During your budget date, review your spending and—depending on your preferred budgeting method—reconcile your spending with your budgeted amounts, and check in with your money goals.

During your meeting ask yourself:

- How do I feel about this month's spending?
- Am I struggling with overspending in any of my budget categories?
- Do I need to modify any of my categories?
- Did I meet my saving/investing/debt payoff goal for the month?

Next, plan for the following month. Review next month's calendar and ask yourself:

- What upcoming events do I have (e.g., birthdays, weddings, dinners)?
- How much should I budget for these events?

- Do I need to modify my budget categories for those areas? If so, by how much?
- Do I have any large expenses that I should budget for (e.g., car registration, day camp deposit, annual membership)?

Once you have answered these questions, create your budget for the upcoming month.

Before you know it, your monthly budget dates will become a *habit* that you look forward to. These regular check-ins with your money will make you more intentional about your spending and exhibit the progress you are making on your financial goals.

My Top Tips for Those Who Have Trouble Sticking to a Budget

Budgeting does not come naturally to most. When I first started budgeting it took me several months to get used to. I found myself constantly going over budget. But I persisted. Since then, I have picked up a few tips.

- **Be realistic with your budgeted amounts:** One of the most common mistakes is being overly aggressive and budgeting too little or too much.
  - *Budgeting too little:* For example, during your financial inventory, you realize that you are spending about $500 monthly on shopping. You decide to cut your budget by 90% and budget $50 for shopping. This sudden deprivation could discourage you and cause you to quit budgeting before giving it a real chance.

    Instead, try cutting your spending in that category by 25% or 30%, and then reevaluate.
  - *Budgeting too much:* You are very ambitious and budget $1,000 for savings, which leaves you with a tight budget for your other expenses.

    Instead, try budgeting a manageable amount (such as $400 or $500) and work your way toward your $1,000 monthly savings goal.

Be honest with your budget and remember that slow and steady habits are more effective than sudden drastic changes.

- **Separate bank accounts:** Keep two checking accounts—one for your bills and necessary expenses and another for your discretionary and personal spending.
  - This allows you to easily see how much you have available in your personal spending account while having the confidence that your necessary expenses are being covered by your other account.
  - Note that these accounts can be with the same bank.
- **Use cash envelopes for discretionary categories:** Identify your "problem" categories—for example, dining out, shopping, entertainment. Assign a specific amount for that category and use an envelope to hold the allocated cash for that category. Once the funds in your envelope run out, that is it for the month. Start fresh the following month.
  - By limiting your spending to the amount available in your cash envelope, you can slowly develop healthier habits with your spending.
  - For those who do not use cash or prefer a digital option, try a virtual envelope system with an app like Goodbudget. The app has a free version that includes 10 envelopes or a paid version ($7/month as of this writing) that includes unlimited envelopes.
- **Automate your financial goals:** Automation is key. Set up automatic transfers to your savings and investments and autopayments to your bills and debts to ensure that you are prioritizing them.
- **Create sinking funds:** Sinking funds are created to save for large or irregular expenses.
  - For example, if you have a trip in five months and expect to spend $1,000, budget and save $200 per month in a "travel sinking fund." We cover sinking funds in detail in Chapter 7.

Let's Get Personal

Why I Still Budget Even after Becoming Debt-Free

When I started my financial freedom journey, I was immediately drawn to the zero-based budget. It gave me the level of detail and discipline that I desperately needed at the time. Years after becoming debt-free, I still budget the same way I did when I started my journey, mainly because I am naturally a spender *and* I have big financial goals. My budget allows me to balance the two.

(continued)

(continued)

> Budgeting gives you the permission to unapologetically spend on what you value. Want to travel? Put it in your budget. Love splurging on fancy restaurants? Put it in your budget. Want to retire early and become financially independent? Put it in your budget.
>
> Knowing that I can spend guilt-free because my budget is simultaneously ensuring that I reach my financial goals is the biggest reason why I have successfully maintained my budget habit.

A solid budget makes room for your everyday spending *and* your financial goals. So, experiment and discover what is best for you and your lifestyle. And remember to pace yourself—take it one month at a time.

MEET MARC RUSSELL

Marc is a foster child turned financial educator. Coming from a low-income family, he put himself through college and paid off $80,000 in debt after graduating. Marc's work has been featured in CNBC, *Time* magazine, Bankrate, Bloomberg: Quicktakes, and *Business Insider*. He is the face behind the BetterWallet social media channel.

Marc spent much of his career at two of the largest financial institutions in the world, where he consulted thousands of households on how to manage their money the right way. Now, the owner and founder of BetterWallet, LLC, Marc teaches people all around the world how to put their money to work.

Q. You went from foster care to Wall Street to financial educator. Can you share the impact that your upbringing had on your financial journey?

A. My childhood had a huge impact on my financial journey. In foster care, you are constantly bouncing from foster home to foster home, group home to group home. Though there was plenty of trauma that came from 13 years of instability, I learned a great deal about different people and different cultures. During this time, I learned how to quickly connect and relate to total strangers—strangers who didn't know who I was, didn't know my background, and oftentimes didn't share my same culture.

When I was finally adopted, I was adopted into a lower-income, small-town family with limited finance acumen. Fast-forward five years, and I went from a small high school to one of the largest college campuses in the country. My strength of relatability helped me build strong relationships on campus and eventually build enough relationships to self-fund my college education.

It didn't stop there. Being able to easily relate to others paid dividends when trying to network my way into a Wall Street firm. This eventually helped me land my first corporate job with The Vanguard Group.

Relatability helped me network with complete strangers online and these same strangers taught me how to budget, pay off debt, and take my passion full-time!

Q. You paid off $80,000 of debt. First, congrats! Second, what role did budgeting have on your financial goals, particularly debt payoff?

A. Budgeting was critical to my debt-free journey. As a kid who didn't come from means, I learned plenty of poor money habits growing up. The only thing I knew about money was how to spend it. Budgeting (specifically zero-based budgeting) helped me build a plan for my hard-earned dollars and put me in the driver seat.

What I love about zero-based budgeting is that you don't have anywhere to hide. Because you are giving *every* dollar a job, if you overspend in one specific category, you have to pull dollars from another category to make up for it. So, for example, if I overspend on restaurants for the month, I'd have to pull funds from my "new clothes" envelope. Doing this held me accountable.

Since I was giving every dollar a job, I could also be more purposeful with paying off my $80,000 of debt. Every two weeks, I had a line item that told me how much money was going to debt payments. Since I knew how much was going to debt, I could do the math and calculate when my debt-free date would be. It was a domino effect.

I can honestly say that budgeting completely changed my financial trajectory.

(continued)

(continued)

Q. What are some of the common mistakes that you see people make with budgeting?

A. One common mistake I see with budgeting is that we forget to budget for variable expenses. Variable expenses include going out to eat, shopping, vacations, and so on. Instead, we budget for our fixed expenses/bills because most of the time we are contractually obligated to pay them. Then, any leftover money we call "spending money."

   This is something I had to unlearn as well. Frankly, not budgeting my "spending money" led to more overdraft fees than I'd like to admit.
   Over time, I learned how to budget for my variable expenses (give every dollar a job) and that made a world of difference.

Q. Your Instagram bio says that you combine culture with financial tips. What does that mean and why is it important?

A. Personal finance can be super dry and boring (unless you're a finance nerd like Cindy and me). To spice it up a notch, I try to balance my finance tips with a little bit of humor and culture.

   For example, loaning money to friends and family is a kind deed but sometimes it can leave you in a financial hole. On my platform, instead of simply providing tips to help people manage this situation, I instead will offer financial tips while highlighting that "one cousin" we *all* have who periodically asks you for $20 until they get paid in a few weeks. Mixing in culture helps make the financial tips more real and (mostly importantly) helps the audience take action.

Q. What does *financial freedom* mean to you?

A. Growing up, oftentimes, spending money in one category meant less money in another. Want to get a new car because your current car breaks down once a week? You have to think about how that new car note will impact your rent payments. Want to take your sister out to dinner after she received a promotion? How will this impact your cell phone payments? Want to go to college and make a better life for yourself? How will this impact your parents, who are barely putting food on the table?

   Financial freedom means moving freely in life without having to think about the financial domino effect. I'm blessed to say that I reached my own version of financial freedom and I'm on a mission to help others do the same!

Chapter 6

Become a Conscious Consumer

For the longest time, I considered shopping a hobby. This pastime started when I got my first job at the Bronx Zoo at the age of 16. I worked for the membership sales department and my pay was based on my hourly rate (I believe it was $7/hour at the time) and commissions. At the end of each shift, my coworkers and I split the commissions, which were based on the number of memberships we sold that day. The more memberships we sold, the more money we made. A bigger paycheck meant I had more to spend on clothes and shoes. The spending habit I developed crept into my college and law school years.

In my freshman year at Stony Brook University, I learned there wasn't much to do on campus during the weekends, but the campus bus was available to take students to the mall. My best friend and I both had on-campus jobs, which meant that we had a paycheck to spend. Paychecks were for spending, not for saving. We knew our way around the nearby Smith Haven Mall like the back of our hand. After visiting our favorite stores—Forever 21, Wet Seal, H&M, Macy's—we would wrap up our trip at the food court, or The Cheesecake Factory if we felt fancy.

In law school, my spending habit spiraled. My law school classmates were different from my college friends—many had trust funds, an allowance from grandparents, or had worked prior to law school and had some type of savings. I wanted to keep up with my new group of friends. However, I had no disposable income. Because of the demands of law school, I did not have a job during the academic year. I was exclusively living off my student loans and had little to no money to spend on discretionary items. This meant that any nonessential purchases went on my credit cards. Fast fashion purchases were frequent, without any regard for the planet or my wallet.

When I started my career as an attorney, payday meant a trip to Sephora and the many stores on Fifth Avenue—Saks, Jimmy Choo, and J. Crew, to name a few. I browsed, shopped to my heart's content, and impulsively purchased unnecessary items at the checkout line. I ignored my six-figure debt while convincing myself that I deserved to buy these things.

It has taken me years to shift from the mentality of a shopper to that of a mindful spender. Regardless of where you fall on the spending spectrum, we can all improve our finances by becoming more conscious consumers. Let's explore what that looks like.

Consumerism in America

Many experts date the origins of American consumerism as we know it to World War II. The technological improvements that allowed for mass production during the war helped America's economy overcome the Great Depression. The return of American soldiers, an increase in job opportunities, and higher wages created optimal conditions for young adults with a desire to spend. Federal programs, including the G.I. Bill of Rights, allowed young and growing families to purchase homes, cars, televisions, and home appliances.[1] Participating in this consumerism resulted in praise "as a patriotic citizen in the 1950s, contributing to the ultimate success of the American way of life."[2]

A glaring omission from this 1950s idyllic version of American consumerism are non-White people.[3] For example, the G.I. Bill was denied to more than a million Black World War II veterans.[4] Lawmakers engaged in countless tactics to ensure that the New Deal, a series of programs, projects, financial reforms, and regulations enacted by President Franklin D. Roosevelt between 1933 and 1939, benefited as few people of color as possible.[5]

Notwithstanding this historical context, we know that at present two things are true. First, non-White people have more buying power[6] than ever before. Blacks, Asians, Hispanics, and Native Americans have a combined buying power of $3.9 trillion.[7] Second, the power of advertising has significantly increased over the past decades. During the 1950s, the rise of television in American homes meant that advertisers had a new way to reach Americans to promote their products.[8] Since then, the time the average American spends in front of a screen has dramatically increased, especially in the era of social media.

An increase in buying power across all racial groups in an increasingly diverse society and accessibility to advertisements create perfect conditions for more consumption. However, the root of consumerism goes beyond the advertisements we are fed daily. Consumerism is also based on the competition that we have among ourselves. In a *Vox* article titled "Why Do We Buy What We Buy?" sociologist Juliet Schor states:

> We have a society which is structured so that social esteem or value is connected to what we can consume. And so the inability to consume affects the kind of social value that we have. Money displayed in terms

Overcoming Debt, Achieving Financial Freedom

of consumer goods just becomes a measure of worth, and that's really important to people.[9]

Schor takes the view that "marketers have less to do with what we want than, say, our neighbors, coworkers, or the people we follow on social media." The phrase "keeping up with the Joneses"—our desire to emulate what our neighbors have or do[10]—may come to mind.

Our reference groups—those we compare ourselves to and identify with—impact our consumerism and have significantly changed over the decades. Just a few decades ago, our reference groups were limited to our neighbors (the Joneses) and perhaps our work colleagues. However, largely thanks to social media, our current reference groups go beyond our immediate circles and include celebrities and influencers who are paid to promote lifestyles and products that are unrealistic, unnecessary, and/or not within our budgets.

Despite the global COVID-19 pandemic (over two years in as of the time of this writing), Americans are spending more than ever.[11] The rise in consumerism, and the often-accompanying consumer debt, undoubtedly impact our financial goals. So, how can we become more conscious consumers, without deprivation? Here are four strategies that have helped me.

Practice Value-Based Spending

As we discussed in the previous chapter, budgeting gives you the permission to spend on what you *value*. Value-based spending is the practice of spending on what is important to *you*. If you do not value something—that is, it does not matter to you—then do not spend money on it (or spend little). When we adapt value-based spending, we become intentional consumers by allowing our personal values to guide our spending decisions.

Adapting value-based spending is especially important given our era of online shopping. Advances in technology allow us to purchase goods with the click of a button thanks to algorithms that study our preferences, stored payment information at our favorite websites that ensures a seamless checkout process, and the promise of fast shipping.

Let's look at a former client of mine, "Julia." During our coaching session, we discovered that Julia was spending $300 on beauty and over $200 on Amazon monthly. Her instinct was to dramatically cut back on both categories. I advised against that. Drastically cutting back could be counterintuitive because if Julia started feeling deprived, she would be less likely to stick to her budget. Instead, I asked her to review her individual transactions and to describe how she felt about those purchases.

Her personal spending included a biweekly nail appointment that cost $100 with tip. She explained that her nail appointment was her time to unwind and relax and that she genuinely enjoyed keeping up her nails, especially for her client-facing work setting. On the other hand, her Amazon purchases were usually from boredom or late-night internet browsing. Her bathroom and kitchen were full of gadgets that she never used. Ultimately, we kept her beauty budget as it was but cut her Amazon budget in half.

How to Practice Value-Based Spending

1. Review your credit and debit card transactions for the past three months (you did this in Chapter 4!). If you are short on time, at least review the past month.

2. Make a list of things that you value and things that you do not. To determine whether you value something, ask yourself:

   a. Is this important to me?

   b. How does this make me feel?

   c. Does this get me closer to the type of life I want to build?

3. Budget for what you value and cut out the rest.

4. Spend guilt free! Your budget functions as your spending plan, so if something is within your budget, give yourself the permission to spend on that without hesitation.

Let's Get Personal

How I Practice Value-Based Spending

As a natural spender, shifting my mindset from "budgets are boring and restrictive" to "my budget gives me the permission to spend on this" has been transformative. Value-based spending means asking myself whether I truly care about something that I am tempted to purchase.

When I go out to eat, I do not usually spend money on drinks. Here in New York City, a drink can cost anywhere from $12 to $25. But the cost alone is not the main driver of my decision to opt for a water with lemon. I personally do not value drinking the way that others may. But I do value food and trying new dishes, which is why I will almost always order an appetizer or dessert with my meal. If I gave into the societal pressure of ordering a fancy drink (or multiple drinks) with my meal even though it

---

Overcoming Debt, Achieving Financial Freedom

is not something that I care for, I would be spending in a way that does not align with my values.

Here is a list of other things that I do and don't spend money on.

Things I spend money on	Things I do not spend money on
Designer bags	New cars
A well-rated hotel	First- or business-class airplane seats
Michelin star restaurants	Takeout (a rare purchase in my household)
High-quality, whole foods	Expensive beauty products or treatments
Quality furniture	Seasonal home decor

Create your own list that reflects your personal values! By mindfully spending on what you value, you can spend on your lattes, manicures, or sneakers, while achieving your financial goals.

Embrace Minimalism (or Minimalism-ish)

After I graduated law school and assimilated into my role as a junior attorney, I came to the stark realization that I owned way too much stuff. I lived in a small studio apartment and had enough possessions to fill a spacious one-bedroom apartment. My closets did an excellent job at concealing my books, papers, linens, unused body care products, clothing, handbags, and over 50 pairs of shoes.

Marie Kondo's book *The Life-Changing Magic of Tidying Up: The Japanese Art of Decluttering and Organizing* had been gaining popularity, so I decided to purchase it. In it, the author teaches how to effectively get rid of the accumulating clutter in our homes by discarding, cleaning, and organizing. Importantly, the book teaches how to be intentional with the items you choose to keep and bring into your home.

That book changed my life. After reading it, I conducted a thorough declutter of my 400-square-foot apartment. I donated and tossed several large trash bags full of more than half of my shoe collection. The effects were instant. Not only was my physical space clearer, so was my mind. I felt calmer, more at peace.

Less stuff → less to clean and maintain → less stress

I implemented the book's teachings by regularly asking myself whether a purchase would serve a purpose and add value to my life.

■ ■ ■

Before we define *minimalism*, let's get clear on what it is not. Minimalism is not about owning a specific number of items or owning as few things as possible. It is not a plain white and gray aesthetic (although, if that's your style, please by all means incorporate it into your home design). Minimalism is not about restricting ourselves or rejecting consumerism in its entirety.

Instead, "[m]inimalism is a tool to rid yourself of life's excess in favor of focusing on what's important—so you can find happiness, fulfillment, and freedom."[12] It is about being intentional with what you own or bring into your life. Minimalism runs against our society's obsession with consumption by encouraging us to be mindful about our life's choices, including our everyday purchases.

Declutter

A great way to embrace minimalism is to declutter your space. Decluttering is the process of getting rid of (donating or discarding) items that no longer serve a purpose. When we declutter our space, we must decide whether to hold onto or let go of our belongings.

Decluttering's benefits go beyond a tidier space. Decluttering:

- Reveals how much stuff you have
- Reveals how much stuff you do not use
- Allows you to rediscover items you love but have neglected
- Reminds you to use up items before your next purchase (I'm looking at those unburned candles and unused lotions accumulating in your closet)
- Frees up both your physical and mental space
- Helps you save money by not buying duplicates of things you already own
- Makes cleaning your home a lot easier (less stuff → less maintenance → less stress)

Five Steps to Declutter Your Home

1. **Set aside time to declutter:** Decluttering takes time. If you have never decluttered your home, carve out at least a few hours across

a few days. Write down your planned time blocks in your planner or calendar to ensure that you honor your commitment.

- Pace yourself. Cramming an entire home declutter in one day will likely burn you out, which will lead you to resent the process or give up. Set a realistic time frame with a deadline to complete your declutter—for example, "I will declutter my home over the next 30 days or before I leave on my vacation in six weeks."

2. **Create a declutter game plan:** Determine how you will declutter your home. I recommend doing so by room.

- For example, "One day I will focus on my kitchen, the next day I will declutter the bathroom, the next day my office, and so on."

3. **Clear out and clean the area:** To effectively declutter, clear out the space in its entirety.

- For example, if you are decluttering your kitchen, this means completely emptying your cabinets and junk drawer. This is also a perfect time for a deep clean.

4. **Create three piles: (1) keep, (2) donate, and (3) toss (recycle, if possible):** Instead of placing everything back in its place, review each item and ask yourself: "Does this add value to my life?" Marie Kondo recommends asking yourself, "Does this item spark joy?" I prefer asking whether something adds value because utilitarian items such as utensils seldom spark joy (for me, at least).

- Now is also a good time to check the expiration dates on consumables and to toss expired items.

TIP: Skincare and makeup products usually have a small period-after-opening symbol on the back of the product with the item's lifetime after opening, such as 12 months, 24 months.

---

5. **Give everything a home:** All your items should have a home. If something does not have a home, it will cause clutter.

- Use storage solutions that you already have or get creative by repurposing items you already own. Only purchase storage items as needed and make sure that it is functional and not just for aesthetic purposes.

If a full-blown minimalist lifestyle is not for you, consider adapting aspects or principles of minimalism—call it minimalism-lite or minimalism-ish.

77

For example, if the thought of an entire home declutter overwhelms you, start small! Declutter your nightstand, the junk drawer in your kitchen, or your medicine cabinet. Small progress is still progress.

Calculate Cost per Use

Clearing our space of clutter is a great first step. But, in an ever-increasing consumeristic society, we must also pay attention to what we bring into our homes. This is why I recommend creating your own rules to guide your purchasing decisions. One of my guiding rules/questions is: *What is this item's cost per use?*

Cost per use (CPU) is an analysis that goes beyond simply looking at an item's price. Instead, you evaluate the price *and* how much use you will get out of the item.[13] CPU follows a simple formula:

Cost of the item ÷ Number of times you expect to use it = Cost per use

Example: Kate's New Laptop

Kate needs a new laptop. After some browsing, she finds the perfect one for $1,200. Her past laptops typically have lasted around five years. She uses her laptop at least five times per week. The number of times she expects to use her laptop is 1,300 (5 times per week × 52 weeks × 5 years). Her CPU is as follows:

$$\$1,200 \div 1,300 \text{ uses} = \$0.92$$

Kate's CPU for a new laptop is less than $1! Satisfied with this number, she decides it is a smart purchase.

Example: My Sister's KitchenAid Stand Mixer

An item's CPU is unique to the purchaser.

My sister has a KitchenAid Stand Mixer, which retails for about $400. She is an avid baker and has used her stand mixer at least 120 times over the past five years (that's about twice per month).

My sister's KitchenAid Stand Mixer CPU:

$$\$400 \div 120 \text{ uses} = \$3.33$$

I, on the other hand, typically limit my baking to the holidays (around four times a year, at most). My expected CPU for a KitchenAid Stand Mixer would therefore be significantly higher.

My expected KitchenAid Stand Mixer CPU:

$$\$400 \div 20 \, uses = \$20$$

A beautiful stand mixer on my kitchen counter is not only impractical in my small New York City kitchen, but the CPU is not worth it to me. Instead, my $30 electric hand mixer does the job and suits my needs just fine.

Cost per Wear

Cost per wear (CPW) is CPU's sibling and applies to items you wear (e.g., clothes, bags, shoes):

Cost of the item ÷ Number of times you expect to wear it = Cost per wear

---

Let's Get Personal

In college, I often purchased inexpensive dresses and shoes that I would wear one or two times before getting rid of them. Now, I invest in higher quality items that I know will last for years. Let's compare inexpensive party shoes that I bought in college to one of my current favorite sandals.

A pair of inexpensive, uncomfortable party shoes that I wore just a few times:

$$\$30 \, (total \, cost) \div 3 \, (wears) = \$10$$

My favorite Tory Burch sandals that I have owned for six years and wear every summer and on vacation (about 20 wears each year: 20 wears × 6 years = 120 wears):

$$\$200 \, (total \, cost) \div 120 \, (wears) = \$1.67$$

Calculating your next purchase's CPU or CPW conserves your resources—time, energy, physical/mental space, and money. Experiment with this simple formula the next time you make a purchase.

Curate Your Wardrobe

One noteworthy industry that has significantly benefited from American consumerism at the expense of our environment is fashion. The fashion industry's impact on our environment is alarming. It accounts for nearly 10% of global carbon emissions and 20% of wastewater.[14] In fact, the fashion industry takes up more energy than the aviation and shipping industries *combined*.[15] Every year, microfibers—equivalent to 50 billion plastic bottles—are dumped into the ocean. Because these microfibers cannot be extracted from water, they spread throughout our food chain.[16]

A principal driver of this environmental impact is overconsumption. The fashion industry encourages customers to keep up with trends and purchase new items per microseason.[17] The average person buys 60% more clothing than he or she did in 2000.[18] Yet, only 40% of clothing that is purchased gets used.[19] This means that most of the clothes that we purchase are discarded, many of which end up in our landfills.

Capsule Wardrobe

One way that I have become more conscious about clothing is by adopting a capsule wardrobe. A capsule wardrobe is a curated wardrobe with versatile pieces that complement each other. Some equate capsule wardrobes to a uniform. As someone who attended Catholic school for 13 years, I assure you that capsule wardrobes allow for much more versatility than an ordinary uniform. In fact, the argument that we should aspire to wear the same pair of pants and shirt the way [insert name of billionaire] does makes me cringe. I like variety!

A capsule wardrobe consists of items that you love, that flatter your body, that make you feel confident, and that reflect your personality and style. It saves you money because you are not purchasing items for the sake of fulfilling an imaginary void. It also removes decision-making fatigue. Instead of wasting time thinking, "I have nothing to wear today," you know that you have your go-to looks that you can effortlessly pull together.

Because I live in New York City, I rotate my capsule wardrobe seasonally. For example, my summer capsule includes T-shirts, tank tops, dresses, and sandals, whereas my winter capsule includes sweaters, coats, and boots. Although there is no rule for the number of items to include in your capsule, mine typically includes 30–40 items (clothes and shoes included). 80% of my wardrobe consists of everyday items; 20% is reserved for special occasion and trendy items.

Five Steps to Create Your Capsule Wardrobe

1. **Gather all your clothing:** Take everything out of your closets, dressers, and storage. If you have clothes in multiple rooms in your home, pick a designated location to gather your items. This may seem overwhelming, but it is worth the effort.

2. **Sort your clothing:** Sort your items into these piles:

   - **Keep:** These are items that you love and that fit you and your lifestyle.

   - **Maybe:** These are items that you like but do not necessarily love. Items with tags (we all have them) should go in this pile. Store these in a box or shopping bag. Give yourself a deadline by when to wear these items—for example, "If I do not wear these items in the next 60 days, I will sell or donate them."

   - **Sell:** Let go of items that no longer fit you or your taste. You can list your items on secondhand websites like Poshmark, ThredUp, Tradesy, or The RealReal. This is also a great way to make extra cash. My general rule of thumb with reselling clothes is that if an item has not sold in 60 days, donate it.

   - **Donate:** Donate to local shelters, foster homes, churches, or secondhand shops. Schedule time for your drop-off, so that your donation bags do not linger in your home.

   - **Toss:** This last-resort pile should be reserved for clothing that is damaged or badly stained.

3. **Organize your "keep" items:** Put everything in your "keep" pile back in your closet or dresser. Store any seasonal items.

4. **Evaluate your wardrobe:** Take a moment to review what you have kept.

   - What do you like?
     - Notice the types of styles, fabrics, and colors that you gravitate toward. For example, when I first created my capsule wardrobe, I realized how much I love simple silhouettes, as well as neutral colors and blues. Something you will not find much of in my closet: loud prints, florals, and warm colors. Don't be afraid to get honest about your *personal* style!

   - What do you need?
     - Are you missing a little black dress? Do you need a new pair of running sneakers? Do you need a new everyday work bag?

5. **Stick with it:** The next time you are tempted to make a spontaneous purchase, ask yourself whether this item complements your current capsule wardrobe, what void it would be filling, and of course calculate the cost per wear! This way, you can add new pieces, including trendy items, but you will do so more mindfully.

Note that there is also no rule for what colors, item types, or style to include in your capsule wardrobe. A mom who works in an office is going to have a different wardrobe than a full-time graduate student.

Sustainable Fashion Efforts

Regardless of whether a capsule wardrobe is right for you, as consumers, we can all work toward more sustainable efforts. Consider the following:

- **Focus on quality rather than quantity:** Quality does not have to mean expensive!
  - Look at the fabric label: Natural materials such as cotton, wool, leather, and silk often last longer and have less of an environmental impact than synthetic fabrics.
  - Look at the stitching: Gently tug at the fabric and notice whether there are loose threads.
- **Do your research:** Before supporting a brand, take a moment to research their sustainability efforts. Consumers are increasingly holding brands accountable, which has led to the growing popularity of "slow fashion" brands such as Everlane, ABLE, and The Curated.
- **Rent:** Instead of buying a new dress for your friend's wedding that you will only wear once, rent from companies like Rent the Runway or Armoire.
- **Follow a "one in, one out" rule:** If you are going to purchase something new, get rid of something similar from your closet.
- **Shop secondhand:** Consider thrift shops or online secondhand websites.
- **Clothing swaps:** These events are a great way to freshen up your wardrobe while giving your items a new home. Be sure to create a plan for any items that go unclaimed, such as donating to a local shelter.
- **Repair your clothing:** Before letting go of an item because of a lost button or broken zipper, repair it! For just $8, my local tailor repaired a hole in one of my favorite wool sweaters. Good as new.

- **Remove your credit card information from your favorite websites:** Increase the friction between you and a purchase. This barrier gives you the time to consider whether something is worth the cost.
- **Wear your clothes:** Groundbreaking, I know. But consider this: "the average number of times a piece of clothing is worn decreased by 36% between 2000 and 2015. In the same period, clothing production doubled."[20] I'll say it again: wear your clothes.

Let's Get Personal

A few years ago, I spotted a denim jacket at a store for $120. A quick Google searched revealed that the same jacket was listed as preowned but "like new" for $40 on Poshmark. Years later, that jacket is still a staple in my spring/summer capsule wardrobe.

Consuming less and differently has a significant impact on our environment, and our pockets.

Meet Brittany Polanco

Brittany is a work-from-home parent of one in Hudson Valley, New York. She is passionate about simple living, minimalism, and childhood development. Since becoming a parent, she has homed in on how the three relate to help lead a more fulfilling life.

Q. What does *minimalism* mean to you? Would you describe yourself as a minimalist?

A. *Minimalism* to me is being, owning, and doing what truly makes you happy. It's consciously deciding not to fall into the trap of what you "should" have and instead having what genuinely fits you and your lifestyle. I would describe myself as a minimalist. But that's not to say that I own little to nothing. Rather, I am happy with what I have because it serves a purpose for my family's lives.

(continued)

Q. You have lived in some of the most expensive parts of the country (New York and California). How do you curb the temptation to spend and acquire material possessions?

A. Curbing the temptation to spend on material possessions is difficult, especially when you've grown up in a culture where having nice, designer things is what people strive for—which there's absolutely nothing wrong with, if that's what you enjoy. But I have found that figuring out who I am, and remaining true to that, has stopped my mindless consumption. I ask myself, "Do I want this because I've seen someone else with it? Or would it add value to the life I intend to lead?"

Q. What role has conscious consumerism played on your money journey?

A. Being a conscious consumer is something that anyone can benefit from. When I stopped impulse buying and took the time to consider our purchases, it made a huge impact on our finances. I didn't "need" as much money as I thought I did because I wasn't buying things I hadn't needed or even wanted in the first place. Inadvertently, that trickled into a new feeling of freedom for my family. Since I have been able to curb mindless consumption, I can work less and stay home with our son. Less consumption has led to less clutter, more money, and more freedom.

Q. I am truly impressed by how you have incorporated minimalism in your everyday life, especially as a wife and as mom to a young child. What are some ways that individuals and parents can adapt minimalism in their day-to-day lives?

A. Ask yourself what your values are, not what society or your peers expect. Ask yourself what is truly important to you. How are the things you are buying adding value to your life? Do they align with who you are? Stay true to those values daily, especially when making purchases. Also, ensure that your new items will have a place in your home. Parents have so much on their plate already. The mental load is real and to add clutter from things that don't bring you joy doesn't make your life any easier. In fact, it does you a disservice. There is so much calm in a clear space for yourself and for your children.

Q. What does *financial freedom* mean to you?

A. Before becoming a mom I thought *financial freedom* meant having enough money to retire and never needing to work again. Now I believe that *financial freedom* means having the ability to work less while still being able to meet financial goals. We aren't living the lavish lifestyle we see in the media, but we know that life wasn't for us anyway. We've learned to want for less but are happier overall because what truly matters to us is raising our family on our terms. That's what freedom means to me.

Chapter 7

Save with a Purpose

My dad has always stressed the importance of saving money. *Cindy, hay que ahorrar* (Cindy, you must save), he would say. Although his advice was well-founded, it took me decades to understand *why* and *how* to properly save.

Does any of this sound familiar?

- You tell yourself that you will save whatever is left at the end of the month. The end of the month rolls around and you either (i) did not save at all or (ii) saved less than you wanted.

- You have ambitious moments where you deposit a significant amount into your savings account but find yourself chipping at that amount with frequent withdrawals.

- You consider your savings account similar to your checking account.

- You are not a stranger to bank fees (e.g., failing to maintain the minimum required balance in your savings account).

- You do not create annual or monthly savings goals.

- You sometimes question your savings efforts, perhaps wondering: what is the point of this?

- You hoard money in your savings account and hesitate to spend it because of fear, your upbringing, a previous experience, or because you simply do not know what to do with it.

- You have had your savings account with the same bank for years, without any real thought as to whether that bank is the best option for you.

For most of college and law school, I used the same savings account that my dad helped me open when I was in high school. You might assume that by the time I graduated law school (at age 26), I had built a sizable savings cushion, right? Wrong. Here is what would inevitably happen to my money:

- I would transfer what I had left over, or some arbitrary amount, from my checking account to my savings account.
- I would then go out to eat or shopping with friends and realize I had limited funds in my checking account.
- I would run to the ATM to withdraw money from my savings account or, thanks to technological advances in mobile banking, immediately transfer money from my savings account to my checking account at the click of a button.

And this explains why I had little to no savings by the time I graduated law school. Looking back, I realize that the reason my saving efforts failed is because my savings lacked purpose.

Purpose-Driven Savings

You likely understand that saving money is a good thing, that we should all strive to become better savers, and that being a good saver means that you have some semblance of financial stability. All these are true, but they do not provide the *why*, *how much*, *where*, and *how* of saving money.

Which of these statements is more effective?

"I am going to save money every month."

---

or

"I have a savings goal of $10,000. This money will protect me in the event of job loss or some other financial emergency. I am going to save $300 every month toward this goal by setting up an auto deposit of $150 per paycheck from my checking to my savings."

The key to effectively saving money is to save with a purpose. You must tie your savings to a goal. This requires you to shift from saving for the sake of saving to getting specific and intentional.

Take a moment to ask yourself why you want to save money. Give yourself the opportunity to brainstorm, get creative, and think about your future self.

Don't just save for the sake of saving;
save with a purpose.

The Emergency Fund

How would you handle an unexpected $1,000 expense—for example, a medical expense, a flight home to tend to an ill family member, or a car or home repair? What about a loss in income, such as a pay reduction or job loss? How do you handle financial emergencies?

How Americans Pay for Emergencies

According to Bankrate, only 4 in 10 Americans have enough savings to cover a $1,000 unexpected expense.[1] This means that most Americans cannot cover such an expense and would need to look for alternative ways to cover it.

So how do most Americans cover unexpected expenses? They:

- Use a credit card
- Cut back on spending
- Borrow money from family or friends
- Take out a personal loan[3]

Rather than having to resort to these measures, consider an *emergency fund*.

What Is an Emergency Fund?

An emergency, or rainy day, fund is exactly what it sounds like. It is money in a savings account that you can use to cover an expense in the event of an emergency. Your emergency fund serves as your financial cushion.

Have you ever heard someone say that they carry a credit card in case of an emergency? I sure have. I owned a car in college and, as car owners are aware, car expenses are unavoidable. I had a false sense of security that if something went wrong, I could simply swipe my credit card. I ignored the fact that such an expense on my credit card—with its 29% interest rate—would be extremely costly and detrimental to my financial future.

Looking back, I wish I could tell my 20-year-old self that a credit card is not a substitute for an emergency fund and that the time to save in an emergency fund is *now*.

Three Steps to Build Your Emergency Fund

Everyone needs an emergency fund. This is one of the few things that I will say is nonnegotiable. You should treat saving your emergency fund with the same importance that you place on your obligatory bills like rent, internet, or your cell phone.

Imagine the process of saving your emergency fund as three tiers:

Step 1: Starter Emergency Fund

To start your emergency fund, save $1,000 as quickly as possible.

Let's revisit the Bankrate statistic: most Americans cannot cover a $1,000 emergency. I do not want you to be like most Americans. I want you to be among the 44% of Americans who *can* cover this type of expense. Having a $1,000 starter emergency fund means that you will be ahead of the curve.

Once you have your $1,000 saved, move on to Step 2.

Example: Amira's Starter Emergency Fund Amira currently has $800 in her savings account. She needs to save an additional $200 to meet her $1,000 goal. She will direct $100 from her next two paychecks to her savings account to complete Step 1.

Example: Jolene's Starter Emergency Fund Jolene does not have an emergency fund. In fact, the first time she hears of one is from reading this book. She makes a plan to save her first $1,000 over the course of the next three months:

Month 1: save $300

Month 2: save $300

Month 3: save $400

Step 2: One-Month Emergency Fund

The goal for this step is for your emergency fund to be able to cover one month of necessary living expenses.

Note: One month of *necessary living expenses* does not mean one month of *income*.

Unlike Step 1's flat $1,000 rule, the amount for Step 2 will depend on your specific expenses. To calculate your number, determine how much you need in order to cover one month of necessary living expenses. The easiest way to think of this is to ask yourself, "If I lost my job tomorrow, what are the expenses that I must be able to cover?"

At a minimum, I recommend including:

- Housing
- Utilities
- Cell phone
- Transportation
- Groceries
- Health (insurance, medication)
- Minimum debt payments

Once you have completed Step 2, you are ready to move on to the last step.

Example: Amira's One-Month Emergency Fund Amira's necessary expenses include the following:

One-Month Necessary Expenses.

Rent	$1,200
Utilities	$100
Cell phone	$100
Transportation	$200
Groceries	$300
Credit card payment	$100
Student loan payment[3]	$300
TOTAL	**$2,300**

Amira should aim to have **$2,300** in her emergency fund to satisfy Step 2. This means that she needs to add an additional $1,300 to her already existing $1,000 emergency fund (from Step 1).

Example: Jolene's One-Month Emergency Fund Jolene's necessary expenses include the following:

One-Month Necessary Expenses.

Rent	$1,000
Utilities	$70
Cell phone	$80
Transportation	$250
Groceries	$300
Credit card payment	$50
Student loan payment	$250
TOTAL	**$2,000**

Jolene's Step 2 amount is **$2,000**. She needs to add an additional $1,000 to her emergency fund to meet her Step 2 goal.

Step 3: Fully Funded Emergency Fund

Your ultimate goal should be for your emergency fund to be able to cover three to six months of necessary living expenses. Think of this as your "hashtag goals" (#goals) amount.

The formula is straightforward:

Step 2 amount × # of months = fully funded emergency fund

To determine your goal amount for a three or six-month emergency fund, calculate:

Step 2 amount × 3 = three-month emergency fund
Step 2 amount × 6 = six-month emergency fund

Whether you aim to cover three months, six months, or something in between, your emergency fund amount will depend on your personal comfort level and circumstances. Consider the following when deciding how much you should aim for:

Three-Month Emergency Fund	Six-Month Emergency Fund
Strong job security	Less job security
High-demand industry	Lower-demand industry
No dependents	Dependents
Dual-income household	Single-income household
No current health concerns	Health concerns (i.e., greater likelihood of medical expenses)

92

Example: Amira's Fully Funded Emergency Fund Amira works in healthcare and has worked for her employer for five years. She has strong job security and knows that employment opportunities are plentiful in her industry. She is single and has no dependents. She occasionally helps her parents financially. Given these factors, Amira is comfortable with a four-month emergency fund:

$$\$2,300 \,(\text{Step 2 amount}) \times 4 \text{ months} = \$9,200$$

Amira needs to save an additional $6,900 to have a fully funded emergency fund:

$$\$9,200 \,(\text{fully funded emergency fund goal}) -$$
$$\$2,300 \,(\text{amount saved from Step 2}) = \$6,900$$

Example: Jolene's Fully Funded Emergency Fund Jolene works as a freelance graphic artist. Her income took a significant hit during the start of the global pandemic but has since recovered. Even though she does not have any dependents, she feels comfortable with a six-month emergency fund.

$$\$2,000 \,(\text{Step 2 amount}) \times 6 \text{ months} = \$12,000$$

Jolene needs to save an additional $10,000 to have a fully funded emergency fund:

$$\$12,000 \,(\text{fully funded emergency fund goal}) -$$
$$\$2,000 \,(\text{amount saved from Step 2}) = \$10,000$$

How to Save Your Emergency Fund

Regardless of your emergency fund amount, approach it as follows:

- **Break it up:** Large numbers are intimidating. Break up your number into small, manageable amounts and take it one step at a time. For example, if your ultimate goal is a $10,000 emergency fund, aim to save $100 per paycheck until you reach your goal.
- **Put it in your budget:** Once you have determined how much you will save monthly, include that amount in your money plan.
- **Keep it separate:** Your emergency fund should be separate from other savings goals. For example, do not commingle your emergency fund with your savings goals for travel or a house down payment.

- **Label it:** Words have power. If your bank allows it, rename the account that holds your emergency fund.
  - When I first started saving my emergency fund, I named it "DO NOT TOUCH."
  - Here are some other examples:
    - o "[YOUR NAME]'s emergency fund" (a classic choice)
    - o "I love me fund"
    - o "Future me fund"
    - o "Future me will thank me for this"
    - o "If **** hits the fan"
- **Start now:** Don't overthink it. Your emergency fund is a high-priority financial goal that you should work on *even if* you have debt. And remember that it is okay to start small.

TIP: As life changes, so should your emergency fund. Check in at least twice a year to ensure that your emergency fund accurately reflects your current needs and circumstances.

Let's Get Personal

When I first calculated my emergency fund number, I was stumped. The minimum payment on my student loan alone was $3,000.[4] Add that to my other necessary living expenses and I was looking at a fully funded emergency fund of $30,000. Once I got over the shock, I broke my number into smaller, manageable goals. Ultimately, it took me about five years to save my emergency fund and, although that time frame may seem long, my present-day self is so grateful that I did this.

Once you have completed saving in your emergency fund, you can move on to building other financial goals!

The Family Emergency Fund

Much of the traditional financial advice ignores the reality that many children of immigrants or of low-income backgrounds face: we are our family's emergency fund. And, if you are anything like me, these emergencies occur beyond our immediate family here at home (parents and siblings) and can extend to our family abroad (grandparents, uncles/aunts, cousins).

Let's Get Personal

Since graduating from law school, my family emergencies have looked as follows:

- Family member experiences job loss
- Family member needs medication or medical treatment
- Major appliance gives out after decades of use
- Necessary home or structural repairs
- Death in the family requires immediate travel
- COVID-19 global pandemic (and the many economic hardships that created)

As a first-generation daughter of immigrants, it is a privilege to be able to provide for my family in this way. But I also recognize the importance of balance and ensuring that these situations do not derail my own personal financial goals. For this reason, I strongly recommend creating a *family emergency fund*.

The family emergency fund is a fund that you can use to help provide for family members who may need financial assistance. How much you decide to save depends on your own financial needs and goals, the overall needs of your family, and your level of comfort.

Here are some tips for creating your family emergency fund:

- **Include it in your budget and save regularly:** Add "Family Emergency Fund" to your budget and remember that small amounts make a big impact (e.g., $10/week = over $500 saved in one year).

- **Keep it separate from your personal emergency fund:** At any given moment, you should be able to easily identify how much is in your personal emergency fund as opposed to your family's.

- **Do not feel obligated to inform family members about this fund:** If a family member knows that you have this fund, they may unnecessarily ask you for money. No one wants to admit that this happens, but it does. These requests can put you in the uncomfortable position of having to explain that the money is reserved for emergencies only. It is okay to implement boundaries.

Sinking Funds

What types of expenses tend to throw off your monthly budget? Here are a few that have thrown me off:

- Baby shower and wedding gifts
- Annual Amazon subscription (I always forget about this)
- Annual renter's insurance payment
- Donations (e.g., GoFundMe requests, friend's fitness fundraiser)

Now think about large life expenses that are bound to come up in the next year, five years. Here are some of mine:

- Technology upgrade (computers, phones)
- Travel
- Down payment for a home

These inevitable expenses *that are not quite emergencies* can easily derail our financial goals. A budget that does not account for these realities ignores our complete financial picture.

Cue *sinking funds*.

What Are Sinking Funds?

A sinking fund is a savings account that you use to cover your irregular or large expenses. The goal is to save money in these accounts *incrementally* (i.e., weekly, biweekly, monthly).

Unlike the emergency fund, which is one dedicated savings account for life's emergencies, you can have numerous sinking funds (although one or two are just fine) to cover your irregular and large expenses. Irregular expenses are those that do not necessarily come up on a monthly basis. Large expenses are those significant life purchases that you reasonably expect will come up in the future.

Here are some examples of sinking funds to include in your budget:

Sinking Funds for Irregular Expenses	Sinking Funds for Large Expenses
Car repairs	Travel
Gifts (birthdays, weddings, baby showers)	New apartment (security deposit, furniture)
Personal grooming (facials, haircuts)	New car
Seasonal clothes shopping	Wedding
Kid expenses (school trips, book fairs)	Down payment on a home
Pet expenses (medical, specialty food, toys)	Holiday season (gifts, decor, food, travel)

Sinking Funds Formula

Use this simple formula to budget for your sinking funds:

Total cost for the goal or expense

÷

The number of months you have until you incur that expense or reach that goal

=

The amount that you should be saving monthly

Once you determine your amount, add it to your budget! Let's look at some examples.

Example: Francesca's Dog

Francesca has a dog named Luna. Francesca adores her dog, but does not love the expenses that come with being a dog owner. These expenses are often sporadic and are anywhere from $200 to $400 at a time. Francesca calculates that she spends about $1,200 annually on Luna.

How much should Francesca save in her sinking fund?

$$\$1,200 \div 12\,\text{months} = \$100$$

Francesca should save $100 monthly in a "Pet (or Luna) Sinking Fund" and add it to her monthly budget.

Example: Wanda's Wanderlust

Wanda dreams of backpacking through Europe. This will be the trip of a lifetime, so she is prepared to save for it over the next two years. Wanda estimates that her trip (flights, hotels, food, and excursions) will cost $5,000. She has already saved $200.

How much should Wanda save in her sinking fund?

$$\$4,800 \div 24 \, \text{months} = \$200$$

Wanda should save $200 monthly in a "Travel Sinking Fund" and add it to her monthly budget.

Example: Shanitra and Steve's Wedding

Shanitra and Steve recently got engaged and plan on getting married in one year. They anticipate spending $20,000. They manage their finances separately (i.e., separate budgets and bank accounts). They have agreed to split the costs and are not expecting any financial help from family.

How much should Shanitra and Steve save in their sinking funds?

$$\$20,000 \div 12 \, \text{months} = \$1,667$$
$$\$1,667 \div 2 = \$833$$

Shanitra and Steve should *each* aim to save $833 in a "Wedding Sinking Fund" and add it to their monthly budgets.

Example: Patricia and Ariel's Home Down Payment

Patricia and Ariel have been married for one year. They would like to purchase a home in the next four years. The average price for houses in their area is $500,000. They plan to put 10% down ($50,000) and want to have money for closing costs and furniture. They decide on a goal of $70,000. They already have $10,000 saved for their home purchase.

How much should Patricia and Ariel save in their sinking fund?

$$\$60,000 \div 48 \, \text{months} = \$1,250$$

Patricia and Ariel should aim to save $1,250 monthly in a "House Sinking Fund" and add it to their monthly budget.

■ ■ ■

Sinking funds allow you to break up large and overwhelming expenses and goals into small, manageable amounts.

How to Manage Your Sinking Funds

The questions that I inevitably get after sharing the joys of sinking funds include "Where should I save this money?" and "How do I keep track of so many different funds?"

First, you do not need a dozen sinking funds. I personally have three: travel, gifts, and Christmas. Second, where you keep them and how you track them is up to you.

One Bank Account and a Spreadsheet

You can keep all your sinking funds in one bank account and manually track the money that goes in and out with a spreadsheet. For example, if you are saving monthly for car repairs ($100) and a wedding ($500), you would deposit that money ($600) into that one bank account.

If this option is for you, be sure to:

1. Open a savings account separate from your emergency fund to hold your sinking funds.

2. Update the spreadsheet tracking your sinking funds at least once a month.

Multiple Bank Accounts

You can open several savings accounts that correspond to the number of sinking funds you have. For example, if you have four sinking funds, you can open four savings accounts (in addition to and separate from your emergency fund, of course).

If this option is for you, be sure to:

1. Ask your bank about their policy on how many bank accounts you are permitted to open. They may have limits.

2. Be mindful of any bank maintenance fees or fees for minimum required balances.

3. Understand that the more bank accounts you have, the more paperwork you will have to keep track of.

Save with a Purpose

One Bank Account that Allows You to Save for Multiple Goals

Some banks offer savings accounts that allow you to separate your goals to track your progress and easily manage your savings in just one account. This is my personal preference.

I use Ally Bank, an online high-yield savings account (more on this in the next section). Ally has a feature called "savings buckets." Their savings bucket options include emergencies, vacations, special occasions, and tax payments, or you can create and customize your own. You can withdraw money from and deposit money to the specific bucket of your choice. I have one savings account with one account number. However, when I sign into my account via the mobile app or on my desktop, I can easily see my various savings buckets with their respective amounts.

Other banks that allow customers to save for multiple goals include:[5]

- Capital One 360
- Betterment
- Wealthfront

Given the attractive nature of these accounts, I predict that more banks will roll out similar features in the near future.

Optimize Your Savings Strategy with the Right Bank Accounts

I touched earlier on the type of bank account that I use for my emergency fund and sinking funds, but let's take a deeper dive.

FDIC-Insured Banks

Your emergency fund and sinking funds should be kept in a savings account at a bank. Keeping them in a drawer at home or under the mattress simply will not do. The main reason is security.

Regardless of which company choose to bank with, you should ensure that they have FDIC insurance:

> The Federal Deposit Insurance Corporation (FDIC) is an independent agency created by the Congress to maintain stability and public confidence in the nation's financial system. The FDIC insures deposits; examines and supervises financial institutions for safety, soundness, and consumer protection . . . .[6]

You have likely seen "FDIC" signs or stickers at the entrance of your local bank or on the front page of a bank's website. "[T]he FDIC protects your money in the unlikely event of a bank failure"—up to "$250,000 per depositor, per insured bank, for each account ownership category."[7] This insurance is automatically applied to your account (no purchase required).

FDIC insurance helps establish trust with those who may be hesitant about keeping their money at a bank. Notably, the percentage of unbanked (i.e., not having an account with a bank) households varies significantly across racial groups. In its 2019 survey, the FDIC found that 13.8% of Black households and 12.2% of Hispanic or Latino households are unbanked. Although these numbers have improved over the past decade, they are in stark contrast to the percentage of unbanked White households (2.5%).[8]

The cause for this distrust in financial institutions, particularly within historically disadvantaged communities, is due to numerous reasons, which we cannot possibly dive into at length in this book, that include:

- Racism: banks historically discriminating against Black borrowers and depositors[9]
- Sexism: women did not obtain the right to open a bank account until the 1960s[10]
- Fraud and corruption: immigrants with trauma caused by their native country's corrupt economic systems

Regardless of our sex, race, or socioeconomic background, we should all endeavor to educate ourselves on our options and keep our hard-earned money secure with a reputable banking institution.

High-Yield Savings Account

My favorite type of account for my savings is a high-yield savings account (HYSA).[11] The HYSA is a savings account that pays its customers a higher interest rate than traditional banks do.

When you deposit your money at a bank, the bank uses that money for its business needs and financial products, which include loans that it issues to other customers. In return, most traditional banks pay their customers an annual percentage yield (APY). This APY varies but is typically around 0.01% at traditional banks.[12] That means that for every $1,000 deposited, a customer can expect to receive about 10 cents annually from the bank.[13] On the other hand, with a HYSA, that APY can be around 1.0%.[14] That means that for every $1,000 deposited, a customer can expect to receive about $10 annually from the bank.

Will a HYSA make you rich? Unlikely. But as your savings grow, so will your returns. And, as my mom says, *algo es algo* (something is something).

In addition to providing a higher APY, many banks with high-yield savings accounts also offer:

- No monthly maintenance fees[15]
- No minimum deposit requirement to open your account
- Innovative features (e.g., Ally's savings buckets)

Because most HYSAs are through online banks, a potential drawback is that they are not as easily accessible as traditional banks. Traditional banks provide customers with the option to withdraw funds from physical branches or bank-specific ATMs. On the other hand, if customers want to withdraw money from their HYSA, the easiest way to do so is typically to transfer the funds from their HYSA to their checking account.[16]

As someone who has banked with online banks for years, the lack of a physical branch has never been an issue for me. In fact, I would argue that the lack of easy access has made it easier for me to reach my savings goals because of the extra friction between me and withdrawing money from my savings. When I need to access my funds, a transfer to my everyday checking account typically takes one to two business days.

But, if you prefer to exclusively bank in person (like my parents do), a traditional bank that is FDIC insured will do the job just fine.

How to Open a Bank Account

If you do not yet have a bank account, now is a great time to get one! Have the following information ready:

1. **Proof of identity:** For example, a driver's license, passport, or other government-issued identification
2. **Proof of address:** For example, a driver's license or municipal identification, utility bill, or apartment lease
3. **Identification number:** For example, a Social Security Number (SSN)
   a. **Undocumented immigrants:** Some banks permit customers to open an account with a passport or an Individual Taxpayer Identification Number (ITIN). The ITIN is a tax identification number issued by the IRS to those who are not otherwise eligible

to obtain an SSN.[17] Such banks include Chase, Bank of America, and Capital One.[18]

TIP: Before opening a new bank account, inquire about any promotions or monetary incentives for new customers.

Smart Banking Tips

To improve your banking experience:

- Review your bank accounts regularly to curb fraudulent activity.
  - o Immediately contact your bank if you detect any suspicious activity.
- Set up text or email alerts for purchases above a certain amount (e.g., purchases above $50).
- Set up alerts if your account falls below a certain amount. This will minimize the likelihood of overdraft.
- Contact your bank if you are charged an unexpected or overdraft fee. Banks often grant customers courtesy waivers.
- Research competitor banks. The bank that served you a decade ago may not be the best fit for you today.

My Top Tip to Build Your Savings: Automate

We have discussed at length the importance of budgeting and including your savings goals—both emergency fund and sinking funds—in your budget. I always encourage clients to include "Savings" at the top of their budgets and to treat their savings with the same importance they place on their monthly obligations like rent and utilities. To ensure they honor the commitment to save, I recommend that they *automate* their savings.

Automating your savings simply means that you create a system to automatically deposit money into your savings accounts. For example, you can:

- Contact your employer's human resources department and direct a specific percentage of each paycheck (e.g., 15% or 20%) to your savings account.

103

- Set up automatic transfers across your existing bank accounts (e.g., every other Friday on payday, automatically transfer $200 from your checking to your high-yield savings account).

- If you have an inconsistent income, decide on a minimum amount that you will automatically transfer to your savings (e.g., $50 every other week) and, when you receive your pay, determine whether you can transfer an additional amount to your savings.

Automation is all about effortlessly managing your money. It reduces decision-making and the friction between the money in your checking account and your savings account. Taking the time to set up these systems will make it easier for you to reach your savings goals.

Remember to always tie your savings to a goal.

Meet Rita Soledad Fernández-Paulino

Soledad is a queer Mexican-American and the founder of Wealth Para Todos, a company with a mission to ensure that more BIPOC (Black, Indigenous, people of color), women, and LGBTQ+ (lesbian, gay, bisexual, transgender, questioning, and others) folk have a financial plan to retire early. Soledad wants us working because we want to, not because we have to.

Q. You view financial literacy as a social justice issue. Tell us more.

A. Financial literacy is a gatekeeper to financial independence. The more Latinas committed to learning about how to live below our means, cash flowing expenses, and investing to build wealth, the more financially secure we can all become.

Financial security enables us to walk away from toxic environments, pay for preventive healthcare, care for loved ones, and advocate for others. The fact that we are not all taught how to build wealth in the United States continues to perpetuate the wealth gap and impacts who considers themselves able to become financially independent.

And yet financial literacy is not enough. There are systems of oppression that impact one's ability to build wealth. Although we can learn how to build wealth, it's important that we understand how

---

racism, paths to citizenship, colorism, transphobia, ableism, fatphobia, sexism, rising costs of higher education, lack of quality affordable healthcare, and other forms of oppression interfere with equitable access to financial security.

While we can and must nurture our agency, it's important for us to advocate for those who are still consumed with surviving financially in a society that had no intentions of ensuring that BIPOC, women, and LGBTQ+ had a path to becoming financially independent.

Q. How do you balance saving your emergency fund with other goals, including as an individual, wife, and parent of two children?

A. The key to reaching any financial goal is to be proud of progress that happens *poco a poco* [little by little]. People often think they need to save the same amount of money from each paycheck and if something unexpected happens they feel defeated about not being "consistent."

Instead, people need to focus on taking pride in every contribution toward an emergency fund, big or small. If I had focused on being "consistent" with contributing to my emergency fund, it would have taken my family 18 months to save our six-month emergency fund.

Instead, I told myself we are going to save *poco a poco*. I'm going to be open to learning about all the challenges that interfere with saving and come up with a way to prevent them from happening in the future. When I got into a car accident while trying to save an emergency fund, I decided that moving forward I was going to make sure to always have a sinking fund that would have money to cover my deductible. When my mother asked for a few thousand dollars, I realized I needed to make sure to have a Loved One Emergency Fund. When I found myself jealous of friends traveling to Mexico with their kids while I was saving for our emergency fund, I made sure to start saving for travel in a sinking fund.

I was able to save money toward an emergency fund and sinking funds by decreasing the amount I spent on things I care very little about. I would rather walk a longer distance than pay for parking. I love wearing "new to me" clothing but don't care about owning them permanently so I rent most of my clothes and collect hand-me-downs

(*continued*)

(continued)

for my children. I also sold everything I didn't love, including my "mom van," to make sure our *dinero* [money] was going toward things we really wanted. By cutting down on parking fees, what my family spent on clothes, and selling things we didn't love, we had more cash flow to put toward savings.

Ultimately, we made the most progress toward saving an emergency fund by focusing on increasing our incomes. Once we had a sustainable budget that reflected our "ideal" lifestyle, we were able to increase our income without increasing our expenses, which allowed us to save $30,000 in six months. We didn't save $5,000 each month; rather, we saved what we could when we could *con orgullo* [with pride]. Some months that meant between $250 and $1,500, and one month it meant $10,000 because we used our tax refund and a hiring bonus to complete our emergency fund.

When you focus on reaching a bigger goal like early retirement, then you start to realize the importance of creating sustainable financial habits instead of just sacrificing until you reach some milestone. Focus on creating a lifestyle that you enjoy so you can have the resilience it takes to pay off debt, save an emergency fund, invest toward early retirement, and explore ways to increase your income.

Q. You teach your audience about the "loved one emergency fund." Can you tell us about that? What recommendations do you have for those who want to set up something similar?

A. A "Loved One Emergency Fund" is a sinking fund you keep in a high-yield savings account that you can pull from when a loved one is in need. This is a way to provide support without sacrificing your own financial security.

If you know that you would want to help a parent, sibling, cousin, *abuela* [grandma], *amiga* [friend], or anyone you love during a challenging financial time, I recommend you start saving money for it now.

How much you decide to save, give, or lend, is up to you. Here are some things to consider for your Loved One Emergency Fund:

1. ***How much do you want to save in total?*** It's important to set boundaries around how much you will use to support your loved ones during each season of your financial journey. You may have less to give when

you are paying off debt, building your own emergency fund, saving to buy a property, or if you have a child on the way. The amount you keep in this fund may change over time and that's more than okay.

2. ***Who are you willing to give money to from this fund?*** There may be some people in your life who you do not expect to pay you back or certain circumstances where you prefer to just gift money to loved ones. Identify these people and circumstances ahead of time so that you can prepare for them.

3. ***Who are you willing to lend money to from this fund?*** I recommend that you only lend money that you can afford to never see again. I think it's better to give someone an amount of money that is less than what they are asking to borrow rather than lend an amount that they don't have a plan to pay back. With that said, there may be people who you trust will pay you back—who are those people?

4. ***How much money are you willing to give/lend to any specific person?*** It's important to reflect on how you plan to budget the money in your Loved One Emergency Fund. Just because you have the money doesn't mean you need to give/lend it to someone. If you have a lot of loved ones like me, you may set a lower amount of money to give/lend since multiple people may need it. If there are few loved ones that you would give/lend money to, then you may be okay with letting one person have 50% of your Loved One Emergency Fund.

Q. What does *financial freedom* mean to you?

A. *Financial freedom* means being at *paz* [peace] with how my *dinero* can support my lifestyle, my loved ones, and my community. It means knowing at a spiritual and financial level that I have more than enough *dinero* to live life on my terms, *comiendo afuera de la casa cuando quiero* [dining out when I want] and especially *descansando cuando quiero* [resting when I want].

Chapter 8

Create Your Debt Payoff Plan

One of the most significant parts of my money story is that I paid off $215,000 of debt in four years. When I share this, I am usually met with a variety of reactions:

- Expressions of awe at this feat.
- Skepticism because how is that possible?
- Wonder on why I would rush to pay off my debt when I could have instead enjoyed my money (this reaction was common, especially among my colleagues in the legal community).
- Dismissive attitudes and eye rolls accompanied by statements like: "Well, of course, you did. You're a lawyer."

These are all fair reactions. Paying off a significant amount of debt in such a short period of time is uncommon and, to be frank, took a great amount of financial privilege (namely, my six-figure attorney salary). But to stop the conversation there ignores what I have learned about debt, the strategies that I implemented to become debt-free, and what I have taught others.

Since becoming debt-free in December 2019, I have coached hundreds and taught thousands on how to create an effective debt payoff plan— regardless of income or debt amount.

My clients have spanned all parts of the income spectrum, including:

- A part-time barista earning $20,000 annually
- A teacher with a $70,000 salary
- A software engineer with a $150,000 salary
- A physician with a $300,000+ salary

My clients' debt amounts have similarly mirrored their income diversity:

- A recent college graduate with a $10,000 loan
- A single mom with $40,000 of credit card and medical debt
- An MBA graduate with $150,000 of student loans and $20,000 of credit card debt
- A married couple with a combined $400,000 of student loans and two car notes

Reflecting on my clients' and students' journeys, as opposed to just my own, drives home the larger point that regardless of your income or debt amount, anyone who has debt can, and should, create a debt repayment plan. This does not mean that you must pay off your debt in any specific time period. All it means is that *you* have a plan to pay off *your* debt on *your* time.

Before we create a debt repayment plan, let's cover some basics.

Understanding How Debt Works

Debt's Main Components

Debt is money that one party borrows from another. The borrowing party promises to repay the lender at a later date, typically with interest.[1] Debt generally consists of two parts: the principal and the interest.[2]

- **Principal** is the amount that you borrowed from the lender.
- **Interest** is what you agree to pay the lender in exchange for borrowing the principal. This is typically expressed as a percentage of the loan.

Example: David's Undergraduate Loan

David took out a $40,000 loan to fund his undergraduate degree. His loan has a 5% interest rate. This means that *in addition* to repaying the $40,000 principal to the lender, David must also repay the lender 5% interest ($2,000).

Simple versus Compound Interest

The two main types of interest that we see with debt are simple interest and compound interest.

- **Simple interest** is interest that grows only on top of the principal— the original loan amount.

- **Compound interest** is interest that grows on top of the principal amount *and* the interest that has accrued. Think of this as interest that grows on top of interest . . . that grows on top of interest.

Most student loans use a simple interest calculation.[3] On the other hand, most forms of credit card debt use compound interest.

Example: Danielle's Personal Loan[4]

Danielle takes out a $1,000 personal loan. The interest rate for the loan is 10%. Let's compare how the loan would look with simple interest versus compound interest:

Simple Interest

If Danielle takes out a one-year loan, she will repay $1,100 ($1,000 principal + $100 interest):

$$\text{Year 1 interest} : \$1,000\,(\text{principal}) \times 10\%\,(\text{interest}) = \$100$$

If Danielle takes out a two-year loan, she will repay a total of ***$1,200*** ($1,000 principal + $200 interest):

$$\text{Year 1 interest} : \$1,000\,(\text{principal}) \times 10\%\,(\text{interest}) = \$100$$
$$\text{Year 2 interest} : \$1,000\,(\text{principal}) \times 10\%\,(\text{interest}) = \$100$$

Compound Interest

Like the simple interest loan, at the end of Year 1, Danielle will repay $1,100 ($1,000 principal + $100 interest) because no interest has accrued. Thus, no compounding *yet*.

$$\text{Year 1 interest} : \$1,000\,(\text{principal}) \times 10\%\,(\text{interest}) = \$100$$

However, we see a difference with a two-year loan. Because the interest compounded, the Year 2 interest grows on top of the principal *and* Year 1's accrued interest:

$$\text{Year 1 interest} : \$1,000\,(\text{principal}) \times 10\%\,(\text{interest}) = \$100$$
$$\text{Year 2 interest} : \$1,100\,(\text{principal} + \text{Year 1 interest}) \times 10\%\,(\text{interest}) = \$110$$

This means that Danielle will repay a total of ***$1,210***.

Although in this example the difference between simple and compound interest is small ($10), the larger the debt amount and the longer the loan term, the greater impact this difference has.

111

Create Your Debt Payoff Plan

Because compound interest grows not only on top of the principal, but also on top of the interest that has accrued on the debt, it is more expensive than simple interest. The more *time* interest has to compound—or the longer it takes you to repay the debt—the more you will ultimately repay.

Interest Capitalization

One thing that I wish I had understood about student loans before graduating from law school is interest capitalization.

Even though student loans generally use a simple interest calculation, there are times when the interest compounds. Interest capitalization is when unpaid loan interest is added to your principal balance. Capitalization can happen during deferment, a grace period, or even consolidation.[5]

To avoid capitalization, you can pay the interest while you are in school. But that's not always the best option.

- Depending on the loan type, your loan may or may not be subject to capitalization. Not all loans are![6]

- Your loan repayment strategy may make repaying unpaid interest during school futile—for example, if you pursue a loan forgiveness program or opt for a repayment plan that does not capitalize the interest.

- If you have little to no income while you are in school, your focus may be on covering necessary expenses and building a small emergency fund, if possible.

Let's Get Personal

While I was in law school, I was unaware that interest was accumulating on my student loans. I did not realize that my unpaid interest during the period that I was in school (a deferment period) would later get added to my principal. That unpaid interest that had accumulated on my debt increased the outstanding principal amount that I owed when I graduated.

For example, let's say that the amount that I borrowed for law school was $150,000 (the principal) and during my three years of law school, $20,000 of interest accrued on my principal. After graduation, that unpaid interest capitalized—it was added to my principal. Thus, my new "principal" amount—or the amount that interest would now be charged on moving forward—was $170,000 as opposed to the $150,000 that I had originally borrowed.

Fixed versus Variable Rates

Debt is generally subject to a fixed or variable interest rate.

- **Fixed rate** means that your interest will remain the same throughout the life of the debt. The interest that you agree to when you take on the debt will remain the same until you pay it off.

- **Variable rate** means that your interest can increase or decrease throughout the life of the debt. This is because variable interest rate "is based on an underlying benchmark interest rate or index that changes periodically."[7]

If you are presented with the choice to pick between the two, consider the following:

	Fixed Rate	Variable Rate
Pros	• Predictable and consistent payments. Your monthly payment amount generally remains the same until you repay your loan (assuming you do not take on additional debt). • Predictable total repayment amount.	• Low and attractive introductory interest rate.
Cons	• Interest rate may be higher than a variable rate option, which can ultimately make for a more costly debt.	• Rate may increase significantly. • Unpredictable total repayment cost. • Unpredictable and inconsistent payments. Your monthly payment amount can increase or decrease due to the variable interest rate, which can affect how much you budget toward debt.

Create Your Debt Payoff Plan

Installment versus Revolving Debt

Debt generally falls under one of two categories:

1. **Installment debt** gives borrowers a lump sum loan with a fixed payment schedule. The borrower makes payments until the loan is paid in full. These can include student loans, personal loans, car loans, and mortgages.

Example: Maureen's Car Loan

Maureen recently purchased a car for $30,000. She put $10,000 down and took out a loan for the remaining $20,000. Her car loan has a 3% interest rate. Her loan repayment time frame is 60 months, or five years. Her monthly payments are $360 until her loan is paid in full.

2. **Revolving debt** allows borrowers to borrow a certain amount, repay that debt, and borrow again as often as needed. This typically includes credit cards.

Example: Maureen's Credit Card

In addition to her car loan (installment debt), Maureen has a credit card (revolving debt). Her credit card has a $5,000 limit. This means that she can borrow up to $5,000, repay that debt, and borrow $5,000 again as often as she needs.

Maureen currently owes $3,000 on her credit card. Because her credit limit is $5,000, she can charge another $2,000 to her card. However, she refrains from doing so because that will dramatically increase her credit utilization rate, which can affect her credit.[8]

Impact on Credit Score

Did you know that revolving debt has a greater impact on your credit score than installment debt?

Installment debt shows that you can pay back what you borrow consistently over time. However, revolving debt shows that you can borrow varying amounts every month and manage your personal cash flow to pay it back. This is why credit cards typically have a greater impact on your credit score than student loans.

We discuss credit in greater length in Chapter 9.

What School Didn't Teach You about Student Loans

As a senior in high school, I understood student loans as a rite of passage. If you wanted to go to college, you had to take on debt—unless you were fortunate to receive grants, scholarships, or familial help. Although my undergraduate years were minimally funded by loans, I was unable to avoid them when I applied to law school. Signing up for $150,000 of debt for my law degree felt like a natural part of the process of becoming a lawyer—a sentiment shared by many in and out of the legal field.

Here are a few things that I wish I had known about student loans when I signed my name on that dotted line.

Student Loan Basics

Federal Loans versus Private Loans

Student loans generally fall under two categories: federal and private. Roughly 92% of student loan debt is federal and 8% is private.[9] Here are some notable differences between federal and private loans:

Federal Loans	Private Loans
Issued by the federal government	Issued by private companies (e.g., banks, credit unions)
Terms and conditions are set by law	Terms and conditions are set by the lender
Fixed interest rates[10]	Fixed and variable interest rates
Income-driven repayment plans	Repayment terms are set by the agreement with the lender
May qualify for certain forgiveness programs	Usually excluded from forgiveness programs

A **promissory note** is an agreement—a contractual obligation—that a borrower signs, agreeing to repay the loan at a future date. For example, if you take on a private loan, the lender will ask you to sign a promissory note to memorialize that you agree to its loan's terms and conditions. The **Master Promissory Note** (MPN) is the agreement detailing the terms and conditions for *federal* loan(s). Borrowers sign the MPN promising to pay the loan, interest, and applicable fees to the U.S. Department of Education.[11]

Regardless of the agreement, be sure to review the following:

- The principal (the amount you are borrowing to fund your education)
- The interest rate, including whether it is fixed or variable
- The expected monthly payment (your lender may or may not provide this information)
- The total cost of borrowing (your lender may or may not provide this information)

If you have questions about the documents that you are signing, contact your lender!

Subsidized Loans versus Unsubsidized Loans

Federal loans are either subsidized or unsubsidized.[12]

Subsidized Loans	Unsubsidized Loans
Available to undergraduate students with a financial need.	Available to undergraduate and graduate students. There is no requirement to demonstrate financial need.
The U.S. Department of Education pays the interest on your loans: - While you are in school at least half-time - For the first six months after you leave school (this is called the grace period, but note that there are certain exceptions) - During deferment (postponement of payments)	You are responsible for paying the interest on your loans during all periods. Most federal loans for graduate degrees are unsubsidized.

Let's Get Personal

Because most of my student loans were for law school, the majority of my debt was *unsubsidized*. This meant that the interest accrued *while* I was in school rather than holding off until I graduated. Thousands in interest accrued on my debt, capitalized, and was added to the principal after I graduated law school.

Federal Loan Repayment Options

Federal loans offer a variety of repayment options:[13]

- **Standard Repayment Plan**
  - All borrowers are eligible for this plan.
  - Payments are a fixed amount.
  - The plan ensures that your loans will be repaid in 10 years.
  - Borrowers usually pay less over time with the standard repayment plan than with other plan options.

- **Graduated Repayment Plan**
  - All borrowers are eligible for this plan.
  - Payments are lower at first and then gradually increase, usually every two years.
  - The plan ensures that your loans will be repaid in 10 years.
  - Borrowers will pay more over time with a graduated repayment plan than with the standard plan.

- **Extended Repayment Plan**
  - Borrowers with more than $30,000 in outstanding Direct Loans are eligible.
  - Fixed or graduated payments are available.
  - The plan ensures that your loans will be repaid in 25 years.
  - Although your monthly payments will be lower than they would be under the 10-year plans, you will ultimately pay significantly more due to growing interest with the extended repayment time frame.

- **Income-Based Repayment Plans**
  - These repayment plans depend on the borrower's income. Payments are usually 10–20% of the borrower's discretionary income.
  - Some borrowers qualify for loan forgiveness, where the outstanding balance is forgiven after a period of time.
    - o Note that borrowers *may* have to pay income tax on the amount that is forgiven.
  - Some borrowers who work in the public sector may qualify for the Public Service Loan Forgiveness (PSLF) program.
    - o Loan amounts forgiven under PSLF are *not* considered taxable by the Internal Revenue Service (IRS).[14]

117

Create Your Debt Payoff Plan

- The terms for qualifying for an income-based repayment plan vary for each plan, so visit Federal Student Aid at studentaid.gov for complete details.

IMPORTANT: If you are pursuing Public Service Loan Forgiveness, make sure that you are under the correct repayment plan. Not all repayment

---

Let's Get Personal

When I graduated law school, the balance on my *federal* student loans was roughly $150,000.[15] I opted for the Standard Repayment Plan because, from what I understood at the time, it provided the shortest time frame (10 years) and a lower amount that I would have to ultimately repay (as opposed to the Graduated Repayment Plan).

But my monthly loan payments were high. My monthly minimum payment for my federal student loan was approximately $1,700. *Additionally*, I had an approximate $300 monthly minimum payment for my private student loan.

Although I am glad I chose the Standard Repayment Plan, I wish I had been more knowledgeable about the minimum payment amount that I would be expected to pay before I graduated law school. My monthly minimum payment for my student loans was more than my New York City rent at the time!

---

plans qualify for PSLF. See the next section for more.

Loan Forgiveness Programs

Loan forgiveness is when borrowers are released from repaying their debt, either partially or fully. Here are some loan forgiveness program options to consider:

- **Public Service Loan Forgiveness (PSLF):** This is a popular federal loan forgiveness program. Those who have federal loans and work in the public sector may be eligible to receive forgiveness if they meet certain requirements:
  - They are employed by a U.S. federal, state, local, or tribal government or not-for-profit organization (federal service includes U.S. military service);
  - They work full-time for that agency or organization;

- They have Direct Loans (or consolidate other federal student loans into a Direct Loan);
- They repay their loans under an income-driven repayment plan; and
- They make 120 qualified payments.[16]

TIP: Since the global COVID-19 pandemic, the federal government has made changes to the PSLF program, some of which have greatly benefited borrowers. If you are pursuing PSLF, it is imperative that you stay up to date on federal policy changes and changes to the program.

- **State and local forgiveness programs:** Most states offer various student loan forgiveness programs for their residents.
  - For a detailed list of programs, review Investopedia's "Student Loan Forgiveness by State."[17]
- **Employers:** Some employers offer forgiveness programs, usually contingent on a minimum time period of employment.
  - Ask your employer if the company offers loan forgiveness. If it does, be sure to understand the terms and conditions of the program.

Let's Get Personal—Friend Edition

Loan forgiveness is possible! Several of my friends—teachers, social workers, nurses, and human resource professionals—have received loan forgiveness through the state of New York or through their individual employers. But this information is not always public, so be sure to do your research and talk to friends and colleagues about loan forgiveness![18]

A National Debt Crisis

Now that we have some of the basics out of the way, let's discuss the student debt crisis in the United States. Americans owe $1.76 trillion in student loans.[19] Most of that debt consists of federal loans, which stand at $1.61 trillion. Over 43 million people have some type of federal student loan debt, with an average balance of $37,000.

The average debt amount varies by debt type, significantly increasing from undergraduate degrees to those with doctorate degrees.

Average Student Loan Debt Amounts[20]

Debt Type	Average Debt
Bachelor's degree debt	$28,950
Graduate school debt	$71,000
MBA school debt	$66,300
Law school debt	$145,500
Medical school debt	$201,490
Dental school debt	$292,169

Notably, the average debt, payment amount, and impact on ability to build wealth varies significantly across racial groups. Consider a few statistics:[21]

- Black college graduates owe an average of $25,000 more than their White counterparts.
- Black borrowers are the most likely to be financially burdened by their student loans.
- 40% of Black borrowers have debt from graduate school compared to 22% of White borrowers.
- American Indian and Alaskan Native borrowers have the highest monthly payments.
- Hispanic and Latino borrowers are the most likely to delay getting married and having children due to their student loan debt.
- Asian college graduates repay their debt fastest and are the most likely to earn a salary that exceeds their loan balance.

Rapidly increasing student debt—a near 100% increase in just the past decade[22]—and the global COVID-19 pandemic have heightened the demand for government action. Lawmakers and borrowers nationwide have called for executive action or legislation that will release borrowers, either partially or fully, of their federal student loans.

In addition to student loan forgiveness, sustainable long-term legislation addressing student loans should account for the following:

- **Rising cost of higher education:** According to an analysis of data from the National Center for Education Statistics and the U.S. Census

Bureau and Bureau of Labor Statistics, from 1980 to 2019, the cost of college increased by 169% while the pay for workers between ages 22 and 27 only increased by 19%.[23] Measures that address the exponential price tag of higher education and affordability are necessary.

- **Interest rates:** We have all heard of someone (or perhaps we are that someone) who owes more on their student loans than they originally borrowed—sometimes despite making consistent payments! Have you ever wondered why that happens? One word: interest. If the borrower's monthly payment does not at least cover the interest owed, then that interest and overall loan balance are growing each day.[24] Policies addressing the interest rates imposed on student loan debt, including their accrual during periods of deferment (e.g., while in graduate school) will significantly impact the total cost of borrowing.

- **Financial literacy:** Students are unfortunately ill-equipped with the knowledge needed to take on student loans. Before signing any promissory note, elementary and high schools should prepare students with the basics of debt, how student loans work, what repayment will look like, options beyond the expensive private schools our guidance counselors tend to push, and a thorough understanding of funding options. Although financial literacy alone will not eliminate a student's need to take on debt, ensuring that borrowers are educated is a necessary first step.

This nationwide economic issue requires our collective involvement. We need sound legislation that addresses both the root and unfortunate consequences of the student loan debt crisis. Keep this in mind the next time you head to the polls to vote for your elected officials!

How to Create an Effective Debt Repayment Plan

Have you ever thought:

- I will never pay off my debt.
- This debt is crushing me.
- I feel like I am drowning.
- No matter how much I try, my debt keeps increasing.

If you said yes to any of the above: Do you have a debt repayment plan? I am not talking about simply paying what your lender requires of you. I am talking about a personalized written plan that *you* created, with repayment deadlines for each of your debts.

If you do not have one, that is okay! It's time to create your debt repayment plan and to crush debt once and for all.

Step 1: Create Your Debt Overview

For each of your debts, gather these four pieces of information:

1. **Type:** What kind of debt do you have?

   For example, credit card debt, student loan, medical debt, personal loan, car loan

2. **Account balance:** How much do you owe on that debt as of today?

3. **Interest rate:** What is the interest rate on your debt?

   This might be reflected as the annual percentage rate (APR) on your account statement.

4. **Minimum payment:** What is the minimum amount you are required to pay monthly?

   If this amount varies, use your latest payment amount.

Regardless of whether you have 1 or 10 debts, carve out the time necessary to gather this information.

Example: Kathy's Debt Overview

Kathy has a car loan, student loans, and two credit cards. She wants to become debt-free and is ready to create her personalized debt repayment plan.

Her debt overview is as follows:

Type	Balance	Interest Rate	Minimum Payment
Toyota car note	$10,000	3%	$300
Federal student loans[25]	$20,000	5% (average rate)	$350
Chase credit card	$1,000	20%	$50
Bank of America credit card	$3,000	25%	$100

> **TIP: Review your credit report to ensure that you are capturing all your debts.**
> **Your credit report will show the debts that are under your name. You can access your credit report for free at annualcreditreport.com.**

Step 2: Calculate Your Additional Payment Amount

Making additional payments—beyond what your lender requires—is *key* to paying off your debt. For this step, refer to the budget that you created in Chapter 5. Your budget will tell you exactly how much you can direct toward your debt as an additional payment.[26]

Example: Kathy's Additional Debt Payment Calculation

After creating her monthly budget and accounting for her (i) net income, (ii) emergency fund and sinking funds, (iii) expenses, and (iv) minimum debt payments, Kathy determines that she has an additional $400 that she can direct to her debt.

Kathy's budget is as follows:

Monthly Net Income	**$4,800**
Savings (emergency fund and sinking funds)	**$1,000**
Expenses	**$2,600**
Debt (minimum payments)	**$800**
Toyota car note	$300
Federal student loans	$350
Chase credit card	$50
Bank of America credit card	$100
Additional Debt Payment	***$400***

Note: Monthly net income ($4,800) – monthly spending ($1,000 [savings] + $2,600 [expenses] + $800 [minimum debt payments]) =
$4,800 – $4,400 = $400 (additional debt payment).

Use Online Debt Repayment Calculators to See the Impact of Your Additional Payment

My favorite tool for easily seeing the impact of an additional debt payment is Credit Karma's Debt Repayment Calculator.[27] Simply plug in the information that you have already gathered for Steps 1 and 2 and let the calculator do the work for you. There are many other free online calculators that can also help you with this task.

Let's look at two examples that demonstrate the impact of an additional debt payment.

Example: Khalil's Additional $400 Payment to His Credit Card

Khalil has a credit card with a $3,000 balance and 22% interest rate. He has struggled with paying off this card since graduating college. But he is now determined to pay it off once and for all. After creating his budget, Khalil decides to direct an additional $400 monthly payment to his card.

Let's analyze the impact that Khalil's additional $400 payment will have:

Repayment Strategy	Credit Card Standard Repayment	Additional $400 Monthly Payment
Estimated monthly payment	$100	$500
Time frame	37 months	7 months
Total principal paid	$3,000.00	$3,000.00
Total interest paid	$1,144.89	$234.05
Total debt paid	**$4,144.89**	**$3,234.05**

Source: Calculations made using the Credit Karma Debt Repayment Calculator.

Khalil's additional $400 monthly payment to his credit card cuts his repayment time frame from 37 months to 7 months and saves him over $900 in interest! This simple, but intentional, change to his debt repayment strategy will save Khalil both time and money.

But do not underestimate the power that even a small additional payment can have on your debt!

Example: Christian's Additional $100 Payment to His Student Loan

Christian recently graduated with $30,000 of student loans. His interest rate is 6%. He selects a standard 10-year repayment plan, which comes with a $333 minimum payment.

After reviewing his budget, Christian decides that he can direct an additional $50 per paycheck, or $100 monthly, to his student loans.

Let's analyze the impact that Christian's additional $100 monthly payment will have:

Repayment Strategy	Standard 10-Year Repayment Plan	Additional $100 Monthly Payment
Estimated monthly payment	$333	$433
Time frame	120 months (10 years)	73 months (6 years + 1 month)
Total principal paid	$30,000.00	$30,000.00
Total interest paid	$9,967.38	$ 5,918.83
Total debt paid	**$39,967.38**	**$35,918.83**

Source: Calculations made using the Credit Karma Debt Repayment Calculator.

By simply making an additional $100 monthly payment (think of it as just $25 per week!) to his student loans, Christian can shave nearly four years from his student loan repayment and save over $4,000 in interest!

Not only is he saving money, but he is also saving time.

TIP: Any time you receive extra income (e.g., overtime pay, work bonus, tax refund), determine how much you will direct to your debt as an additional payment.

For example, if you receive a bonus at work, you can follow a 70/30 rule, where 70% of the money goes to your financial goals and 30% goes to your personal spending (treat yourself!). Of the 70% for your financial goals, determine how much you will deposit in your savings, how much you will invest (more in Chapter 10), and how much you will send as an extra payment to your debt.

Step 3: Choose Your Debt Payoff Strategy: Snowball or Avalanche

If you have more than one debt, you may be tempted to split your additional debt payment amount across your various debts. For example, if you have three credit cards and can afford to throw an additional $300 to debt, you might divide that amount by three and do an additional $100 payment to each card.

There's a better way.

Focus on *one*. Rather than spreading your efforts across all your debts, focus your energy on one debt at a time (while making your minimum payments on your other debts, of course).

Pick one of two strategies: the debt snowball or the debt avalanche.

Debt Snowball

The debt snowball method involves making minimum payments on all your debts, except the smallest debt. Follow these steps:

1. List your debts from smallest to largest balance. Your focus for this strategy will be the debt with the smallest balance.

2. For the smallest debt, make the minimum payment *and* add your additional debt payment.

3. For all other debts on the list, make the minimum payment.

4. Once you have paid off your smallest debt, *roll over to the next debt on your list*:

   (i) the smallest debt's minimum payment and (ii) your additional payment.

5. Repeat until you are debt-free!

An advantage of the debt snowball method is that it gives you quick wins by knocking out your small debts, keeping you motivated throughout the journey. A disadvantage of this strategy is that it could cost you more than the alternative because you might be pushing off your debts with the highest interest rates to the bottom of your list. The higher the interest rate, the more a debt will ultimately cost you.

Debt Avalanche

The debt avalanche method involves making minimum payments on all your debts, except the one with the highest interest rate. Follow these steps:

1. List your debts from highest to lowest interest rate. Your focus for this strategy will be the debt with the highest interest rate.

2. For the debt with the highest interest rate, make the minimum payment *and* add your additional debt payment.

3. For all other debts on the list, make the minimum payment.

4. Once you have paid off your debt with the highest interest rate, *roll over to the next debt on your list*:

   (i) the debt with the highest interest rate's minimum payment and (ii) your additional payment.

5. Repeat until you are debt-free!

An advantage of the debt avalanche method is that it could save you the most money because you are prioritizing your debt with the highest interest, which costs you the most. A disadvantage of this strategy is that, if your debt with the highest interest rate also has a large balance, it may take you a while to pay it off. You may become discouraged or lose steam if the initial debts in your journey take you a long time to pay off.

How to Pick the Best Strategy

The inevitable question: *Which strategy should I choose? Snowball or avalanche?*

Answer: *Whichever strategy gets you to pay off the debt.* Seriously. The "best" strategy is going to be the one that you believe will keep you motivated.

With that said, I recommend using simple, free, online tools that help you compare both strategies. NerdWallet has an excellent debt repayment calculator that allows you to plug in the information you gathered for your debt overview.[28]

Example: Kathy's Debt Snowball versus Debt Avalanche

Let's revisit Kathy's debt overview and the additional payment that she calculated from her budget.

Kathy's Debt Overview

Type	Balance	Interest Rate	Minimum Payment
Toyota car note	$10,000	3%	$300
Federal student loans	$20,000	5% (average rate)	$350
Chase credit card	$1,000	20%	$50
Bank of America credit card	$3,000	25%	$100

Kathy's additional payment amount: $400

Kathy plugs in her various debts and additional payment amount into a calculator comparing the debt snowball and avalanche methods.

Debt Payoff Strategy	With No Additional Payment	Debt Snowball (with $400 additional payment)	Debt Avalanche (with $400 additional payment)
Debt payoff order	N/A	1. Chase credit card 2. Bank of America credit card 3. Toyota car note 4. Federal student loans	1. Bank of America credit card 2. Chase credit card 3. Federal student loans 4. Toyota car note
Time frame	66 months	30 months	30 months
Total principal paid	$34,000	$34,000	$34,000
Total interest paid	$5,328	$2,369	$2,229
Total debt paid	**$39,328**	**$36,369**	**$36,229**

Source: Calculations made using the NerdWallet Debt Snowball Calculator.

In this example, the time and monetary differences between the debt snowball and avalanche methods are small. With either method, Kathy is projected to be completely debt-free in 30 months. Compared to the debt snowball, the debt avalanche is estimated to save Kathy an additional $140 in interest.

Regardless of the strategy that she chooses, Kathy will:

- Be debt-free *three years earlier* (66 months versus 30 months); and
- Save nearly $3,000 in interest.

thanks to her thoughtful, written, debt repayment plan!

Let's Get Personal

When I started my debt-free journey in January 2016, I had yet to learn about the debt snowball or avalanche methods. I decided to first tackle my credit card debt because of its oppressively high interest rate (about 29%). In hindsight, because my highest-interest debt also happened to be the debt with the smallest balance (about $13,000), I guess you can say that I implemented a hybrid strategy!

Regardless of the chosen strategy (snowball, avalanche, or hybrid), consistency is essential.

Step 4: Implement Your Strategy

Now that you have gathered your debt information, determined your additional debt payment amount, and selected either the snowball or avalanche method, it is time to execute your plan.

Contact Your Lender

Before making an additional payment to your debt, review your lender's policies. Additional payments for credit cards are ordinarily easy to make via the credit card company's website. However, other debts may require more. For example, *your lender may*:

- Require that you cover any outstanding interest before they direct your additional payment to the debt's principal;
- Treat additional payments as an early payment for the following month rather than applying the extra payment to your principal; and/or
- Require that you specify in writing that your additional payments should be applied to your debt's principal.

To avoid any confusion, contact your lender and ask them about their policies and process for directing additional payments to your debt's *principal*.

Put It in the Budget

Once you are clear on your lender's additional payment policies, include your additional debt payment amount in your budget. Remember that you will be making minimum payments on all your debts except the one that you have chosen to focus on (either the smallest debt or the one with the highest interest rate).

Consistency is key. Even if you have a month in which you are unable to apply as much as you had planned, go back to your plan and pick up where you left off. Slowly but surely, you will crush your debts!

Refinancing and Balance Transfers

Refinancing Your Debt

Refinancing is the process of revising and/or replacing the terms of an existing debt, such as a car loan, student loan, or mortgage. The refinancing process typically involves a borrower taking on a new agreement with their same lender or a new lender, which replaces the borrower's original debt agreement.[29] The reasons for refinancing include taking advantage of a lower interest rate (which reduces the total debt cost), a shorter repayment period (which brings you closer to paying off your debt), and other more favorable terms.

The Refinancing Process

Here is what the refinancing process typically entails:

Step 1: Get clear on your goal: Why do you want to refinance your debt? Are you looking for the lowest possible interest rate, an adjusted repayment time frame, more favorable terms? Answering these questions will help you understand the type of lender and plans to look for.

Step 2: Conduct research: Do your homework! Refinancing is not an overnight process. Find out whether your current lender offers refinancing options to borrowers. Research external lenders, which can include online banks, traditional banks, and credit unions. Compare their interest rates, fees, and repayment terms.

Step 3: Prepare your documents: In order to refinance, you must first be approved.

- Check your credit: Now is a great time to review your credit. If you refinance with your current lender, the company may rerun a credit check or may approve you based on your repayment history. However, a new lender will almost always check your credit to assess your riskiness as a borrower.[30]

- Gather your documentation: Lenders may ask for a variety of documents including government-issued identification, Social Security number, proof of employment, income, residency, and degree (some student loan refinancing companies request this).

Step 4: Select, wait for approval, and sign: Once you have selected your new lender, submit your documentation and wait until you are approved. If you are approved, carefully review your new agreement's terms and conditions.

Step 5: Have your old lender confirm in writing: After you have completed the refinancing process, tie up any loose ends with your old lender. Have the company confirm in writing that your obligations have been fully satisfied and that you no longer have a balance, nor any outstanding interest or fees owed.

Questions to Ask a Prospective Refinancing Lender

- **Process:** *What is your refinancing process?*
  Call and ask prospective lenders to walk you through their refinancing process. This is also a great way to test their customer service support.

- **Interest:** *What interest rates are you offering? Are these rates fixed or variable?*
  A lower interest rate is usually the key factor for refinancing, so get clear on your options.

- **Autopay deduction:** *Do you offer an autopay deduction?*
  Many lenders offer borrowers a deduction on the interest rate (e.g., 0.25% or 0.50%) if the borrowers set up an automatic payment for their monthly bill. This is a great way to save money and effortlessly automate your debt payments.

- **Loan term:** *How long is the loan repayment term?*
  Confirm that the proposed time frame aligns with your goals.

- **Loan origination fee:** *Are there any origination fees?*
  Inquire whether you will be charged a loan origination fee.

- **Monthly minimum payment:** *What is the monthly minimum payment?*
  If your new monthly minimum payment is higher than your old payment, consider how this will fit into your budget. Run the numbers!

(continued)

(continued)

- **Total cost of borrowing:** *What is the total cost of borrowing?*

  Many lenders provide the total cost of borrowing, which breaks down your principal and the total interest that you will pay the new lender over the loan term.

- **Additional payments:** *What is your policy for additional payments made to the loan?*

  Get clear on the lender's additional payment policies. Some lenders require borrowers to submit written approval for additional principal payments. This may be referred to as a "standing payment instruction."

- **Late fees and hardship policies:** *Can you describe your policies on late payments? Do you offer any assistance to borrowers that are unexpectedly unable to satisfy their payment obligation?*

  Life happens, so be sure to understand what your lender's policies are on late payments and the process if you are unable to make payments.

Note: It may be a better idea to first research this question via the lender's website and other materials if you believe that directly asking this question may reflect negatively on your loan application. Because it is simply a question, it should not, but you may want to err on the side of caution.

- **Reviews:** Read reviews of prospective lenders. Refinancing is a serious process, so customer feedback can help you decide whether a lender will suit your needs.

Example: Shannon's Loan Refinance

Shannon has a personal loan with a $20,000 balance and a 10% interest rate. She has five years left to repay her loan. Her current monthly payment is $425.

Shannon believes that her interest rate is high, so she explores refinancing. She reviews her credit report, credit score, and loan repayment history and is confident that she can lock in a lower interest rate with a new lender. After some research, she decides to refinance her loan through her local bank, which offers her a 4% interest rate.

Her local bank pays off her loan with her old lender, which releases Shannon from her old lender. She now has an agreement with her local bank to repay the debt. Her monthly payment remains the same at $425.

Repayment Strategy	Personal Loan with 10% Interest Rate	Refinanced Loan with 4% Interest Rate
Estimated monthly payment	$425	$425
Time frame	60 months (5 years)	49 months (4 years + 1 month)
Total principal paid	$20,000.00	$20,000.00
Total interest paid	$5,496.45	$1,708.99
Total debt paid	**$25,496.45**	**$21,708.99**

Source: Calculations made using the Credit Karma Debt Repayment Calculator.

By refinancing, Shannon has shaved 11 months off her repayment time frame and has saved nearly $3,800 in interest!

Refinancing May Not Be for You

Although refinancing has its benefits, it is not the best option for everyone.

For example, refinancing *federal student loans* with a private lender means that you no longer have federal loans; you instead now have a private loan. This means that you will no longer have access to the benefits federal student loans provide, including income-based repayment plans and forbearance/deferment options.

Critically, and relevant to those in the public sector, refinancing your federal student loans with a private lender removes you from loan forgiveness eligibility. This means that you will be ineligible for a federal loan forgiveness program such as Public Service Loan Forgiveness (PSLF), and if the federal government cancels or forgives federal student loans, you will not be eligible for those benefits.

Let's Get Personal

In early 2017 (a year after I had started repaying my student loans), my law firm circulated a brochure advertising student loan refinancing with a company called SoFi.[31] SoFi is a finance company that provides a variety of products, including loans, banking and investment solutions, and credit cards.[32]

(continued)

(continued)

> At the time, the interest rate on my student loans averaged about 8%. Because I had a high debt balance (well over $150,000), I knew that even a small reduction in my interest rate could mean significant savings. After doing my research, I learned that refinancing would allow me to lower the interest rate on my loans, save me tens of thousands, and cut my repayment term in half.
>
> SoFi allowed me to make additional payments to the principal, which I took full advantage of during bonus and tax season. I also took advantage of an autopay discount (which lowered my interest rate even further) and cut my repayment time frame even further.
>
> ***Ultimately, I shaved six years off my original debt repayment (from 10 years down to four years) and saved nearly $40,000 in interest.***

Refinancing played a major role in my debt-free journey and although it is not the right choice for everyone, it is an option that I encourage people to explore.

Balance Transfers

A balance transfer is when you move your debt balance from one account to another. Like refinancing, borrowers typically do a balance transfer to obtain a lower interest rate, adjusted repayment term, or other favorable terms.

We often see balance transfers in the form of credit card balance transfers. These are credit card transactions in which a new credit card pays off the balance on one (or more) credit cards. The borrower now has an obligation to the new credit card. The new credit card typically offers the borrower a low or 0% introductory interest rate, which can result in significant savings. A balance transfer is a great option for those who are looking to make their high-interest credit card debt more manageable.

However, balance transfers are not right for everyone:

- *First*, a balance transfer does not close your old credit card(s). If you continue to use your old cards without paying them off in full, you will rack up new debt—in addition to the debt that you now have with your new credit card. Racking up debt on the old cards, while attempting to pay off the new card with the balance transfer defeats the purpose of using this strategy.
- *Second*, a successful balance transfer requires a repayment strategy. If you do not have a clear plan to pay off your debt in full during the

low or 0% interest introductory period, your outstanding debt *could be subject to an even higher interest rate* than you previously had once the introductory period expires.

If you are considering a balance transfer, keep these in mind:

- **Credit check:** Like refinancing, balance transfers typically require a credit check. Review your credit score and report to ensure that you are in a good position to get approved for a balance transfer. The credit card company that you seek approval from will also likely run a credit check, which may impact your credit score.

- **Interest rate:** Many balance transfer cards offer an introductory APR of 0% for 12 to 18 months. Ideally you want a card that offers you the lowest possible interest rate.

- **Balance transfer fee:** Some cards charge a one-time fee to conduct the balance transfer. These fees usually range from 3% to 5%. For example, if the balance that you want to transfer is $10,000, a 3% fee means that you will have to pay $300. Aim for a card that does not charge a balance transfer fee.

- **Annual fee:** Some cards charge an annual fee, which typically ranges from $50 to $200. Aim for a card that does not charge an annual fee.

Balance transfers can be an excellent tool in your credit card debt payoff strategy. However, it is critical to have a written plan with deadlines by which to pay off your balance. This will ensure that you maximize this strategy's benefit.

Example: Tiffany's Not-So-Wise Balance Transfer

Tiffany had a credit card with a $5,000 balance and 20% APR. Let's call this Card 1. She was approved for a balance transfer card with a 0% APR for 18 months. Let's call this Card 2.

Unfortunately, after Tiffany transferred Card 1's balance to Card 2, she did not use Card 1 responsibly. Rather than using it for purchases that she could immediately pay off (e.g., a utility bill) or temporarily ceasing any purchases, she started charging travel and other discretionary expenses to Card 1. Card 1 went from having a $0 balance to $3,000 over the course of a year.

As for Card 2, Tiffany has only made the minimum payment because she has relied on the card's 0% interest rate.

The 0% APR 18-month introductory period will expire soon. Tiffany now realizes how quickly her debt has accumulated. Once the introductory period expires, Tiffany will have more debt than she started with, subject to a high-interest rate.

Example: Patricia's Wise Balance Transfer

Like Tiffany, Patricia also has a credit card with a $5,000 balance and 20% APR. She too gets approved for a balance transfer card with a 0% APR for 18 months.

Patricia is eager to take advantage of this opportunity and plans to pay off her balance in full before the 0% APR offer expires. To determine her monthly minimum payment, she divides her $5,000 balance by 18 months.

$$\$5,000\,(\text{card balance}) \div 18 \text{ months}\,(0\% \text{ APR period}) = \$278 \text{ monthly payment}$$

She incorporates her $278 monthly payment into her budget.

	Card 1 with 20% APR	Balance Transfer with 0% APR
Estimated monthly payment	$100 (minimum payment)	$278.00
Time frame	60 months (5 years)	18 months (1.5 years)
Total principal paid	$5,000.00	$5,000.00
Total interest paid	$2,948.17	$0.00
Total debt paid	**$7,948.17**	**$5,000**

Source: Calculations made using the Credit Karma Debt Repayment Calculator.

Without a balance transfer, and making only the minimum payment, Patricia would have repaid a total of $7,948.17. But, by wisely using a balance transfer, Patricia instead pays a total of $5,000, saving her nearly $3,000 in interest and reducing her debt repayment time frame from 5 years to 1.5 years!

More Debt Repayment Tips

- **Request a lower interest rate:** Contact and direct your lender to your positive repayment history, and ask if you can get a lower interest rate. Always review the terms and conditions for a lowered interest rate.
- **Refrain from incurring more debt:** During your debt payoff journey, avoid adding to your debt as much as possible. This seems

obvious, but many fail to realize the impact that accumulating debt during your payoff journey has on both your debt payoff goal and stamina.

- **Hide your cards:** If you are struggling with credit card debt, temporarily put them away or cut them up. This does not mean that you should close your credit card, which can hurt your credit score. All this means is that you will refrain from using them while you pay off your cards.

  - Note that some banks will close a card after a certain period of nonuse (e.g., a year), so check your bank's policies.

- **Use your emergency fund:** If you find yourself in a tight spot, use your emergency fund, rather than debt, to cover your expenses—that's what it's there for!

- **Do not ignore your debt:** Ignoring your debt can result in legal action from your lender, collection agency letters, and a damaged credit score.

- **Reward yourself along the way:** The debt-free journey can be long. Celebrate milestones (e.g., every $5,000 or $10,000 paid) by treating yourself to something that brings you joy. This does not have to be anything expensive, simply something that will encourage you on the journey.

- **Do not follow one-size-fits-all advice:** Your debt-free journey is unique to you. Ignore any advice that shames or argues that everyone should follow the same approach. Apply the tips you have learned from this chapter as appropriate to your circumstances.

- **Write down your debt-free date:** Remember that words have power. Grab a sticky note or your planner, and write down the month and year that you expect to become debt-free!

- **Keep your "why" in mind:** Your why will keep you motivated during times of discouragement or frustration. Write it down, make it your screensaver. You've got this!

Debt repayment is only a part of your financial freedom journey. It is a chapter, not your story.

Meet Nika Booth

Nika is an award-winning debt expert, personal finance content creator, and the founder of Debt Free Gonnabe. She's on a journey to slay her six-figure debt and has so far paid off over $70,000. Nika created Debt Free Gonnabe to document and share her journey, and now teaches women how to better manage their money and pay off debt without sacrificing fun. She won the 2021 Plutus Award for Best Debt Freedom Content and has been featured by Meta and CNN Audio, as well as CNBC, Yahoo!, GoBanking Rates, *Vox*, *Mic*, and more.

Q. You are currently tackling over $200,000 of debt and have already paid off $70,000! What made you decide to embark on a debt-free journey?

A. I started and stopped this journey a number of times before I really got serious. I was tired of knowing that I made decent money, but I never seemed to have any for myself, especially when it came down to saving money, paying down my debt, investing, giving, and so on. Every time I got paid, the money was gone almost immediately because every time I turned around, I was owing someone else money. I felt stuck and out of control.

However, the thing that really lit a fire under me was when the federal government shut down for 35 days between December 2018 and January 2019. During that time, I received partial pay and had no idea how much each paycheck would be. There was so much uncertainty about my financial future and once the shutdown was over, I said, "never again!" Never again would I allow someone else to have that much control over when I got paid, how much I got paid, and my ability to take care of myself. I knew that in order to make that happen, I would have to change my mindset and habits around money and get rid of my debt.

Q. How do you balance debt payoff with enjoying life?

A. I make sure that I budget for fun as much as I can. I don't believe in the "all or nothing" approach when it comes to tackling debt and that you have to sacrifice fun and be miserable while paying off debt. So, I never eliminated spending money on the things that bring me joy and that matter to me. Instead, I spend my money on those things according to a budget or spending plan. Of course, it doesn't look the same way it did when I was racking up debt because in order to make real progress in tackling debt, you have to give up the behaviors that got you into debt in the first place.

Enjoying life while balancing debt payoff looks like eating more meals at home but budgeting for eating out or happy hour with friends once every two weeks, or not swiping my credit card for plane tickets impulsively but setting aside money every payday into my vacation sinking fund and then paying for the trip in full.

I still get to do the things I enjoy with the people I love but now there are boundaries in place when it comes to my money. Those boundaries help to ensure that I'm able to meet my financial goals while still enjoying life.

Q. What advice would you give to someone who is having a difficult time forgiving themselves for past money mistakes, particularly with regard to debt?

A. Remember that those past money mistakes were made based on the information, resources, and money management tools you had *at that time*. You did the best you could with what you had and what you knew then. There's nothing you can do about what happened in the past and you can't live in the past. However, you can take the information, resources, and money management tools that you have *today* to correct those mistakes and set up your future self for financial success.

Q. What is one piece of debt management advice you would give your younger self?

A. Look at purchases and how you spend money as time worked or based on the amount of time you have to spend working in order to pay for something. Looking at spending this way can help reduce the likelihood of getting into debt or digging yourself deeper in debt.

I learned this lesson the hard way. I now must work extremely hard to tackle my six-figure debt. However, because I didn't value my purchases based on the time I would have to give up, I can hardly remember everything I went into debt for.

(*continued*)

(continued)

Q. What does *financial freedom* mean to you?

A. *Financial freedom*, to me, means having options. The option to give to the people and initiatives that I care about. The option to spend as much time as I want or need doing what brings me joy. The option to do what I want with my time and my money. The option to do work that matters to me and the option to create the terms upon which I work.

Chapter 9

Master Your Credit and Your Credit Cards

It was spring 2007, and I was a senior in high school. A credit card company came to my school and set up outside the cafeteria. Their eye-catching table allowed students to sign up for what would be, for most of us, our first credit card. I completed a simple form that asked for my personal information and signature. I was given the option to personalize my card with a variety of images—I chose a puppy on a blue background. A few weeks later, my credit card arrived in the mail in a discreet envelope. I beamed with pride as I signed my name on the back of the card. I was stepping into adulthood.

My credit card had a limit of $250, so I told myself that I would only put small purchases on the card and immediately pay it off. I also told myself that I would never get into credit card debt. Those promises were quickly broken when I started college just a few months later.

In the fall of 2007, I started my freshman year at Stony Brook University. I began to regularly use my credit card for purchases for my dorm room and funding regular trips to the mall. I wasn't alone in this. My classmates and newfound friends were all signing up for credit cards on campus. On Wednesdays, my school had "Campus Life Time"—a two-hour time block where students could enjoy free events, food, fairs, and giveaways. Credit card companies also made their way to Campus Life Time. Much like the company that had visited my high school, these companies would set up tables with goodies—mugs, pens, stickers, and T-shirts—to incentivize students to sign up for a credit card. If you are unfamiliar with these practices, it is likely because you attended high school or college after federal and state laws greatly limited credit card companies from promoting their products on school campuses.[1]

Instead of immediately paying off my card as I had promised myself, I only made the minimum payment and allowed my debt to grow. My credit card company increased my credit limit from $250 to $500, and then to $1,000, which meant a greater opportunity to spend. Something else that increased: my APR. The 0% introductory APR on my card eventually skyrocketed to 29%—yes, you read that correctly. The compounding interest coupled with my poor spending habits made getting to a $0 balance impossible.

My credit card debt was ever present throughout college and law school. I was stuck in a vicious cycle: pay the minimum (sometimes a little more), swipe the card, accrue more debt, and repeat. My lack of a budget and proper money management skills had led to accumulating high-interest and expensive credit card debt. My credit score had also taken a hit. It took me nearly a decade to completely free myself of credit card debt and improve my credit score.

In the spring of 2016, I fully paid off my $13,000 credit card debt. A bonus with that milestone: my credit score hit 750, which placed it in the "very good" range. Even though I had yet to fully understand how intertwined credit cards are with credit, I would soon develop a healthy relationship with both my credit and credit cards.

Since becoming debt-free, my credit score has increased to above 800, placing it in the "exceptional" range. I still regularly use my credit cards for most of my purchases—in a responsible way, of course—and have discovered how to maximize them for my benefit. In this chapter, I teach you how to do the same.

Credit Basics

What Is Credit?

Credit establishes a relationship between a creditor (the lender, such as a bank) and a borrower (the debtor, such as a customer). This relationship allows the borrower to purchase goods or services using the lender's money before repaying the lender. It is based on the *trust* that the borrower will repay the lender in the future.

Think of credit as a rating that you are assigned. Having "good" credit, or a high rating, indicates to lenders that you are likely to be a responsible borrower. Having "bad" credit, or a low rating, indicates that you are less likely to be a responsible borrower and more likely to default on your payments.

Credit means that you are being trusted with debt to purchase goods or services.

A borrower's credit report contains information on their credit history and current credit profile. The three national credit reporting bureaus—Experian, Equifax, and TransUnion—regularly collect and update this information.

Think of your credit report as your "report card."

A borrower's credit score is a three-digit number that measures your credit risk—the lower your number, the higher the risk; the higher your number, the lower your risk. This number is based on information pulled from your credit report at a certain point in time.

Think of your credit score as your "GPA."

Why It Matters

Credit impacts your ability to qualify for credit cards and loans.[2] It also impacts the terms the lender will offer you, including interest rate and credit limit. Credit can impact your ability to:

- Buy a car
- Buy a home
- Buy insurance
- Open a new credit card
- Refinance your student loans

Credit can also impact your ability to secure a job. Certain employers, particularly those in the financial services industry, may request a prospective hire's credit information. Employers will use this information to assess how responsible a candidate would be with sensitive company or customer information and will look for signs of financial distress (e.g., high credit utilization, excessive debt) that could increase the risk of fraud or theft.[3] An employer must notify you of their intention to check your credit and obtain your written permission to do so.[4]

Credit can also impact your ability to get approved for an apartment. Landlords, including those in my home of New York City, often require that a credit check accompany your lease application to determine whether you will be a reliable tenant who will pay your rent on time.

Credit Score Ranges

Most credit scores fall under two types of scoring models: FICO® and VantageScore®.[5] These models use a score range of 300–850, with 300 being the lowest credit score and 850 the highest.[6] The differences between the two scoring models are minor. That is, if you have a strong FICO® score, you likely have a strong VantageScore®, and vice versa. For purposes of this chapter, we will focus on the FICO® score, which is the most common credit score.[7]

143

FICO® Score Ranges

The FICO® score ranges are as follows:

Score Range	Rating	Description
<580	Poor	Your score is well below the average score of U.S. consumers and demonstrates to lenders that you are a risky borrower.
581–669	Fair	Your score is below the average score of U.S. consumers, although many lenders will approve loans with this score.
670–739	Good	Your score is near or slightly above the average score of U.S. consumers; most lenders consider this a good score.
740–799	Very Good	Your score is above the average score of U.S. consumers and demonstrates to lenders that you are a very dependable borrower.
800+	Exceptional	Your score is well above the average score of U.S. consumers and clearly demonstrates to lenders that you are an exceptional borrower.

Source: "What Is a FICO® Score?" myFICO, https://www.myfico.com/credit-education/what-is-a-fico-score (last accessed July 25, 2022).

Credit Score Impact on Loan Terms

As just discussed, your credit score can significantly impact the terms that a lender offers you, including the interest rate.

Example: The Impact of Different Credit Scores

Paola and Monique are sisters. They each wish to purchase a car. They each have saved $5,000 in cash as a down payment and expect to take out a loan to finance the rest.

Paola has a 760 credit score, which is considered "very good." Her bank has approved her for a $20,000 loan with a 3.0% APR and 60-month term.

Monique has a 590 credit score, which is considered "fair." Her bank is reluctant to issue her a loan but ultimately approves her for a $20,000 loan with a 10.0% APR and 60-month term.

Here is how that 130-point credit score difference will impact the sisters:

	Paola's Car Loan	Monique's Car Loan
APR (interest rate)	3.0%	10.0%
Monthly payment	$359	$425
Time frame	60 months (5 years)	60 months (5 years)
Total principal paid	$20,000.00	$20,000.00
Total interest paid	$1,562.43	$5,496.45
Total debt paid	**$21,562.43**	**$25,496.45**

Source: Calculations made using the Credit Karma Debt Repayment Calculator.

Not only is Monique's monthly car payment higher than Paola's, but her loan will ultimately cost her nearly $4,000 more!

The Factors that Impact Your Credit Score

Your credit score is calculated by analyzing the information in your credit report at a specific point in time. This means that your credit score is not a static number. For example, your score this month may look different than it did a few months prior. It can increase or decrease depending on your debt management activity.

The data in your credit report is grouped into five categories, which make up your credit score.

Category	Percentage	Description
Payment history	35%	This shows whether you have paid your past accounts on time.
		Lenders want to know that you are going to pay your debt on time. Aside from affecting your credit, missed payments can result in late fees and interest.
Amounts owed	30%	This shows how much debt you owe relative to the amount of credit that you have available. This is also known as credit utilization.

(continued)

(continued)

Category	Percentage	Description
		This does not necessarily mean that a high debt amount (e.g., student loans or a mortgage) will negatively impact your score. Rather, it means that lenders want to know if you are overextending yourself with the debt that has been made available to you, which can put you at risk of default.
Length of credit history	15%	The longer a credit history you have, the better.
		This will look at the age of your credit accounts and will consider the age of your oldest and newest accounts.
New credit	10%	This shows the new credit accounts that you have opened.
		This looks at whether you have opened several accounts in a short period of time. That type of activity could indicate financial distress and flag you as a greater risk.
Credit mix	10%	This considers the various types of credit accounts that you have, including revolving debt (e.g., credit cards) and installment debt (e.g., student loans).

Source: "What's in My FICO® Scores?" myFICO, https://www.myfico.com/credit-education/whats-in-your-credit-score (last accessed July 25, 2022).

Building Your Credit

One of the most popular questions that I get regarding credit: "Cindy, how do I increase my credit score?" Here are three steps to get you started.

Step 1: Review Your Credit Report

The first step to building and improving your credit score is to understand the status of your credit. The best way to do this is to obtain your credit report. Not only will your credit report inform you of your credit health, but it can also help you catch signs of identity theft.

Federal law allows you to obtain a *free* copy of your credit report every 12 months from each of the three national credit reporting bureaus: Experian, Equifax, and TransUnion. You can easily obtain your free reports through AnnualCreditReport.com by providing the following to verify your identity:[8]

- Name
- Address
- Social Security number
- Date of birth

When you pull your credit reports, carefully review them to ensure that your information is accurate and complete. Specifically, look out for the following:

- **Personal information:** Confirm that your personal information is correct (e.g., name, date of birth, address, Social Security number).
- **Financial accounts:** Review your "open accounts" and confirm that you own these and that they are still open. Review your "closed accounts" and confirm that these accounts were all under your name and are now closed. Review your payment history and ensure that it has been accurately reported.
- **Inquiries:** Confirm that you authorized any inquiries that are listed. For example, if you recently opened a new credit card or sought a car loan, that may appear on your report.
- **Public records:** Confirm that the information on any lawsuits, bankruptcy filings, judgments, or liens filed against you is accurate.

Address Inaccuracies in Your Credit Report

The Fair Credit Reporting Act requires that credit bureaus ensure that the information they collect about you is accurate. Credit bureaus must also provide you with the opportunity to correct any mistakes.[9] If you identify an error on your report, contact both the credit bureau and the business reporting the error. For example, if your Experian credit report shows that you missed a payment for your Chase credit card, contact both Experian and Chase to correct the error.

Do not neglect to report errors!

147

Master Your Credit and Your Credit Cards

Seemingly small errors can have a significant impact on your credit report and score, so do not neglect to report errors!

Another potential risk of failing to review your credit report is identity theft. Identity theft can result in significant financial, legal, and emotional harm. With your personal information, thieves can steal money from your bank accounts, charge purchases to your credit cards, open new lines of credit, steal your tax refund, and more. If you suspect identity theft, visit IdentityTheft.gov to report it and obtain a personalized recovery plan.[10]

Let's Get Personal

I recommend helping loved ones obtain their credit reports—with their clear consent, of course. A few years ago, I pulled my mother's credit report for the first time. My mother speaks limited English and does not use a computer (although she loves her iPhone and WhatsApp—if you are the child of immigrants, you know exactly what I mean), so she welcomed my help with this task. To our relief, the information on her reports, including her personal information, payment history, and information on past and current accounts, was accurate.

But this is not always the case. Far too often, people, particularly members of our older population and non-English speakers, fall victim to identity theft. Therefore, it is critical to ensure that not only our credit but that of our loved ones is accurate.

Step 2: Review Your Credit Score

Even though you are entitled to a free annual credit report, there isn't an entitlement to a free annual credit score.[11] However, a credit bureau might provide you with a free credit score. Many banks, credit unions, and credit card companies also offer their customers free credit scores. For example, I can access mine through most of my credit card accounts. Keep in mind that providers may offer either the FICO® or VantageScore®, so review their site for complete details.

Companies that offer a paid credit monitoring service may also offer customers with a free score. However, before signing up for a credit monitoring service, review their terms and conditions, particularly as related to their fees.

Here are free resources to obtain your credit score:[12]

- Experian: Experian.com; FreeCreditScore.com
- Credit Karma (scores from TransUnion and Equifax): Creditkarma.com
- Discover Credit Scorecard: CreditScorecard.com

Step 3: Focus on the Five Factors

Let's revisit the five factors that make up our credit score and consider the following strategies to maximize each of those factors.

Category	Percentage	Tips
Payment history	35%	**Pay your bills on time.** If you accidentally forget a payment, pay your bill immediately and contact your lender. Remember that your lender may report missed payments to the credit bureaus. Explain to your lender your mistake and direct them to your otherwise positive payment history. Politely ask your lender if they can grant you a courtesy waiver.
		Set up text/email notifications and calendar reminders. Many lenders allow customers to set up notifications of upcoming due dates. If your lender does not provide this feature, set aside an hour of your time to set up recurring calendar reminders for your bills.
		Set up automatic payments. Most companies allow you to set up automatic bill pay by linking your checking account. With automatic payments, you can avoid missed payments.
Amounts owed	30%	**Calculate your credit utilization rate (CUR).** To calculate your CUR, divide your outstanding debt by your credit limit.
		For example, if your credit limit across two credit cards is $10,000 and you owe $4,000, your credit utilization is 40%:
		$$\$4,000 \div \$10,000 = .4 \text{ or } 40\ \%\ CUR$$
		Keep your CUR less than 30%, ideally less than 10%. The general rule of thumb is to keep your CUR less than 30%. However, many experts recommend keeping your CUR less than 10% for the best credit score.[13]

(continued)

Master Your Credit and Your Credit Cards

Category	Percentage	Tips
		Ask for a higher credit limit. After a certain period and positive payment history, many companies automatically provide borrowers with an increased credit limit. If yours has not, ask for a credit limit increase.
		For example, if your credit limit across two credit cards is $10,000 and you owe $2,000, your credit utilization is 20%. If your credit limit is increased to $15,000, your credit utilization drops to 13.3%.
		Note that this *may* result in a temporary decrease to your credit score *if* the lender conducts a hard inquiry to determine whether you are eligible for a credit increase. When in doubt, ask your lender about their process for increasing your credit line.
Length of credit history	15%	**Keep your oldest accounts open.** Keeping your earliest accounts, such as your first credit card, open shows creditors a longer credit history.
		• **Patience.** If you are new to credit, you likely do not have a long credit history. A 32-year-old with a 12-year credit history is more likely to have a higher score than a 22-year-old with a 2-year credit history (all other things being equal) because of their longer credit history.
New credit	10%	**Be mindful of how many new lines of credit you are opening and when.** Applying for multiple lines of credit—for example, new credit cards, a car loan, and/ or a personal loan—during a short time frame may hurt your score.
Credit mix	10%	**Understand the types of credit you have.** Having a mix of installment and revolving debts shows creditors that you are good at managing various types of debt.

To be clear, this *does not* mean that you should take on unnecessary debt. In full transparency, I only have one type of debt (which I pay off every month)—credit cards—and my credit score is over 800.

Let's Get Personal

Remember the credit card I told you about at the beginning of this chapter—the one that I got in high school with a 29% APR? Well, I closed it after paying the balance in 2016.

Why would I close my oldest credit card? Several reasons:

- **29% APR:** As a matter of principle, I could not support a company that charged such an onerous interest rate, despite my repeated requests to decrease the rate.

- **Annual fee:** The credit card had a $99 annual fee and provided no rewards or benefits.

- **Miscellaneous fees:** I started to notice random monthly fees for $3 or $5 on my credit card statement and was never able to obtain a clear reason for the charges.

Although I knew that closing the card would impact my score by affecting my credit utilization (my overall credit limit would decrease with the removal of a card) and length of credit history (it was my oldest card), I was confident with my decision. At the time, I had four other credit cards with a positive payment history, combined high credit limit, and decent average age of credit.

Even though my credit score temporarily decreased, it quickly increased because of my new and improved debt management practices. Although this move may not be the best for everyone, it was right for me.

Credit Cards

The Impact of Credit Cards on Credit

A credit card is a form of payment issued by a bank or other financial institution that allows users to purchase goods and services. In return, the user agrees to repay the borrowed funds with applicable interest and fees.

You may have noticed that credit cards are heavily intertwined with credit. Proper credit card use is a great way to improve your credit score. But poor credit card use is a surefire way to hurt your score.

Proper credit card use is key to obtaining, building, and maintaining credit.

Your Credit Card Statement

When was the last time you reviewed your credit card statement? Here are a few things to look out for:

- **Total credit limit:** The total amount of credit that your credit card company has made available to you.
- **Balance:** The amount that you owe your credit card company.
- **Available credit:** Your total credit limit minus your current balance. It tells you how much you can charge to your credit card before maxing it out (which I do not recommend!).
- **Minimum payment:** The minimum amount that you must pay your credit card company to avoid a late or penalty fee.
- **Payment due date:** The date by which you must make your minimum payment to avoid a late or penalty fee.
- **Statement opening and closing dates:** The dates of your billing cycle.
  - Your credit card company typically reports the balance and payment information to the credit bureaus on the closing date.
- **Purchase APR:** The interest applicable to purchases.
- **Cash advance APR:** The interest applicable to cash advances. This rate is typically higher than the APR on purchases.
  - A cash advance is when you withdraw cash from your credit card account.

Managing Your Credit Cards

Pay Your Balance by the Payment Due Date

One thing that I wish I had understood about credit cards during my college and law school years: if you pay your balance *in full by the payment due date*, then you will not be charged interest.

However, if you only make the minimum payment by the due date, then interest will accrue on the remaining balance. Because credit card interest typically accrues *daily*, debt accumulates quickly!

Pay your credit card balance in full by the payment due date to avoid interest.

Example: Yusuf's Credit Card Statement

ABC Bank Credit Card Statement—February	
Balance	$1,200
Total credit limit	$10,000
Available credit	$8,800
Minimum payment	$50
Payment due date	March 11
Statement closing date	March 18
Purchase APR	20%
Cash advance APR	26%

If Yusuf pays off his $1,200 balance by March 11, he will not owe any interest. However, if he pays less than his complete balance—for example, if he only makes the minimum payment of $50—20% interest will start accruing on the remaining balance. Luckily for Yusuf, he reads this book and pays off his credit card balance in full by the payment date!

Aim for a Credit Utilization Rate Less than 10%, but Not 0%

Credit card use requires a delicate balance. We have already discussed that keeping your credit utilization rate (CUR) to less than 30%, ideally 10%, will help your credit score. However, if your CUR is 0%, some credit score models might interpret that to mean that you are not using your cards, which *may* be unhelpful to your score.[14]

Let's Get Personal

I use my credit cards the way I would use a debit card. I put my everyday purchases on my cards—groceries, household items, entertainment,

(continued)

(continued)

transportation, and so on. Rather than attempting to keep track of my credit cards' various closing dates (the date my credit card companies typically use to report my balance and payment information to the credit bureaus), I simply make sure that their balances are paid in full by their payment due dates. This way, I am confident that:

1. I will not accrue interest because the balances have been paid in full; and

2. The credit bureaus will see that I regularly and responsibly use my credit cards.

The delicate balance of a low credit utilization, but not quite 0%, can look like using your credit card for everyday purchases but making sure that the card is paid off in full by the payment due date.

Example: Yusuf's Credit Card Use

Recall the previous example.

Yusuf uses his credit card for his everyday purchases. He pays off his balance ($1,200) by the payment due date (March 11). After paying off his balance, he puts $800 of purchases on his card. His credit card company reports that $800 balance to the credit bureaus. This means that the credit bureaus will calculate Yusuf's credit utilization as 8%.

$$\$800 \text{ balance} \div \$10,000 \text{ credit limit} = .08, \text{ or } 8\% \text{ CUR}$$

Yusuf's credit utilization is less than 10% but more than 0%.

If you currently have credit card debt, focus on paying down the debt and getting your CUR to less than 10% and watch your credit score improve!

Credit Card Rewards

Aside from helping build your credit score, credit cards can also offer users with numerous benefits, including rewards. These rewards provide users with cash, free flights and hotel stays, free goods from merchants, and more. Credit card rewards come in several forms, including:[15]

- **Cash back:** Users earn a certain percentage of cash based on spending and/or payments. Cash back can typically be redeemed as cash via direct deposit in your checking account or check, or it can be applied as a credit to your credit card statement.
  - For example, ABC Credit Card offers 2% cash back on all purchases. This means that users will earn $2 cash back for every $100 spent on the card.
- **Miles:** Users can earn rewards from credit cards that are affiliated with their favorite airlines. Users can redeem these rewards for flights, free checked bags, hotel stays, and even other forms of transportation such as ride shares.
  - For example, ABC Airline offers its customers a card that will give them 50,000 miles upon approval. The card allows users to accumulate miles for every purchase made. When the user is ready to redeem their rewards, they can apply the miles toward discounted or free flights.
- **Points:** Users can accrue points and use the points to purchase goods or services.
  - For example, ABC Credit Card Company offers 50,000 points to new users. It also offers three points for every $1 spent on groceries and one point for every $1 spent on all other purchases.
    - o If you recently signed up for the card, and spend $100 on clothing and $100 on groceries, you will have 50,400 points (50,000 points when you sign up + 100 points on clothing purchase + 300 points on groceries).

Before taking advantage of credit card offers promising attractive rewards, keep the following in mind:

- **Credit score:** Even though most credit cards do not expressly state their credit score requirements, it is a good idea to:
  - Check your credit report
  - Check your credit score
  - Get a sense of the credit card company's score approval range (you can usually find this information online)
- **Review the terms and conditions:** Reward programs have their unique set of rules, including whether there is a minimum amount that you are required to spend on the card. Programs might also have limitations on when users are allowed to redeem the rewards.

Master Your Credit and Your Credit Cards

- **Pay off your cards in full:** In order to make the most of your rewards, pay off your balance in full. Otherwise, you risk having interest accrue, which can outweigh the benefits that you receive from the cards.

    - For example, if you receive 2% cash back on your credit card purchases, but you are paying 20% interest on your credit card's outstanding balance, you are losing more than you are gaining.

Let's Get Personal

Earlier I mentioned that I use my credit cards, rather than my debit card, for my everyday purchases. In addition to helping me maintain an "exceptional" credit score, responsibly using my credit cards has resulted in thousands (over $10,000, in fact) earned through cash back, miles, and point programs.

Over the past few years, I have followed this simple strategy to ensure that I am maintaining my 800+ credit score while maximizing my credit card benefits:

1. I pay off my credit card balances *in full* every single month.

2. I always pay my credit cards (and other bills, e.g., rent, utilities) *on time*.

3. I keep my credit utilization generally in the 2-5% range.

Credit Cards for Those with No or Poor Credit

Now that we understand the impact of credit cards on credit, as well as the benefits they provide, you may be eager to apply for one. But what if you have limited credit history or a poor score? Can you use credit cards to help repair or build your credit score?

Yes, and I have two options for you to consider.

Authorized Users

A primary cardholder is the owner of a credit account. An authorized user is someone who is added to the primary cardholder's account. The authorized user is issued their own card and is allowed to use it for purchases. However, the authorized user is not responsible for making any payments and is usually not allowed to make any changes to the account (such as requesting a credit limit increase).

Why would anyone want to have an authorized user on their account if the authorized user can run up charges on the card without being responsible for payment? Because of the benefits to the authorized user.

When an authorized user is added to a cardholder's account, the primary cardholder's credit activity—information on their credit utilization, credit type, timely payments, and so on—gets reported to the credit bureau for the authorized user. This means that if the authorized user has no credit history or poor credit, positive credit activity can improve their credit.

Anyone—such as a spouse, partner, sibling, child,[16] friend—can be an authorized user. But allowing someone to be an authorized user is a serious matter. The primary account holder should consider their relationship with the prospective authorized user, ensure that they are trustworthy, and must remain vigilant about their credit card statements, payments, and activity.

If you are thinking about adding an authorized user to your account, or want to be added as an authorized user to someone else's account, consider the following:

- **Confirm that credit activity will be reported:** The primary cardholder should ask the credit card issuer whether the credit activity will be reported to the credit bureaus for the authorized user. If the whole point of being an authorized user is to piggyback onto the primary cardholder's good credit management activity, then you want to make sure that the activity is being reported.

- **Ask about fees:** Inquire with the credit card issuer whether they charge an authorized-user fee.

- **Set clear terms:** Regardless of the primary cardholder and authorized user's relationship, establish clear terms on how the card will be used, what types of purchases are allowed, spending limits, and how and by when the card will be paid.

- **Understand the consequences of being removed as an authorized user:** The primary cardholder has the right to remove an authorized user from their account at any time. An authorized user may also be able to remove themselves from the account. But being removed as an authorized user may hurt the authorized user's credit score if they do not otherwise have credit accounts of similar age, have a low credit limit, and so on.

TIP: *If you have a positive credit history, consider giving the child in your life a great head start on building credit by adding them as an authorized user to your cards.*

Master Your Credit and Your Credit Cards

Being an authorized user is a great way to build credit from a young age. For example, if a parent (with good credit habits) adds their 16-year-old child to their credit card, that child will start building credit at the age of 16 rather than having to wait until they can apply for their own card. Naming the child as an authorized user, along with providing proper credit and credit card education and establishing ground rules, can give that child a head start on mastering their credit.

Also, keep in mind that you do not have to give the child their own card until you deem it appropriate.

Secured Credit Cards

Traditional credit cards are considered *unsecured* debt. This means that they are not backed by collateral. Collateral is "an asset that a lender accepts as security for a loan."[17] In order to get approved for a traditional credit card, there is no need for you to offer your assets like cash or your car to provide the credit card issuer assurance that you will repay your card. (Although you will, of course, sign an agreement promising to repay any debt, interest, and fees.)

Secured debt, on the other hand, is backed by collateral. For credit cards, this collateral comes in the form of a cash deposit from the cardholder. In order to get approved for a secured credit card, the user must put down a certain amount of money, which will also serve as the credit limit for the card. For example, if the user puts down a $200 deposit with the secured credit card application, that card will have a $200 credit limit. The deposit is held by the credit card issuer in the event that you do not pay your bill.

"But, Cindy, why would anyone want to do that?"
It's simple: to repair or build credit.

If someone has no or poor credit, a secured credit card is a great way to build credit from scratch or to rebuild damaged credit. The credit card issuer reports the user's activity to the credit bureau. After a certain period of time, the issuer may offer to upgrade the card from a secured card to an unsecured card and return the deposit to the user.

If you are interested in applying for a secured credit card:

- **Research:** Research the best options via popular websites like NerdWallet, WalletHub, or Bankrate. Look for cards with no annual fees. Also be mindful of other fees that may not be so obvious, like activation fees, monthly maintenance fees, and balance inquiry fees.

- **Apply and deposit:** Submit your application and, upon approval, deposit the required cash amount (e.g., $200).

- **Exercise good credit management:** Pay off your balance in full and on time and maintain low credit use.

- **Request an upgrade:** Many credit card issuers automatically offer an upgrade to an unsecured credit card. However, if your issuer does not, contact them about upgrade eligibility. If you are approved for an upgrade, your credit card issuer will return your deposit (assuming you do not have any charges outstanding).

Using a secured credit card requires patience and consistency. However, if you use it responsibly, you will slowly see an improvement in your credit, making the process worth the trouble.

Debunking Credit Myths

Before we wrap up this section, let's debunk some popular credit myths:

- **Myth #1: Checking your credit score will hurt it:** Checking your credit is considered an "inquiry," but not every inquiry will affect your score. In short, hard inquiries can affect your credit score; however, a soft inquiry will not.

  - *Hard inquiries:* These are inquiries made by a lender to determine whether you will be approved for credit (a loan, credit card, mortgage, etc.).

  - *Soft inquiries:* These can be inquiries that you make when you check your own credit. These can also include inquiries by creditors that are monitoring your credit or that prescreen you for a credit offer.

- **Myth #2: Carrying a balance on your credit card will help your score:** A balance is the outstanding amount that you owe on your credit card. If you do not pay off your balance by the due date, it will carry over to the next billing cycle where you can be subject to interest charges. A high balance can also negatively impact your credit score by increasing your credit utilization rate (CUR).

  - In short, pay off your balance in full to avoid interest charges and lower your CUR.

- **Myth #3: Married couples have a combined credit score:** There is no such thing as a joint or combined credit score. Everyone should build and maintain their individual credit.

Master Your Credit and Your Credit Cards

- However, one spouse's credit can affect the other's ability to obtain credit. For example, if a couple applies for a mortgage, one spouse's poor credit history can impact the couple's ability to get approved for the loan or to receive a competitive interest rate.

- **Myth #4: Closing your credit cards after paying them off will help your score:** *Paying off* your credit cards is great because it will reduce the amount that you pay in interest and improve your CUR. However, *closing* a card may impact your CUR and age of credit.

  - A suggestion to those who have paid off a card but want to keep it active: charge a small recurring subscription to the card and set up an automatic payment by the due date.

  ### Example: Kiana's Recently Paid Off Card

  - o Kiana recently paid off a credit card that she has had since college. She has had issues with overspending, so she wants to avoid using her card. But, because it is her oldest card and has a high credit limit, she decides to keep it active.

  - o Kiana budgets $9.99 monthly for her favorite music streaming subscription. She sets up an automatic monthly payment from her checking account to her credit card for $9.99.

  - o This strategy allows Kiana to keep her card active while effortlessly ensuring a timely monthly payment, which will help improve her credit score.

- **Myth #5: Late or missed payments will always stay on your credit report:** Although late or missed payments can stay on your credit report for up to seven years, they will not be there forever.

  - Additionally, the older negative information is, the less significant it will be. For example, a missed payment from five years ago will matter less than a missed payment from five months ago.

Meet Yanely Espinal

Yanely was born and raised in Bushwick, Brooklyn, to Dominican immigrant parents. She is a proud product of New York City public schools who credits her teachers and older sisters for her admission to Brown University on a full scholarship. Due to a lack of financial education, she racked up $20,000 of high-interest credit card debt in and after college. She began her career as a classroom teacher and quickly felt stuck when she couldn't keep up with her monthly payments.

Yanely committed to reading books and blogs and watching TED Talks about personal finance and money. She became debt-free in 2015, after 18 months of strict budgeting and following the debt avalanche repayment method. Unable to keep all this knowledge to herself, Yanely decided to help empower others by creating YouTube videos and offering financial workshops in her community with the channel name "MissBeHelpful." Her channel has been viewed over 3 million times and her podcast and book share the title *Mind Your Money*. Yanely serves on several advisory boards at nonprofits and tech companies and is a member of the CNBC Financial Wellness Council.

Q. You serve as a director of educational outreach with Next Gen Personal Finance and as a personal finance content creator on YouTube. What made you decide to become a financial educator and what has been your greatest accomplishment?

A. My experience as a classroom teacher led me to financial education! I was teaching students how to read, write, and do math—all critical topics for young students to learn. However, there was nothing in the curriculum about money and the role it plays in society and in our lives. I knew that my students would be doomed to repeat the same mistakes I had made with money if there was no educational intervention.

My students were predominantly Black and Latinx children of Caribbean immigrants. Like me, many had families that lacked access to financial education. I was afraid that no matter how successful I was at preparing my students academically, many of them would go on to sign up for student loans, credit cards, car loans, and more with little to no understanding of the terms and conditions. Would I really be able to view myself as a successful teacher if that turned out to be the case? I couldn't sit around and allow the next generation to repeat the mistakes I most regretted.

When I discovered that a small nonprofit, Next Gen Personal Finance (NGPF), was on a mission to get a full semester of personal finance into every U.S. public high school, I was drawn to their mission. It was my opportunity to do more than offer workshops or the occasional coaching sessions. It was my opportunity to truly create systemic change within the American education system. I joined as director in 2018, and since then the number of states with a stan-

(continued)

(continued)

dalone personal finance course required for high school graduation has more than doubled, from 5 to 13!

Q. Why is it important, for communities of color specifically, to learn about proper credit management?

A. Due to a lack of generational wealth, communities of color tend to not have sufficient cash available to make large purchases like buying a house or car without borrowing money. Many White families in America have access to financial capital in addition to social capital, which means grandparents or parents can help navigate the process of applying to college, applying for a mortgage, or establishing a strong credit score early on. For many Black families, however, redlining may have prevented parents, aunts, uncles, or grandparents from accessing federally insured home loans, and therefore older generations may lack the experience and knowledge regarding borrowing to pass down to the next generation. For many immigrants and first-generation Americans, the entire U.S. credit system is brand-new, overwhelming, and even confusing.

There are little to no culturally relevant resources available for understanding and navigating credit. Since most individuals of color will need to rely on banks and other institutional lenders to access loans to buy a house or pay for a child's college education, we have an immediate and urgent need for financial education, specifically about proper credit management and savvy methods for debt repayment.

Q. What would you say to those who believe, or have been taught, that credit does not matter?

A. I would say they are correct, to a certain extent! Credit does not matter to most incredibly wealthy individuals because they have large sums of cash available to pay for big-ticket items like a house, car, or a college education. If spending hundreds of thousands of dollars does not put a dent in your budget, then you probably do not care about your credit score right now. However, that would put you in a group with a very small percentage of Americans.

The annual average income for American workers in 2022 was $53,490, according to data from the U.S. Bureau of Labor Statistics. That's just over $1,020 per week, which doesn't leave much cash for big-ticket items after all monthly bills are paid. For everyday people, credit matters a lot! As a matter of fact, having no credit file or a thin credit file is seen as a big risk for lenders when they consider your loan application. That means you might not get approved for a home mortgage, car loan, personal loan, or education loan. If you do happen to get approved with a poor credit score, then you can expect to pay very high interest rates, which compound over time and tend to eat away at your chance to build real wealth.

Q. What is the quickest way to improve your credit score?

A. For revolving credit accounts like credit cards and lines of credit, the quickest way to improve your credit score is to make a large payment toward any outstanding debt you have so that your outstanding balance moves closer to zero. Ideally, you want to make a large enough payment that any remaining debt would be equal to less than 10% of all the credit available to you. Of course, this depends on whether you have wiggle room in your budget to free up enough extra money to send.

As for installment debt, where you make payments until the balance is at zero and then the account is closed, the goal would be to continue making consistent payments on time every month until the term of the loan ends. You can make additional payments if you would like, but first make sure that there is no penalty on your specific loan for early repayment. If you do not have any outstanding debt and are looking to increase your score, the fastest way would be to have a trusted family member or friend with excellent credit add you as an authorized user to their oldest credit card. This is a big decision that involves the authorized user getting a credit card with access to the primary card holder's credit limit, but if used properly it can be a powerful tool for improving or building credit quickly.

Q. What does *financial freedom* mean to you?

A. *Financial freedom* is time freedom. Maybe that's the reason why the phrase "time is money" is so popular! Having financial freedom trans-

(continued)

(continued)

lates to having enough money to not have to work if you don't want to. Instead, you can do whatever you would like to do with your time, at *all* times. On a random weekday afternoon, you can choose to relax for hours if that's what you desire. You can read, do yoga, sweep your yard, play with your kids, volunteer, go for a long walk, listen to your favorite music, watch a movie or television show, take a hot bubble bath, meditate, or do anything else that brings you peace and joy because you no longer have to worry about generating enough money to cover the cost of your needs and even some or all of your wants.

Chapter 10

Invest for Future You

It was my first day of work as a junior associate at the law firm I would call home for the next six years. A human resources staff member handed my colleagues and me a stack of papers to review and sign. One of those sets of papers was for employee retirement benefits. I skimmed the pages and saw unfamiliar terms: 401(k), brokerage, index funds, match, vesting schedule. Instead of asking my firm's benefits department or a colleague to explain what I had just been handed, I smiled, nodded, and put the papers away inside my desk.

I didn't touch those papers for two years.

It wasn't until I started becoming financially literate that I realized the importance of the forms I had been handed. I had missed the opportunity to start investing two years sooner because I had been too embarrassed to ask. But I have learned to give myself grace. My parents had never invested and had never spoken about investing. None of my friends spoke about money, let alone investing. How could I have known?

Fast forward to the present and investing is one of my favorite personal finance topics. I didn't understand the meaning of "make your money work for you" until I started investing. Investing consistently has been key to making my money grow and building a six-figure net worth.

Thanks to the knowledge that I gained from and encouragement that I found in personal finance books, podcasts, and social media, I finally opened my retirement investing account through my employer. I didn't stop there. I also opened my first *nonretirement* investing account with a robo-advisor. I started small, but was proud to start.

Investing is one of those topics where the overwhelming amount of information can debilitate us from acting. So, in this chapter we cover some basics and the two simple strategies that I used to start investing: (i) investing through a tax-advantaged retirement account and (ii) investing in a "regular" nonretirement account with a robo-advisor.

Investing Basics

What Is Investing?

Investing is putting a resource, such as money, into something or someone and expecting to gain from that act. Your expectation is that your investment will grow and that at a future date, you will receive back your original investment plus profit.

For example, you might invest money in a company, with the expectation that your investment will contribute to that company's growth. You might invest in real estate, with the expectation of generating rental income or re-selling the property in the future at a higher price. You might invest money in your small business, with the expectation that it will scale in the next decade.

In Chapter 7, we discussed saving in an emergency fund and sinking funds. To recap, an emergency fund serves as your financial cushion in the event of an emergency, such as a loss of income. Sinking funds allow you to save incrementally for irregular and large expenses, such as a vacation or a down payment on a house. Once you have created a plan for your emergency and sinking funds, it is time to put your money to work and invest!

If you want your money to grow, saving alone is not enough.
You need to invest.

Investing Terminology

For purposes of this chapter, we will focus primarily on investing in the stock market. Before diving any deeper, let's cover some important terminology. I realize that reviewing this type of terminology can be a bit dry, but stick with me!

The Magic Ingredients for Growth

What is it that makes investing so magical? What about this strategy allows your money to *grow* over time?

Rate of Return: This is the gain or loss of an investment over a period of time, expressed as a percentage. It will depend on the investments that you purchase.

To illustrate this point, let's look at an example. For the past century, the average rate of return of the U.S. stock market (how it has performed) has been 10%.[1] This means that, on average, you can expect a 10% return on your investments, if you invest in the U.S. stock market.

Two important things to note:

1. The 10% average return is based on the Standard & Poor's 500 Index (S&P 500). The S&P 500 is an index that tracks the performance of the top 500 companies in the United States. It is often considered the benchmark measure for annual stock market returns.[2]

2. A 10% return is *not* guaranteed. The stock market goes up and down—some years, the rate of return will be higher, and some years it will be lower. For example, during the Great Recession, between October 2007 and March 2009, the S&P 500 fell by 46%.[3] Compare that to 2021, where it performed at over 25%.

Why is this information important? Knowing the average rate of return for the stock market matters because, as investors, we can run projections using this number to estimate the growth of our investments. In this chapter, we will run several projections using an average 10% rate of return. But be mindful that your specific investment projections will depend on numerous factors, including what you decide to invest in, how those investments perform, and your unique time horizon.

Compound Interest: This is "the interest on a loan or deposit calculated based on both the initial principal and the accumulated interest from previous periods."[4] This is interest that grows on your principal (what you invest) plus the interest you have previously earned.

Earlier we spoke about the challenges of compound interest in the context of debt. Compound interest makes debt payoff difficult because debtors are not only paying what they originally borrowed (the principal) but also the interest that has accrued on top of the principal and on top of previous interest.

However, with investing, compound interest is magical. This concept of interest growing on top of interest is what makes our investments grow exponentially over time. Let's look at an example.

Example: Average Rate of Return and Compound Interest Over Time After creating her budget, Stephanie decides that she will invest $300 monthly. She is curious about what her investment will grow to in 5, 10, 20, and 30 years, so she uses the Compound Interest Calculator at Investor.gov and plugs in the following:

Initial deposit (she is starting from scratch): $0

Monthly contribution: $300

Length of time in years: 5, 10, 20, 30 years

Estimated interest rate (she uses the S&P 500 average rate of return): 10.0%

Length of Time	Amount Stephanie Has Invested	Investment Growth Estimate
5 years	$18,000 ($300 monthly × 5 years)	$21,978
10 years	$36,000 ($300 monthly × 10 years)	$57,375
20 years	$72,000 ($300 monthly × 20 years)	$206,190
30 years	$108,000 ($300 monthly × 30 years)	$592,178

Source: Calculations made using the Compound Interest Calculator at Investor.gov.

This example demonstrates that investing *consistently and over time* to allow compound interest the opportunity to work its magic on our money can result in significant growth.

The Three Main Asset Types

An *asset* is something you own that has value. There are many types of investment assets, but let's cover the three main types.

1. **Stock:** Equity, or ownership, in a company. Think of this as owning a fraction of a company. The *stockholder's* (an investor who owns stock) ownership in the company's assets and profits is proportionate to the stocks they own. Returns are typically based on the company's performance.

2. **Bond:** A type of investment where the investor loans money to a borrower such as a government (e.g., U.S. Treasury or municipal bonds) or a company (corporate bonds). Think of the investor functioning similar to a creditor. Returns are typically based on a fixed rate over a specific time frame.

3. **Cash and cash equivalents:** Cash is money (e.g., bills, coins, currency notes). Cash equivalents are investments that can easily be converted into cash. These are very liquid assets. Because of their low levels of volatility, their returns are typically the lowest.

Types of Investments You Can Buy

- **Individual stock:** A share in a single company. For example, if you want to invest in Google, you can purchase a share of Google. By doing so, you have fractional ownership in Google.

- **Mutual fund:** A fund made up of a pool of money collected from investors to invest in assets like stocks or bonds that share a similar trait. For example, if you want to invest in technology companies you might invest in a technology mutual fund that invests in companies like Google, Amazon, and Microsoft.

- **Index funds:** A type of mutual fund that is typically managed by computers that pick stocks or bonds with the goal of matching the market's performance. It is a portfolio of stocks or bonds designed to mimic the composition and performance of a financial market index. Because an index fund could be made up of thousands of stocks, they are a great option for diversification.

- **Market index:** Tracks the performance of a certain group of stocks, bonds, or other investments.

  - We have already reviewed one type of market index—the *S&P 500*, which tracks the performance of the top 500 companies in the United States.

  - Another market index is the *Dow Jones Industrial Average*, which tracks the performance of 30 large, publicly owned, blue-chip companies (companies with a history of strong performance).

  - There is also the *Nasdaq 100*, which tracks the performance of 100 of the largest and most actively traded stocks listed on the Nasdaq stock exchange and includes companies from various industries except for the financial industry.

- **Exchange-traded funds (ETFs):** ETFs are similar to index funds. They package various investments into one investment that you can purchase the same way you would purchase a stock. Like index funds, they typically have great diversification, broad exposure, low expense ratios, and complement a long-term investing strategy.

Where to Find Your Investments

- **Stock market:** Where publicly traded stocks and bonds are issued and traded (i.e., purchased and sold).

- **Investment portfolio:** Your collection of investments; your combination of assets. This collection should work together to achieve your investment goals.

Who Manages Your Investments

- **Brokerage firms:** Financial institutions that purchase and sell investments through financial advisors and/or online trading platforms. Popular brokerage firms include Vanguard, Fidelity, and Charles Schwab.

- **Financial advisor:** Professionals who provide clients with financial guidance to meet their financial goals.

- **Robo-advisor:** Digital platforms that base their financial planning and recommendations on algorithms that assess various factors, including your age, goals, and risk tolerance. Popular robo-advisors include Betterment, Ellevest, and Wealthfront.

- **Expense ratio:** Measures how much of the fund's assets are used for operating expenses (e.g., administrative and management expenses). Because expenses reduce the return to investors, think of an expense ratio as how much it will cost you to own that investment.

Keys for Developing a Solid Investment Strategy

Investing is not one size fits all. Your strategy will depend on your financial goals. For example, someone who wants to invest with the goal of withdrawing their money in the next five years to put toward a down payment on a home is going to have a different strategy than someone who wants to invest for retirement and does not expect to touch their investments for the next 20 or 30 years.

- **Diversification:** An investment strategy to manage and balance your assets in a way that protects against risk. Having a diversified investment portfolio means that you are managing risk by having a variety of investments in your portfolio rather than putting all your eggs in one basket.

- **Asset allocation:** A strategy that involves setting target allocations for asset classes (e.g., stocks, bonds, cash and cash equivalents) that reflect the investor's goals, risk, and time horizon. The investor periodically rebalances how much of those asset classes their portfolio contains as their goals, risk levels, and time horizon change.

- **Time horizon:** The time period you expect to hold your investments. Typically, the longer your time horizon, the more aggressive or riskier your portfolio may be. However, the shorter the time horizon, the more conservative or less risky your portfolio may be.

- **Risk tolerance:** The stock market is volatile—it goes up and down and therefore carries risk. The highs are cause for celebration, but decreases are inevitable. Be honest with how you will handle these highs and lows and focus on diversifying your portfolio to help you manage against this risk.

Five Reasons to Invest

The following are a few reasons to grow your money through investing.

Protect against Inflation

Inflation is the rise in price levels, which causes your money's purchasing power to decrease over time. Inflation is the reason why one dollar today purchases fewer goods than it did 10, 20, or 30 years ago.

The average inflation rate in the United States over the past decades has been around 2%.[5] This means that in order to maintain your purchasing power, you want to earn at least a 2% return on your money. Investing consistently and for the long-term in assets that outperform the rate of inflation will not only maintain your purchasing power, but it will also grow your wealth.

Build Wealth

Some people prefer to save their money in a savings account rather than invest because of the risks associated with investing. Although we should certainly factor our risk tolerance into our investing strategy, we should also recognize that investing is how the rich maintain and grow their wealth.

Saving your way to a million dollars is possible, but it is quite a challenge. On the other hand, investing your way to a million is not only possible but easier than you think.

Example: Saving versus Investing Your Way to a Million

Natasha is 25 years old. She started working after graduating from college at age 22 but has not started investing. She has a three-month emergency fund and two sinking funds for travel and gifts. She is looking for the next step to build wealth but is unsure whether she should save or invest her money. Natasha's big goal is to retire as a millionaire. She uses a compound interest calculator to compare her options.

Natasha's high-yield savings account provides a 0.5% return (which isn't even enough to beat inflation). If she *saves* her money, she will need **to save approximately $1,900 monthly in order to retire with $1,006,822**. Natasha uses the Compound Interest Calculator at Investor. gov to run this calculation:

Initial deposit (she is starting from scratch): $0

Monthly contribution: $1,900

Length of time in years: 40 years (age 65, the average age of retirement)

Estimated interest rate (her bank's current interest rate): 0.5%

On the other hand, if Natasha *invests* her money in the stock market, which has historically returned an average of 10%, she will need to **invest approximately $190 monthly in order to retire with $1,009,111**:

Initial investment (she is starting from scratch): $0

Monthly contribution: $190

Length of time in years: 40 years (age 65, the average age of retirement)

Estimated interest rate (the stock market's average return): 10.0%

For the next 40 years, Natasha can either save $1,900 monthly in a bank account or invest $190 monthly in the stock market to reach her million-dollar goal. The choice is clear.

Earn Passive Income

Growing up, I thought that the only way to earn money was to trade your time for money—that is, the more you work, the more money you will receive. This form of income that we are familiar with is **active income**.

However, there is also **passive income**. Passive income is money that you generate with little to no effort on your part. For example, this could be rental income that you earn from a property or sales from a digital product that you created once, and that now requires little to no involvement on your part. Another example is dividend stocks, which pay their shareholders a percentage based on their profits, typically on a quarterly basis.

Investing is one way to put our money to work for us. Rather than actively trading our time for money, investing in assets that generate passive income allows us to build wealth while working less.

Save on Taxes

Investing in retirement accounts (including through your employer or on your own) can help reduce your taxable income, which can save you money on taxes.

For example, let's say your normal taxable income (this is the income that the government taxes you on) is $50,000. If you invest $6,000 annually for retirement in a pre-tax account, your taxable income will decrease to $44,000. This means that instead of taxing you on $50,000, the government will tax you on $44,000, which means a lower tax bill for you. We discuss tax-advantaged accounts in more detail ahead.

Close the Wealth Gap

Earlier we discussed that the median net worth of White families is $188,200, compared to Black families with a median net worth of $24,100 and Hispanic families with a median net worth of $36,200.[6] Here is another shocking statistic: on average, women in the United States own 32 cents to every dollar owned by men.[7]

Investing is critical for closing the wealth gap. If you are a first-generation wealth builder like me or otherwise belong to a historically marginalized group, having a long-term investing strategy should be nonnegotiable.

Five Reasons We Don't Invest

Even after learning about investing and understanding the benefits and opportunities for growth, the hesitation that I see toward investing is unlike what I see with other areas of personal finance. Allow me to address some of those concerns.

"I Have Debt So I Can't Invest"

As seen from our earlier illustrations on compound interest, one of the most important factors for investing is *time*. If we hold off on investing because we are solely focused on debt repayment, we are losing out on years of compounding interest.

We need to give our money TIME to compound.

A general rule of thumb is to focus on paying off high-interest debt (e.g., credit card debt) before investing. This is because the interest that you are paying on high-interest debt—such as a credit card with a 20% interest rate—is likely more than the average stock market return (10%). Once you

173

have paid off high-interest debt and are tackling lower-interest debts—such as a student loan with a 5% interest rate or a mortgage with a 3% interest rate—*you can balance both your debt payoff and investing goals.*

A few things to keep in mind: (i) this is a *general* rule of thumb—assess as appropriate for your personal situation; (ii) returns in the stock market are in no way guaranteed; and (iii) how you will balance paying off your debt and investing ultimately depends on your comfort level and goals.

Implementing healthy investing habits as early as possible to take advantage of time and compound interest benefits investors in the long run.

"I Don't Have a Lot of Money to Invest"

Would you believe me if I said that you can start investing with just $1? Thanks to advances in technology, many brokerage firms and investing platforms allow you to invest with small amounts.

For example, let's say that your budget tells you that you can currently afford to invest $20 per week. You use a compound interest calculator and plug in the following:

Initial deposit (you are starting from scratch): $0

Monthly contribution: $80 ($20 per week)

Length of time in years: 5, 10, 20, 30 years

Estimated interest rate (you use the stock market average): 10.0%

Length of Time	Amount That You Have Invested	Investment Growth Estimate
5 years	$4,800 ($80 monthly × 5 years)	$5,861
10 years	$9,600 ($80 monthly × 10 years)	$15,300
20 years	$19,200 ($80 monthly × 20 years)	$54,984
30 years	$28,800 ($80 monthly × 30 years)	$157,914

Source: Calculations made using the Compound Interest Calculator at Investor.gov.

Investing just $20 per week consistently over 30 years can grow to over $150,000! This means that the total amount that you actually invest over the course of 30 years—$28,800—can grow over 5 times! Imagine how much more that number can grow the more you invest as you progress financially.

"Picking Stocks Overwhelms Me"

Before I started investing, I thought investing was just about picking the "right" stocks. It's not.

Picking and purchasing specific stocks is certainly one way to invest. You can research the specific company that you are interested in, review their financial statements, and review their performance to assess whether they are the right company for you. But that is not the only way to invest.

If the thought of stock picking overwhelms you (same here!), consider index funds and ETFs. Rather than having to pick a specific company and hope that it performs well, you can purchase an index fund or ETF that bundles hundreds, or even thousands, of companies. Index funds and ETFs provide their investors with:

- **Great diversification:** You buy into many different types of companies.

- **Broad exposure:** Exposure to different companies mitigates your risk.

- **Low expense ratios:** The lower the expense ratios, the less that will cut into your profit.

- **Complementing a long-term investing strategy:** Great for consistent and long-term investing.

For example, index funds and ETFs that track the S&P 500 invest in stocks in the S&P 500 Index. Those index funds or ETFs are made up of the *top 500 U.S. companies*. There are also index funds and ETFs that track the *total stock market*. Those index funds or ETFs are made up of the thousands of companies in the U.S. stock market.

When you invest in index funds or ETFs, no stock picking is required. Why have one company when you can have them all?—or at least as many as are within a specific index.

"I Want to Wait Until the Right Time to Get into the Stock Market"

The perfect scenario for any investor is buying into the stock market when it is "low" and selling when it is "high." Buying in when stocks are at a low price and selling when they are at a high price is ideal for maximum profits. However, *there is no way to predict* how the stock market will perform tomorrow or the day after that. What we do know is that historically the stock market has had an upward trajectory and an average 10% rate of return.

This is why I recommend **dollar cost averaging**. Dollar cost averaging is an investment strategy where you spread what you are going to invest over a period of time to reduce the impact of stock market volatility. For example, say your goal is to invest $3,600 this year. You consistently invest $300 per month, *regardless* of whether the market is up or down.

Time in the market is better than attempting to time the market.

"I'll Get to It Eventually"

Analysis paralysis. You have read all the personal finance books, you have listened to all the podcasts, you follow your favorite personal finance educators on social media . . . but you are frozen.

If you are anything like me, you will never feel like you are the most educated investor in the room. That is okay! Years after first learning about investing, I am still learning. Take what you have learned and implement it. Even if that means starting small, do not overthink it. Just start.

Investing Strategy #1: Invest for Retirement

The first way I got started with investing was through my employer-sponsored retirement account.

Are you already investing in a retirement account? Many do not realize that the money deducted from their paycheck to fund their retirement account makes them an investor! Take a moment to review your paycheck to see if you are already investing.

Regardless of whether you have started, you are self-employed, or you simply want to explore your options, this section covers the basics for investing for retirement.

Isn't It Too Early to Start Talking about Retirement?

Regardless of whether you are in high school, college, in your thirties, forties, or beyond, it is never too early to talk about retirement. When my old firm gave me papers related to retirement, I tossed them aside because I didn't understand their contents and because I thought that a 26-year-old didn't need to worry about retirement. Little did I know that investing for retirement is one of the easiest ways to start investing. In fact, I wish I had started investing for retirement when I got my first job at the Bronx Zoo at age 16!

In the United States, the traditional age of retirement is somewhere between 62 and 67 (we'll say 65 for simplicity's sake). When someone retires, the expectation is that some combination of government benefits, such as Social Security, benefits through their employer, such as a pension plan, and money they have separately saved for retirement will cover their expenses during retirement. However, not everyone has access to these options or enough in savings to allow them to retire comfortably.

How many adults in their sixties and seventies do you know with sufficient retirement savings? Sadly, I personally do not know of many. Not having sufficient funds to financially support them through retirement, having to rely on children and other family members, and/or having to supplement income with work during retirement is a heartbreaking reality for many.

We cannot afford to neglect our retirement. Investing, as opposed to saving alone, is key for a comfortable retirement. And, as we know, *time* is one of the most critical factors for long-term investing. Therefore, we should all create a retirement investing plan—regardless of our age!

What Are Retirement Accounts?

Retirement accounts hold your investments for retirement. Once you reach the age of retirement (starting at age 59.5), you can withdraw money from your retirement accounts to use during retirement.

Consult IRS.gov and a tax professional if you are considering prematurely withdrawing money from a retirement account.

> **TIP: Withdrawing funds before age 59.5 could subject you to taxes and penalties.**

Retirement accounts are funded through contributions. You can contribute to a retirement account through earned income (income from a job or self-employment) and, if applicable, your employer may also contribute to your retirement account. That money then gets invested (into stocks, bonds, etc.) and grows by taking advantage of time, compound interest, and market gains. Once you reach the age of retirement, you can begin to withdraw your money.

Save Money on Taxes

Part of what makes retirement accounts so special are the tax advantages they offer. The federal government provides investors with tax breaks to incentivize us to invest for retirement.

There are two main types of retirement accounts: pre-tax and post-tax retirement accounts.

Pre-Tax Retirement Accounts (tax-deferred, save on taxes today)

Pre-tax money (money from your *gross income*) gets deposited into this account. The money that you are contributing into the account has not been taxed by the government, which means that you save on taxes *today*. At the age of retirement, you will pay taxes on your withdrawals based on your future tax rate.

Example: Ariana's Pre-Tax Retirement Account Ariana's taxable income is $65,000 annually. $400 is automatically taken from her monthly *gross* pay and invested into her pre-tax retirement account, for an annual contribution of $4,800 ($400 × 12).

Rather than being taxed on $65,000, Ariana is taxed on $60,200 ($65,000 – $4,800), which means that she is saving money on taxes *today*. When she retires and withdraws money from her retirement account, Ariana will pay taxes on her withdrawals based on her future tax rate.

Post-Tax Retirement Accounts (pay taxes today, save on taxes in the future)

Post-tax money (money from your *net pay*) gets deposited into this account. The money that you are contributing into the account has already been taxed by the government, which means that you save on taxes *in the future*. At the age of retirement, you will withdraw your retirement funds tax-free.

Example: Joanna's Post-Tax Retirement Account Joanna's biweekly paycheck was just deposited into her checking account. She receives $2,500 after taxes and other deductions. This reflects her *net* pay, meaning that she has already paid taxes on her earnings. She invests $400 monthly from her checking account into a post-tax retirement account.

Because Joanna's contributions were deposited into a post-tax account, when she withdraws money from that account at the age of retirement, she will not pay taxes on her withdrawals.

Investing for retirement is a simple way to invest that lets you take advantage of great tax benefits.

How to Invest for Retirement

The types of retirement accounts that you can access depends on your specific situation. The IRS's website (IRS.gov) is the ultimate resource for information on the various account types, their unique rules, and income and contribution limits. I strongly recommend reviewing its website for more.

Employer-Sponsored Retirement Accounts

Employer-sponsored retirement accounts can only be offered by an employer; you cannot open these on your own. These accounts allow employees to invest for retirement from their employee pay, while benefiting from tax breaks. Employers can offer pre-tax accounts (tax-deferred) and/or post-tax accounts (tax free withdrawals). Here are some common plans:

- **401(k):** Available to employees who work at participating private entities.

- **403(b):** Available to employees who work at participating nonprofit entities, including certain government workers.

- **457(b):** Available to employees who work for certain state and local governments.

One of the biggest advantages of contributing toward retirement through an employer plan is *automation*. Your contributions are made automatically from your pay. This makes for effortless investing!

Employer Match and Vesting Schedule

Another advantage of an employer plan is the possibility of an **employer match**. Through a matching program, an employer will contribute a certain amount to an employee's retirement account, typically based on the amount or percentage that the employee contributes.

For example, if your employer offers a 5% match, you want to ideally contribute at least 5% of your own salary to take full advantage of the match. Your 5% contribution + your employer's 5% contribution = 10% of your salary invested into your retirement plan.

If a match is available to you, take advantage of it.

Do not leave this "free" money on the table!

Employers that offer a match may have a **vesting schedule**. Vesting means ownership. A vesting schedule serves as an incentive program for how and when an employee becomes entitled to the money that the employer contributes to an employee's retirement account. It typically depends on the length of time that an employee is with the employer. If you leave an employer before the contribution "vests"—meaning before you get full ownership of the employer's contribution to your retirement account—you could be missing out on thousands!

179

Invest for Future You

> **TIP: If your employer offers a match, get a copy of the applicable vesting schedule and familiarize yourself with its terms!**

Example: Nathan's Match and Vesting Schedule Nathan's salary is $80,000. His employer offers a 6% match, which means they will match his contributions up to 6% of his salary. His employer's vesting schedule states that after five years of service, the employer match fully vests.

Nathan takes full advantage of the match and invests 6% of his salary. Even though Nathan only contributes $4,800 (6%) of his own pay, a total of $9,600 (12%) gets invested annually into his retirement account:

$$\$4,800 \text{ Nathan's contribution } (\$80{,}000 \times 6\%) +$$

$$\$4,800 \text{ employer contribution } (\$80{,}000 \times 6\%) = \$9,600$$

Additionally, Nathan's five-year anniversary at his job is six months away. At that time, he will have full ownership of the amount that his employer has contributed to his retirement account.

Rolling over Retirement Funds from an Old Employer

If you have changed jobs or are planning on changing jobs, consider rolling over the money in your retirement accounts. A rollover allows you to move money from a past employer's plan into your current employer's plan or into your own retirement account that you personally set up.

By 2021, Americans had left nearly $1.35 trillion behind in retirement accounts that are connected to previous employers.[8] Conducting a rollover from old accounts makes it easier to have control over your retirement funds, while lowering the risk of forgetting about old accounts.

> **TIP: You can roll over funds in old retirement accounts on your own or you can use a free service like Capitalize[9] to conduct your rollover.**

Individual Retirement Accounts

If your employer does not offer a retirement plan, you can open one on your own. Individual retirement accounts (IRAs) allow investors to open and fund their own retirement accounts with a financial institution of their choosing (e.g., Vanguard, Fidelity, Charles Schwab, Betterment, Ellevest, Wealthfront). Here are some account options to consider:

- **Traditional Individual Retirement Account (IRA):** Allows employed or self-employed individuals to contribute pre-tax income toward investments that will grow tax deferred. At retirement, you will pay taxes on your withdrawals based on your future tax rate.

- **Roth Individual Retirement Account (Roth IRA):** Allows employed or self-employed individuals to contribute post-tax income toward investments, which the investor can withdraw at retirement tax-free.

- **Backdoor Roth IRA:** Unlike the IRA or Roth IRA, the Backdoor Roth is not a retirement account; rather, it is a strategy to get around the Roth IRA's income limits.[10] It involves converting a Traditional IRA into a Roth.

  - This strategy can be used by those who want to contribute to a Roth IRA but whose income exceeds the IRS's requirements.

  - Because a Backdoor Roth has tax implications and can be complicated to set up, I strongly recommend consulting with a tax professional.

Retirement Accounts for Entrepreneurs

Finally, in addition to the IRAs just discussed, entrepreneurs have several options for investing for retirement. As with any retirement account, consult IRS.gov and/or a tax professional for recent policies, including regarding contribution limits.

- **One-participant 401(k) (Solo 401(k)):** Available to self-employed individuals, owner-only businesses (and the owner's spouse, in certain instances). Allows a business owner to contribute in two ways: as the "employee" and as the "employer/business."

- **Simplified Employee Pension (SEP IRA):** Allows employers to invest money in retirement accounts for themselves and their employees. Employers are generally the sole contributors of these plans.

- **Savings Incentive Match Plan for Employees (Simple IRA):** Allows employees and employers to contribute to traditional IRAs set up for employees. These accounts do not have the start-up and operating costs of a conventional retirement plan—hence, "simple."

Invest for Future You

> **TIP:** *Regardless of the retirement account that you open, make sure that the money contributed to that account is being invested! This is ONE OF THE MOST COMMON MISTAKES I have seen with respect to retirement accounts (particularly when people open their own). If you are ever in doubt, ask your brokerage or financial advisor to explain what your money is invested in.*

How Much Should You Invest for Retirement?

How much you need to invest depends on what you envision for retirement. What type of lifestyle do you want to have? Where do you want to live? What will your expenses look like—will you have a paid-off mortgage, or will you rent a bungalow abroad? What types of activities will you participate in—travel, sports, volunteer work?

Other factors to consider: how much you have already invested for retirement, how much you are currently contributing, whether your employer offers a match, and, of course, our favorite factor of all: *TIME*.

There is no way to accurately predict what our lives will look like in retirement and the thought of it alone can be overwhelming, so use the following three-step framework to get you started:

Step 1: Review your current numbers

1. How many years do you have until retirement? Use the following formula:

   At what age do you want to retire? – How old are you now? = Years you have until retirement

2. How much do you currently have invested for retirement? (It's okay if you haven't started.)

Step 2: Calculate your retirement number

1. What are your annual expenses?
2. Multiply your annual expenses by 25 to get your retirement number.[11]

Step 3: Run a projection and adjust your budget as needed

1. Use a compound interest or retirement calculator to run your projection.

2. Your projection will tell you how close or far you are to your target. Consult your budget and adjust as needed.

Example: Joanna's Million-Dollar Retirement Goal

Joanna is 30 years old. She opens a Roth IRA and is excited to start investing. She wants to invest $400 monthly from her net pay, but is unsure whether she will be on track to reach her retirement goal. She wants to retire by 65. She follows the three-step framework:

Step 1: Review your current numbers

1. Joanna has 35 years until retirement:

65 (age of retirement) – 30 (current age) = 35 left for retirement

2. She currently does not have any money invested for retirement ($0).

Step 2: Calculate your retirement number

1. Her current monthly expenses are about $4,000, which makes her annual expenses about $48,000.

$4,000 monthly expenses × 12 months = $48,000

2. Her goal retirement number is $1.2 million:

$48,000 annual expenses × 25 = $1,200,000

Step 3: Run a projection and adjust your budget as needed

1. She runs a projection using the Compound Interest Calculator at Investor.gov (as we have done in this chapter).

She plugs in a $400 monthly contribution, 35 years until retirement, and assumes a 10% expected rate of return (recall that the rate of return depends on your investments, how the stock market performs, etc.). This is *only* a projection.

Her projection estimates that her Roth IRA will grow to approximately $1,300,000. And, because she is investing through a Roth IRA (a post-tax retirement account), she will be able to withdraw that money *tax-free*.

2. Joanna is satisfied with her projection and makes "$400 to Roth IRA" part of her regular monthly budget.

Investing Strategy #2: Invest with a Robo-Advisor

The second simple way that I started investing was with a robo-advisor. At the time, I generally understood the investing terminology we reviewed at the beginning of this chapter, including diversification, time horizon, and risk tolerance. I also understood the benefits of diverse investments like index funds and ETFs. However, I was still unsure how to select the right ones for me.

Enter robo-advisors.

What Are Robo-Advisors and Their Pros/Cons?

Robo-advisors are digital platforms that provide automated, algorithm-driven investment services with little to no human supervision. Their investment recommendations are made using data they gather about you, including risk tolerance, time horizon, and investment goals. They take the guesswork out of investing.

Here are some pros and cons to consider:

Pros	Cons
Low fees: Some charge an annual fee as low as 0.25%.	**No personal interaction:** Unlike a traditional financial advisor, you are not going to have a personal relationship with a robo-advisor.
	But note that these services are improving access to their customer support teams and connecting customers to their financial advisors (usually for an additional fee).
Accessibility: If you have access to the internet, you can get started in minutes.	**Less of a tailored service:** Service is automated and algorithm driven.
Low minimums: Some allow you to start investing with just $1.	**Fees:** Although their fees are usually low (as low as 0.25%), their management fees could be avoided if you opt for a self-directed strategy, or DIY investing, where you pick your specific investments.
User-friendly apps: Many have user-friendly applications so that you can review your portfolio and make contributions on the go.	

How and Where to Open an Account

If you decide that investing with a robo-advisor is right for you, have the following information on hand:

- **Contact info:** Name, address, email, phone number
- **Tax identification number:** Social Security number or Individual Taxpayer Identification number (not all robo-advisors accept an ITIN, so review their policies)
- **Bank account:** Checking account to transfer funds to your investment account

Robo-advisors have become increasingly popular over the past decade. Some popular options include Ellevest, Betterment, and Wealthfront. As with anything, research the companies you are considering before you decide to invest with them.

How Much to Invest

Like retirement, how much you should invest depends on your individual goals, risk tolerance, and time horizon. Assess your goals and circumstances, consult your budget, and use a compound interest calculator to determine how much *you* should invest. And remember that it is okay to start small.

Happy investing!

Let's Get Personal

When I started investing outside of my workplace retirement account, I started small—about $40 per paycheck. I set up an automatic biweekly contribution from my checking account to my robo-advisor investment account and I let the robo-advisor do the work for me. I eventually increased that amount to $200 biweekly, which I still invest to this day.

Invest for the Children in Your Life

As someone who had to rely on scholarships, grants, and loans to pay for college and law school, the concept of a college fund or a similar wealth-building account was foreign to me until recently. I had not realized that some parents start investing for their children as early as birth. That something is unrelatable and unfamiliar does not stop me from learning about the options available for the children in my life. After all, isn't generational wealth all about creating opportunities for future generations that you may not have had access to?

If you are a parent, or have a child you love in your life, here are some wealth-building options for you to consider.

College 529 Plan

This is often referred to as a college "savings" plan, although it is an investment account. The money deposited in these accounts is invested and takes advantage of time, compound interest, and market gains. The money can be withdrawn tax free if it is used for qualified education expenses. Effective 2019, the funds can be used for qualified K–12 tuition expenses, in addition to college expenses.[12]

Pros	Cons
Tax benefits: Not subject to federal (and, in many cases, state) taxes so long as the money is used for qualifying education expenses.	**Withdrawal limitations:** Withdrawals that do not qualify as education-related expenses can be subject to taxes and/or a penalty.
Beneficiary flexibility: You can change the plan beneficiary. For example, if one child chooses not to attend college, you can change the beneficiary to another child or you can use it for K–12 expenses.	**Investment option limitations:** Depending on where you open your account, your investment options may be limited.

Custodial Roth/Traditional IRA

Recall that an IRA is an account that holds investments for retirement. With a custodial Roth or Traditional IRA, a custodian opens an account on the child's behalf. Money is contributed post-tax (Roth) or pre-tax (Traditional). That money gets invested and grows tax free (Roth) or tax-deferred (Traditional). At their retirement, the child can withdraw the money to fund their retirement.

The money contributed to these accounts must be from *earned income*, so it is a great option for children who have income from a job source (e.g., a weekend job, babysitting, etc.).

Pros	Cons
Tax benefits: Tax-free growth (Roth) or tax-deferred (Traditional).	**Earned income:** Contributions must be from income from a job or self-employment, *not* gifts made to the child.
No age limit: So long as the child has earned income, a custodian can open an IRA for them.	
Teaching tool: Can teach children the importance of investing at an early age.	

UGMA/UTMA

The Uniform Gift to Minors Act (UGMA) and Uniform Transfer to Minors Act (UTMA) were established as simple ways for a minor to own investments without requiring the preparation of trust documents. You can think of these as "standard" or "regular" investment accounts. These custodial accounts are set up in your child's name. When your child reaches the age of majority, they will have complete ownership and control of the accounts.

Pros	Cons
Tiered tax benefits: Up to a certain amount is tax-free, then taxed at the child's tax-rate, then taxed at the parent's rate.	**Cannot transfer:** Because the specific child named on the account is the legal owner, you cannot transfer it to another child.
Withdrawal and spending flexibility: Money may be withdrawn before retirement and spent as the child wishes.	**Complete discretion:** The child account holder has complete discretion on how to use the funds once they reach the age of majority.
	The parent cannot dictate how that money is used. (This can be perceived as a "pro," depending on whom you ask.)

Invest for Future You

Where to Open

Before opening a 529 account, review the options that your state offers. To do this, simply search "[your state] + 529 plan." For example, for New York there is the NY 529 College Savings Program (nysaves.org). However, note that you do not have to opt for your specific state's 529 program. You can open a 529 in a state other than your own.

You can also open a 529, Roth/Traditional IRA, or UTMA/UGMA account at most brokerage firms, including Vanguard, Fidelity, Charles Schwab, and T. Rowe Price.

Let's Get Personal

I opened a 529 investment account for my nephew and niece before they turned a year old. I started small with what I could afford at the time. I set up an automatic monthly contribution that invests into their account with little effort on my part. For holidays and birthdays, my husband and I contribute an additional amount to their accounts. We also circulate a link to their accounts to family and friends, which allows them to easily contribute at the click of a button. It has been encouraging to see their accounts increase over time!

Although I may not be able to fully fund their college education (especially given the exorbitant cost of college), I am confident that my nephew and niece will be significantly more financially secure than I ever was.

Top Tips for Becoming a Successful Investor

Before we wrap up this chapter, here are some of my top tips for investing and growing your wealth:

1. **Include it in your budget:** Your budget is your money plan, so include the amount that you plan to invest in your monthly budget.

2. **Automate your investments:** After you include it in your budget, set up automatic transfers from your checking account to your investing account(s). This will make for effortless investing so that you can sit back and watch your money grow!

3. **Patience and consistency:** Think long-term! Rather than obsessing over the daily or weekly changes in the stock market, focus on your long-term goals and stick to your plan.

4. **Never stop learning:** I am a proud student of investing and am constantly learning. Read books, listen to podcasts, and subscribe to reputable sources on financial education.

5. **Start today:** Give your investments the time for compound interest and market gains to work their magic. Growth does not happen overnight but by starting *today*, future you will thank you!

MEET DELYANNE BARROS

Delyanne is a nationally recognized money expert and the podcast host of *Diversifying*, produced by CNN. Like many, Delyanne found herself confused and frustrated when it came to managing her money and growing her wealth. She had racked up $150,000 of student loan debt and barely understood her 401(k). In 2020 she became debt-free and launched Delyanne the Money Coach LLC. Her platform educates and inspires Millennials and Gen-Zers to escape the 9-to-5 hamster wheel and build generational wealth.

Delyanne is now a millionaire and on track to retire early, by age 45, and move abroad to Portugal. Her goal is to show investors that they do not need to wait to become debt-free or earn six figures to reach financial freedom. Thousands of students have enrolled in her Slay the Stock Market course. She has been featured on major news outlets highlighting her work in support of financial literacy, including CNN, CNBC, *Business Insider*, *TIME*, and Investopedia. She has built a community of over 350,000 members on TikTok and Instagram. You can find her on social media under the handle @delyannethemoneycoach and on her website, delyannethemoneycoach.com.

Q. You are a self-made millionaire. First, wow! That is an incredible accomplishment. Second, can you share a bit of your money story?

A. I'm Brazilian-American. I was 8 years old when my parents moved to the United States, and none of us spoke a word of English. One thing I recently started sharing was that I was undocumented for many years, and we all lived under this constant fear of deportation.

(continued)

Invest for Future You

(continued)

Not surprisingly, we did not have much money growing up, which made me a very pragmatic person when it came to money. I saw it as a way to solve problems and nothing more. With that in mind, I chose to become a lawyer and plugged away for 14 years at a career that was financially lucrative but unfulfilling. I had $150,000 in student loans that I didn't see myself paying off anytime soon.

When I finally discovered investing and entrepreneurship, my mindset toward money totally changed. I saw how powerful it could be and that sent me down the path of paying off my loans, investing aggressively in the stock market, and eventually launching my coaching business. It's been a year since I left law and I have found my calling teaching people, especially women of color, about the power of investing.

Q. In your experience, what are the biggest obstacles to investing?

A. Many would say financial literacy, which is indeed one major obstacle. But I would argue that income is the biggest obstacle. Most Americans don't even have $400 saved to cover an emergency, so investing is out of the question. This is not because people don't work hard, it's because they are simply not paid enough and there aren't adequate social safety nets to protect them. Failing to acknowledge the wage gap and its effects on people's ability to invest is tone deaf and unrealistic.

Q. Why do women, specifically, need to invest?

A. The gender pay gap is increasing by the day, and we cannot wait around for corporations or the government to remedy it. We should still hold these entities accountable and apply pressure, but change on that level can be painfully slow.

The stock market is one of the few places where a woman's dollar is valued just as much as anyone else's. My share of Apple is worth just as much as any man's. There's no room for gender discrimination to seep in the way it does with corporations during the hiring process. Investing is one way for women to catch up and build the wealth they're entitled to.

Q. What suggestions do you have for a newbie investor?

A. Slow down! Take your time learning this new language that is investing. Just like learning Spanish or Italian, it takes time for the words to
become familiar. It will take practice and many tries, so don't beat
yourself up if you don't understand everything right away. Find a
group to practice your new vocabulary. Whether it's on social media or
friends, finding a group of like-minded people will make this journey
less overwhelming.

Q. What does *financial freedom* mean to you?

A. I now see that money is about having options and building a life on my
own terms and no one else's. That has been the most liberating realization to come out of my money journey. I had been living my life by
society's rules for so long and I lost my way. Now that I see things more
clearly, I have given life to new dreams. I am moving to Portugal where
I will purchase my dream beachfront home and retire my mom.
Financial freedom has given me the permission to dream bigger than
I had ever allowed myself to do.

Chapter 11

Increase Your Income

Despite growing up in a low-income household, I had a unique perspective on money that did not match my circumstances. I believed that money was infinite. This attitude, coupled with seeing my parents take on all sorts of side hustles, shaped my desire to seek income-earning opportunities from a young age.

When I was in the fourth grade, I received a bead kit for Christmas. The kit allowed you to design a variety of items such as people, animals, cars, and fruits using colorful beads on a pegboard. You would then iron over a piece of wax paper covering the beads to fuse them together. I brought my creations to show my friends at school. My friends loved my designs and asked if I could make them their own. I whipped out loose-leaf paper, set my pricing from $1 to $5, and began taking orders. I was so excited to launch my first business. I brought my completed designs to school, collected payment, and built a loyal and satisfied customer base. But my endeavor was short-lived and lasted only about a week—until my teacher's discovery of my underground business.

In high school I worked for the membership sales department at the Bronx Zoo. My pay included an hourly rate and commission that was based on the number of memberships I sold. There was no cap on the amount of commission that employees could earn, which meant that I was committed to selling as many memberships as possible. I even created a skit with coworkers where we would convince those waiting on the admissions line (particularly parents with eager children) to buy a membership by informing them that one of the best perks of purchasing a membership was skipping the park admissions line. (Cue a steady flow of customers.) I will never forget earning over $400 on one spring break weekend, which to any teenager was a whole lot of money.

In college I worked as a switchboard operator, averaging around $8 per hour. Even though my job was simple—directing callers to the appropriate staff or university departments—I went above and beyond my job duties. I planted seeds that would best position me for a promotion and pay raise. When the promotion finally came, a small pay raise of 25 cents per hour accompanied my new title. Rather than get upset or accept my new pay, I wrote down talking points and asked my supervisor for a meeting. After presenting my points, we settled on an additional pay increase of $1 per hour.

To make progress on our financial goals, we must increase the gap between our income and expenses. Much of mainstream personal finance advice focuses on the expenses portion—specifically, on cutting back. But I would argue that rather than simply focusing on what to cut, we should focus on how to increase our income, so that we can accelerate building wealth.

That said, increasing our income is easier said than done. It usually involves some combination of education, hard work, creativity, privilege, and financial literacy. It also entails overcoming societal roadblocks like pay and wealth gaps.

The Pay and Wealth Gap in America

As a first-generation Latina, conversations on the gender pay and wealth gaps and the need to increase income are of particular importance.

The gender pay gap is a measure of what women are paid relative to men, commonly expressed as a percentage. It tells us how much a woman is paid for each dollar paid to a man.[1] As of 2020, women are paid 84 cents for each $1 paid to a man—meaning that women earn roughly 84% of what men earn.[2] This means that a woman must work an extra *42 days* to earn what a man earned in the previous year.

The pay gap is even more pronounced for non-White women:

Average Pay for Every $1 Paid to White, Non-Hispanic Men[3]

Group	Pay Amount
All women	84 cents
White women[4]	79 cents
Asian American, Native Hawaiian, or Pacific Islander women[5]	75 cents
Black women	57 cents
Native women	50 cents
Latina women	49 cents

The fact that the average Latina must work nearly *23 months* to earn what White men earn in *12 months*[6] is alarming and disturbing. I cannot help but think of the many sacrifices my mother made throughout her working life, the pay disparity that my sisters have likely encountered in their careers, and the disparities that I myself have unknowingly encountered and am likely to encounter.

Regardless of how we self-identify, these statistics should alarm us all. The pay gap is not simply about a smaller paycheck or making less in any given year. Compounded over time, the pay gap results in women losing out on hundreds of thousands—if not millions—of dollars over their careers.[7]

Average Lost Income over a 40-Year Career Due to the Pay Gap[8]

Group	Pay Amount
All women	$406,280
White women	$555,360
Asian women	$336,040
Black women	$964,400
Native women	$986,240
Latina women	$1,163,920

The pay gap has the ripple effect of widening the wealth gap, which impacts women's ability to cover their expenses, pay off debt, save, or invest over time. This affects women's ability to build wealth not only for themselves, but for their families as well.

Given the stark disparities in pay and wealth in our communities, we must actively explore ways to increase our income whether through our current employer, a new employer, or our own endeavor.

Ask for What You Deserve In or Out of Your Industry

Increase Your Income through Negotiating

One of my most useful classes in law school was Negotiations. The class taught me to take a collaborative approach when negotiating a deal, while maintaining my client's best interests in mind. Those skills helped me transition into my role as a commercial litigation attorney, where I frequently negotiated with opposing counsel on everything from deadlines and case logistics to monetary settlements. Those skills have also served me in my entrepreneurship journey, where I frequently negotiate everything from my speaking fees to brand partnership deals.

A negotiation is a strategic discussion with the aim of reaching a mutually beneficial agreement. It is relevant to many aspects of our everyday lives: our personal relationships, as consumers, and in the workplace. Negotiating salary and other benefits, including paid time off, remote work, a modified work schedule, parental leave, commuter benefits, professional development funding, and tuition reimbursement can significantly impact your overall income throughout your lifetime, which, in turn, affects your ability to build wealth.

Ask yourself the following:

- When was the last time you asked for a raise?
- When was the last time you received a promotion?
- Did you negotiate your salary for your current job, or did you accept the number and/or benefits that your employer initially offered?

Regardless of how you respond to these questions, here are some practical tips to help you negotiate your pay at your current job or for that new opportunity that you have had your eye on.

- **Keep an accomplishments document:** Create a running document with your workplace accomplishments. This document should contain:
  - Project or task name
  - Date(s)
  - Supervisor or manager
  - Description of work performed, including any quantifiable metrics
  - Results (anything that highlights the value you added to your company's success or growth)
  - Feedback received

    This document will keep a track record of work performed and recognition received. You can use this information when preparing to talk to your boss regarding a raise, during employee evaluation season, or when you are updating your resume. Save your document in an accessible location and update it at least once a month, while your work is fresh in your memory.

TIP: Schedule a recurring monthly hour window in your calendar to remind you to update your accomplishments document!

Overcoming Debt, Achieving Financial Freedom

- **Conduct research:** Research the salary range for your position. Take factors including your industry, experience, and location into account. Consult with colleagues, friends who work in your industry, and internet resources such as LinkedIn, Glassdoor, Salary.com, and Payscale.com. You can then decide on a salary range that includes both "acceptable" and "goal/aspirational" amounts.

- **Create a script:** One of the best practices for a successful negotiation is adequate preparation. Consult your accomplishments document and write out a script with your main talking points. The goal is to state your best case for your salary request. Even though you will not read directly from this script during the actual negotiation, it will help you organize your thoughts. Include information that highlights the value that you bring to the workplace: your qualifications, strengths, top contributions, and any important metrics that have contributed to the company's growth and success.

- **Practice negotiating:** Do not make the discussion with your boss the first time you put your script to the test. Ask a trusted colleague or friend to role-play a negotiation. Is this uncomfortable? Yes. Will it make you a better negotiator? Also yes. You can also practice in front of a mirror. Repeat your talking points until you have internalized them and practice how you will respond to questions or any push back.

- **Be collaborative and get creative:** A successful negotiation leaves both parties satisfied. Approach the discussion in a collaborative manner—be polite, listen to what the other side has to say (their questions, concerns, suggestions), and be friendly (a smile will take you a long way). Also, do not be afraid to offer creative options that will be mutually beneficial to you and your employer.

- **Know when to walk away:** Your salary range should include the lowest number that you would be willing to accept. Because you have conducted adequate research, be confident with your numbers and stand firm in your position. If your employer cannot at least meet your lowest acceptable number, have a plan for your next steps.

Let's Get Personal

When I was at my old law firm, I kept my running accomplishments document saved on my computer's desktop for easy access. (And yes, I regularly emailed it to myself to ensure that I would not lose it.) My

(continued)

(continued)

document included the case or matter name, the supervising attorney (typically the partner), my main responsibilities as well as any notable accomplishments, and how the case or matter concluded. I consulted the document during my firm's annual evaluation period. It was an easy way for me to highlight to my law firm the work that I had accomplished throughout the year.

Increase Your Income by Seeking New Opportunities

If your current job, or even current industry, is not giving you the room to grow and increase your income, it might be time to seek a new and higher-paying opportunity. Studies have shown that often the easiest way to receive a pay bump is to find a new job.[9] In fact, pay increases for those who have switched jobs have outpaced those who have stayed at their employer since 2011.[10]

Before you have the salary conversation with a prospective employer:

- **Update your resume and LinkedIn:** Use your accomplishments document (I told you it would come in handy) to update your resume. Tailor your resume to the position that you are applying for.

    - With an increasing number of recruiters and hiring managers on LinkedIn, update your LinkedIn profile and include your profile's URL (which LinkedIn allows you to customize) on your resume.

- **Evaluate your skills:** If you are looking to pivot into a new role and industry, first evaluate your current skills and determine whether, and to what extent, they complement the new position you seek. For example, if you are in healthcare administration but want to work for a technology company, skills such as supervising employees and preparing inventory records may lend itself nicely to a position in the company's operations department. If the new position you seek demands different or additional qualifications, consider whether taking a course or obtaining a certificate will improve your chances for that new role. Consider online learning websites like Udemy, Skillshare, Coursera, or Masterclass.

- **Practice your negotiation skills:** Implement the negotiation skills we discussed earlier in your new job search.

MEET CINNEAH EL-AMIN

Cinneah El-Amin (pronounced: sin-ee-ah el-ah-meen) is the founder of Flynanced, an online platform that teaches ambitious "9–5 hotties" how to earn more so that we can build wealth *and* claim the lifestyles we want *right now* without shame. Since 2020, Flynanced has grown into a sought-after money and travel advice platform, with over 115,000 community members across social media.

Fed up with her own challenges of living paycheck to paycheck and drowning in debt, Cinneah made the decision to become debt-free in 2020 and paid off over $23,000 of credit card, personal loan, and student loan debt in 12 months. She reached her first $100,000 net worth milestone in 2021 at 26 years old and continues to build wealth in her 9–5 job. She is an avid traveler, visiting 30 countries and previously living abroad in Tulum, Mexico. Cinneah works remotely as a product manager in New York City. Her story has been featured in prominent media like *Good Morning America*, *Business Insider*, *Kiplinger's Personal Finance*, *Fortune*, *Travel Noire*, *Black Enterprise*, and CNBC. She is a graduate of Barnard College of Columbia University and Wake Forest University School of Business.

Q. You have increased your salary by four times (!) in less than five years. Can you tell us how you did that?

A. I've been able to grow my 9–5 income significantly in a short amount of time as a product manager by upskilling, job hopping, and negotiating my salary at every jump. I fell into product management back in 2017, not knowing that it would become a *hot* and *well-paid* career path for someone like me with a nontechnical background. As I progressed in my career, I was intentional about upskilling or adding additional skills and scope to my experience to make me attractive for better-paying jobs.

Additionally, I've job hopped, meaning I've left jobs to pursue more income. Since 2017, I've held four jobs as a product manager across three companies, averaging about two years per company. Finally, I've negotiated my salary each time I landed a new job, which helped me gain massive bumps in salary and total compensation. My tip for negotiation: just ask!

Q. What did your most recent salary negotiation teach you about what you are capable of?

A. My most recent salary negotiation was actually my first time negotiating with a big tech company, so I was already blown away by the

(*continued*)

(continued)

initial offer, which included a high-six-figure salary and five figures of company equity. Still, I know that there's always more money on the table, so I negotiated a five-figure sign-on bonus that was not part of the initial offer. I did this by letting my new employer know that if I accepted the offer, I'd be forfeiting my annual performance bonus. My new employer agreed to the full amount of my ask, making it so much easier for me to eagerly accept the new offer. This experience taught me to always reflect on any money I'd be leaving on the table when I leave a company and to make sure I advocate for myself and my money.

Q. What advice do you have for those who are feeling stuck in their current 9–5 jobs?

A. If your gut is telling you to leave, *listen*! I think many of us, especially those of us who identify as Black or Latina women, have been conditioned to suffer through toxic and uncomfortable work environments for much longer than we need to, out of fear. I promise you there is *better* out there, but you won't know unless you try. I recommend you leverage LinkedIn to source new jobs, connect with other professionals and recruiters who can get you into internal job processes, and believe that you are deserving of more.

Q. How has your relationship with money changed over the past five years?

A. I no longer let scarcity lead me to impulsive money decisions. As a young adult, I never really felt like I had enough money, so that scarcity mindset led me to overspend and self-sabotage. Now, I know I can earn more money whenever I want, in both my business and my 9–5 career, which has helped me overcome impulsive spending behaviors.

Q. What does *financial freedom* mean to you?

A. *Financial freedom* to me means having the leisure to rest and having the agency of choice. I come from a lineage of women who labored their entire lives and never had the choice to rest or do what served their highest desires. By working toward financial freedom, I am giving myself and my descendants a chance at breaking from these chains so that we can show up authentically, create, and simply be as carefree as we choose. That's freedom to me.

Create Your Own Income Opportunities

I have an undergraduate degree in business management. Much of my college studies focused on the traditional workplace—work for a large company, climb up the corporate ladder . . . you know the drill. But I wish that my professors had taught us more about *entrepreneurship*—more about what it takes to start your *own* business. Specifically, I wish I had learned that entrepreneurship is one of the few fields where your income potential is *limitless*.

Entrepreneurship allows you to create endless streams of income and allows you to scale a product or service to reach thousands, if not millions. This does not mean that entrepreneurship is right for everyone, as it certainly has its challenges and risks. But I believe that anyone can take steps—even if they are small—to create their own opportunities for income.

Determine Whether a Side Hustle or Starting a Business Is Right for You

A side hustle is a job that you take on in addition to your full-time work to supplement your income. A small business is a corporation, partnership, or sole proprietorship that is independently owned and operated. Although the two are similar, there are a few differences between them.

One of the biggest factors that will impact whether you choose to start a side hustle or business is *time*. If your full-time job takes up most of your time, leaving little room for anything else, a side hustle or business may not be right at this moment. But if your full-time job allows you to work on the side and/or on a business plan, consider the following when determining if one is right for you.

- **Goal:** Write down your goal for your additional income source. Whether your goal is to earn an extra $200 per month through a side hustle or to be your own boss and earn $20,000 in monthly revenue through your own business, get it down on paper!

- **Time commitment:** Time is our most precious resource. Look at your current calendar and highlight gaps where you can work on your side hustle or business plan. Whether you can dedicate just a few hours or 20+, write it alongside your goal to determine the best course of action.

- **Passion:** Brainstorm what you are passionate about. If you love working with children, babysitting or tutoring might be for you. If you are passionate about languages, working as a translator or language coach might be a good fit.

- **Upfront costs:** Side hustles generally require little upfront costs. For example, taking on weekend work at your local yoga studio or using a freelance platform that connects you to prospective clients likely require few out-of-pocket expenses.

   Businesses, on the other hand, typically require some form of start-up costs. These could include the cost of business formation (e.g., registration fees), insurance, a website, marketing, or inventory. Adequate research into the types of expenses for your business and being financially prepared to take on such expenses are key.

- **Skills:** Look at your skills both in and out of the workplace. For example, if you are an administrative assistant at your full-time job, consider applying for virtual assistant roles. Business owners (myself included) hire virtual assistants to help them with administrative tasks, including email and calendar management. These roles can take anywhere from 5 hours a week (a great side hustle) to 40 hours a week (perhaps you'll start your own virtual assistant business!).

   If you lack the necessary skills to do the work that interests you, do not let that discourage you. As previously stated, courses and certifications, including through online learning platforms, can give you the practical skills that you need to break into your field of interest.

- **Accessibility:** As with anything, it serves to be practical. Look at the types of opportunities that you have access to. If you live in a rural area, remote positions could be perfect for you. If you live in a city, perhaps you can take on dog walking, serving multiple clients at once while getting your steps in.

Increase Your Income through a Side Hustle

If you are ready to earn cash on the side to put toward your financial goals, don't skip the following:

- **Pricing:** Determine how you will price your services. If you are offering your services or creating products to sell via a platform like Etsy, you must determine what you will charge customers. When setting your prices, account for your expenses (materials used, software, etc.), labor, experience, and, of course, your time.

   If you are an independent contractor for a platform that generates revenue through fees (e.g., Uber, Postmates), there may not be wiggle room for setting your own rate. That said, run the numbers on what your payout will be after the platform collects its commission and fees. Determine whether that pay is worth your time.

- **Expenses:** Keep track of expenses made related to your side hustle, as they may reduce your overall tax liability. Best practices include keeping receipts, including a brief note on why the expense was made, and a simple spreadsheet to track your expenses. Consult with a tax professional regarding deductions that you may be able to claim and any required recordkeeping.

- **Taxes:** Additional income means additional tax considerations. Unlike the income you receive from an employer, taxes are generally not automatically withheld from side hustle income. A good rule of thumb is to set aside 25–30% of your income for taxes.[11] I recommend creating a sinking fund line item for taxes in your budget.

  For example, if you earn roughly $500 per month from your side hustle, set aside at least $125–$150 in a "Taxes Sinking Fund." This way you are not left scrambling during tax season. As always, consult with a tax professional to advise you on your specific tax situation.

- **Banking:** To simplify your side hustle income and expense tracking, open a separate checking account for your side hustle. This will make it easier to identify income received and expenses incurred related to your side hustle. This will also be helpful during tax season.

Virtual and In-Person Side Hustle Ideas

Need ideas for a side hustle? Here are some to get you started.

Virtual Side Hustles	In-Person Side Hustles
Freelancer supporting businesses with logo design, website design, social media, email and digital marketing, and/or copywriting	Gig worker: rideshare driver, food delivery, grocery delivery
Virtual assistant	Personal assistant
Data entry	Fitness studio (yoga/spin instructor, front desk assistant)
Resume review	Cleaning (residential, commercial properties)
Translator	Handyperson
Transcriptionist	Clinical trials
Tutoring (can also be in-person)	House sitting
Freelance writing (articles, blogs)	Childcare
Language tutor (can also be in-person)	Dog walking, pet sitting, and boarding

Side Hustle Platforms

Check out these platforms for your next gig:

- Fiverr (freelance jobs)
- Upwork (freelance jobs)
- TaskRabbit (handyperson, moving, delivery services)
- Rover (dog walking, sitters, boarding)
- User Testing (test websites)
- Transcribe Anywhere (a course for those looking to get into transcription services)

Example: Kori's Virtual Tutoring Side Hustle

Kori is a math teacher and decides to use her skills to generate an additional income source. Given the flexibility of remote work, she signs up for a virtual tutoring platform that allows her to set her own price. The platform takes a 20% commission. Kori prices her services at $50 per hour. She signs up for five 1-hour weekly time slots.

Let's get into the numbers behind this side hustle opportunity:

Five 1-hour weekly time slots generate $250 ➔ $50 × 5 slots = $250.

The platform charges Kori 20%, which leaves her with $200 ➔ $250 × 20% = $50.

$250 (total generated) − $50 (commission payment to platform) = $200.

Of the $200 she receives from tutoring, Kori sets aside 25% for taxes ➔ $200 × 25% = $50.

Kori deposits $50 weekly into a "Taxes Sinking Fund."

Because the work is remote, and the only resource required for the work is time, she does not need to set aside money for any related expenses ➔ $0.

This leaves Kori with **$150 weekly** that she can put toward her financial goals such as debt payoff, saving, and/or investing.

Increase Your Income by Starting a Small Business

Your side hustle may evolve into a small business that you run part-time or full-time. Get your thoughts on paper and determine what systems you will need to put into place to ensure your business's success.

Business Plan

Your business plan can be as short or as detailed as you want. The goal is to have an outline that you can easily reference as you work on your business. Here are some topics to get you started:

- **Purpose, mission statement, brand values:** These will serve as your guide and should be the "essence" of your business.

  Ask yourself: What drives your business? What impact do you wish to have? What problem do you wish to fix and who do you wish to serve?

- **Business overview, including product and/or service:** Identify what your business does and what it offers.

- **Industry and competitor analysis:** Provide information on your industry (e.g., consumer goods, education, health and wellness) as well as your competitors.

- **Customer:** Identify whom your business serves. Get as specific as possible with your customer demographics (e.g., college students, young professionals, stay-at-home parents).

- **Team structure:** Identify who will work in your business and what their roles will be. If you are starting as a solopreneur, write down the responsibilities that you will assume as well as any roles or tasks that you might outsource (e.g., you will handle marketing but will outsource bookkeeping and accounting).

- **Marketing:** Identify how you will connect customers to your products and/or services (e.g., flyers, a launch event, popups, email, social media).

- **Revenue sources:** Identify how your business will generate revenue. For example, if you sell homemade candles, your revenue sources may include single orders, bulk orders for events (e.g., weddings, baby showers, parties), and/or virtual candle-making classes.

- **Pricing:** How you price your products and/or services will have a direct impact on how much revenue your business generates. Factor your expenses, labor, experience, and time into your pricing.

- **Business budget:** Include a realistic overview of your expected revenue and expenses. Just as you have a money plan for your personal finances, create one for your business finances as well.

Important Logistics

In addition to creating a sound business plan, there are some logistics that business owners should consider.

- **Business structure:** Three common business structures for small businesses are sole proprietorships, partnerships, and limited liability companies (LLCs). A business attorney can advise you on your business structure and formation.

  - *Sole proprietorship:* A sole owner of an unincorporated business.[12]

  - *Partnership:* A relationship between two or more people, where each person contributes assets (money, property, skill, and/or time) and shares in the profits and losses of the business.[13]

  - *LLC:* A business structure allowed by state law. Each state has different laws, so check with your state's requirements for LLCs.[14]

- **Registration and permits:** Depending on your business type, state, and type of work, you may be legally required to register your business and obtain permits to operate. Consult with a business attorney to ensure compliance.

- **Trademark:** A trademark is a type of intellectual property and "can be any word, phrase, symbol, design, or a combination of these things that identifies your goods or services."[15] It is an important asset to protect as a business owner. Consult with a trademark attorney to discuss your options.

- **Contracts:** As a business owner, you will likely enter into agreements with other parties (e.g., customers, independent contractors). You can consult with an attorney to help you draft agreements. Alternatively, many reputable attorneys offer easy-to-follow electronic contract templates available for download and purchase.

- **Taxes:** As we have discussed, it is generally a good idea to set aside 25–30% of your business revenue for taxes in a sinking fund. An accountant can advise you on federal, state, and local tax obligations, business write-offs, and workers compensation or unemployment insurance requirements (if any).

- **Business banking:** Depending on your business structure, you may be legally required to have a business-specific bank account. Regardless of your business type, it is a good idea to maintain your business revenue/expenses separate from your personal money.

  Most banks allow you to set up a business account with the following:

  - Personal identification: driver's license, passport, or other government-issued identification;

- Tax identification number: Social Security number (SSN), Individual Taxpayer Identification Number (ITIN), or Employer Identification Number (EIN); and

- Business documentation: These vary by bank and state, but may include a business's articles of incorporation, business license, and other related business information.

Create a Plan for Your Additional Income

Now that you have extra income, it's time to create a plan for that income. I recommend having a predetermined percentage breakdown for how you will handle additional income.

When I was paying off debt, I generally followed a 70/20/10 split for additional income that I received such as bonuses and tax refunds. I directed 70% to my financial goals (at the time, my debt and emergency fund), 20% to me (treat yourself), and 10% to giving.

Whether you follow a similar split or a different one, account for both your future *and* current self. Examples:

Aggressive: 80/20 split: 80% to goals, 20% to yourself

Moderate: 60/40 split: 60% to goals, 40% to yourself

Flexible: 40/60 split: 40% to goals, 60% to yourself

Once you decide on a breakdown, include your numbers in your budget!

MEET JANNESE TORRES-RODRIGUEZ

Jannese Torres-Rodriguez is an award-winning Latina money expert and business coach. She became an accidental entrepreneur after a job loss led her to create a successful Latin food blog, *Delish D'Lites*. Now, she helps her clients and listeners build successful online businesses that allow them to pursue financial independence and freedom. Jannese is on a mission to educate marginalized communities on topics like entrepreneurship, investing, and building generational wealth through her personal finance podcast, "Yo Quiero Dinero." The podcast has been featured on *BuzzFeed*, *Telemundo*, *Business Insider*, Yahoo Finance, and more.

(continued)

(continued)

Q. Your platform is named "Yo Quiero Dinero." Can you tell us what that means and why you chose that name?

A. I was inspired by the J. Lo and Cardi B song "Dinero"! The chorus of the song says, "Yo Quiero Dinero," which translates to "I want money," and who doesn't want that? I chose the name because it's unapologetically in your face, and fully aligned with my mission to destigmatize money as a taboo topic in the Latinx and BIPOC communities and to make personal finance fun, relevant, and relatable.

Q. You recently shared that you have grown your net worth to over half a million dollars. Amazing, congrats! What has had the greatest impact on reaching that milestone?

A. Entrepreneurship has allowed me to increase my income way beyond what I thought was possible. Much of the personal finance advice that exists talks about cutting your spending and saving money. I prefer to focus on the discussions around expanding your income. That allows you to reach your money goals much faster.

Q. What advice would you give to someone who wants to start a side hustle but doesn't know where to start?

A. Despite what you may believe, you're already good at something that could become a business. Make a list of your professional and personal skills and determine which you are the most passionate about. Then, research how to turn those skills into a service or product-based business. With the power of the internet, the cost of starting a business is lower and more accessible than ever before.

Q. What are the biggest challenges you have faced as an entrepreneur? How have you overcome those challenges?

A. The biggest challenge is continuing to believe in myself when imposter syndrome sets in. I know it's because I don't see many Latinas in the spaces where I currently am, and I'm paving a path that hasn't existed before. When I start doubting myself, I remind myself that my successes are not the result of random luck, but because I've worked really hard and showed up even when I wasn't sure what the outcome would be.

Q. What does *financial freedom* mean to you?

A. The ability to control your most precious resource: time. *Financial freedom* allows you to opt out of anything that diminishes you—whether it's a relationship or environment. That's the ultimate freedom we all deserve.

Part 3

Implementing the Pillars

Chapter 12

Your Financial Roadmap

Now that you understand the eight pillars to build wealth, it is time to implement them! In this chapter, you will find checklists for each pillar and helpful templates to guide you through your journey to financial freedom.

Pillar 1: Take Inventory of Your Numbers

- Calculate your assets (what you own).
- Calculate your liabilities (what you owe).
- Calculate your net worth.
- Determine how you will track your net worth (e.g., pen and paper, spreadsheet, app).
- Calculate your monthly income.
  - Review your paycheck, including taxes and deductions.
  - Review your revenue sources (if self-employed).
- Calculate your monthly expenses.
  - Review the past three months of credit card and debit/bank transactions.
  - Review your subscriptions and cancel any that no longer serve you.
- Calculate your monthly savings and investments.
- Calculate your monthly debt payments.

Net Worth Tracker Template

Copy this template into a notebook or spreadsheet software to calculate your monthly net worth. Update your numbers once a month, preferably the same time each month.

[MONTH] NET WORTH

ASSETS		LIABILITIES	
Category	**Amount**	**Category**	**Amount**
Checking account	*$2,800*	*Car loan*	*$10,000*
TOTAL ASSETS		**TOTAL LIABILITIES**	

Net worth formula: Total assets – total liabilities = net worth

[Insert Month] Net Worth:

Four Core Monthly Numbers Template

Use this template to get you started on gathering your four core monthly numbers.

FOUR CORE MONTHLY NUMBERS
Step #1: Monthly Income
Step #2: Monthly Expenses
Step #3: Monthly Savings and Investments
Step #4: Monthly Debt Payments

Pillar 2: Choose the Best Budget for You

- Try a 50/30/20 budget if you like following general guidelines or rules of thumb.
- Try a zero-based budget if you are detail oriented.
- Try a reverse budget if you do not like budgeting.
- If your expenses exceed your income, create a plan to (i) decrease expenses and/or (ii) increase income.

Overcoming Debt, Achieving Financial Freedom

- If your income is inconsistent, budget using the lowest reasonable income that you can expect to earn.
- If applicable, include financial help to family and related giving in your budget.
- Determine how you will track your spending (e.g., pen and paper, spreadsheet, app).
- Complete a 30-day spending challenge.
- Set a monthly budget date and add it to your calendar.

50/30/20 Budget Template

Monthly net income: _____

Needs (50%): _____

Wants (30%): _____

Financial goals (20%): _____

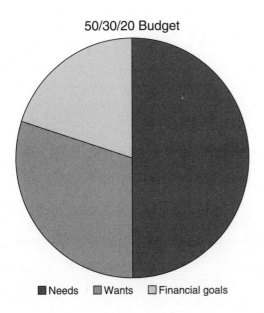

50/30/20 Budget

■ Needs ■ Wants □ Financial goals

Zero-Based Budget Template

Monthly Net Income*	$_____	
Savings/Investments	$_____	
Savings		$_____
Investments		$_____
Expenses	$_____	
Rent		$_____
Utilities		$_____
Cell phone		$_____
Transportation		$_____
Groceries		$_____
Dining out		$_____
Personal/fun/entertainment		$_____
Clothing		$_____
Fitness		$_____
Miscellaneous		$_____
Debt	$_____	
Credit card		$_____
Car loan		$_____
Student loan		$_____
Other debt		$_____
Additional debt payment		$_____
Monthly net income – monthly spending	**$0**	
(savings + investments + expenses + debt) = $0		

*If you are self-employed, or if taxes are not automatically deducted from your pay, budget using your gross income and don't forget to include a "Taxes Sinking Fund" line item in your budget.

Reverse Budget Steps

- Step 1: Assess your monthly cash flow.
- Step 2: List your financial goals and determine how much you will pay yourself.

- Step 3: Create a system for your reverse budget.
- Step 4: Spend the rest.

Spending Tracker Template

- *Use this template to track your spending or to complete a 30-day spending challenge.*

[MONTH] SPENDING TRACKER

Date	Expense	Amount	Category
January 2	*Trader Joe's*	*$84.90*	*Groceries*

Pillar 3: Become a Conscious Consumer

- Budget using value-based spending principles.
  - Make a list of what you value spending money on.
  - Make a list of what you do not value spending money on.
- Create a plan to declutter your home (start small with a specific area or room).
- Calculate cost per use the next time you make a purchase.
- Calculate cost per wear the next time you purchase a clothing item, shoes, or accessories.
- Curate your version of a capsule wardrobe.
- Evaluate your wardrobe and consider how you can be a more sustainable consumer.

Value-Based Spending Template

Use this template to reflect on what you do and do not value spending money on.

Your Financial Roadmap

VALUE-BASED SPENDING LIST

Things I Value Spending Money On	Things I Do Not Value Spending Money On

Cost per Use/Wear Template

Use the cost per use or cost per wear formula for any significant purchases.

COST PER USE/COST PER WEAR FORMULA

Cost of the item

$\div$

Number of times you expect to use/wear the item

$=$

Cost per use/wear

Declutter Template

Use this template to create your decluttering plan. Go through your home by room (e.g., bedroom, living room, kitchen, bathroom) or area (junk drawer, closet, dresser).

DECLUTTER GAME PLAN

Room or Area to Declutter	Date	Notes
Living room	*April 10*	*Declutter entertainment center, coffee table, side table*

Items Needed Template

Use this template after editing your wardrobe to assess what you need to purchase (e.g., little black dress, white button-down, neutral loafers). This will help you shop more thoughtfully.

WARDROBE ITEMS NEEDED

Item	Budget	Notes
Denim jeans	*$60*	*Shop during fall sale or at local thrift shop*

Pillar 4: Save with a Purpose

- ❑ Tie your savings to specific goals.
- ❑ Calculate your emergency fund numbers.
- ❑ Determine where you will save your emergency fund.
- ❑ Create a plan for saving your emergency fund and include it in your budget.
- ❑ Create a family emergency fund (if needed).
- ❑ Calculate your sinking funds.
- ❑ Determine where you will save your sinking funds.
- ❑ Create a plan for saving your sinking funds and include them in your budget.
- ❑ Evaluate your current bank accounts and open accounts if needed.

Emergency Fund Template

Use this template to calculate your emergency fund amounts.

EMERGENCY FUND

Step	Amount
Step 1: Starter Emergency Fund	$1,000
Step 2: One-Month Emergency Fund (one month of necessary living expenses)	
Step 3: Fully-Funded Emergency Fund (three to six months of necessary living expenses)	

Sinking Funds Templates

Use these templates to determine how much you should save in your sinking funds. Think of your sinking funds in terms of time frame (short-term, mid-term, and long-term) and type (known and irregular expenses). Add your monthly budgeted amounts to your budget.

SINKING FUNDS FORMULA

Total cost of the goal or expense

$\div$

Number of months you have until you incur that expense or reach that goal

$=$

Amount that you should save monthly

SINKING FUNDS

Expense Type	Monthly Budgeted Amount	Notes
Vacation	*$300*	*Save $3,000 in 10 months*
Pet expenses	*$40*	*For medical expenses, food, toys, etc.*

Overcoming Debt, Achieving Financial Freedom

Bank Accounts

Use this template to organize your bank accounts.

BANK ACCOUNTS

Account Type	Bank Name	Notes
High-yield savings account	*Ally Bank*	*Open account in two weeks; use for sinking funds*

Pillar 5: Create Your Debt Payoff Plan

- ❑ Review your student loans and compile any relevant information.
- ❑ Review your student loan repayment options.
- ❑ Review any student loan forgiveness options.
- ❑ Create your debt payoff plan.
  - ■ Step 1: Create your debt overview.
  - ■ Step 2: Calculate your additional debt payment amount.
  - ■ Step 3: Choose your debt payoff strategy: snowball or avalanche.
  - ■ Step 4: Implement your debt payoff strategy by incorporating it into your budget.
- ❑ Determine whether refinancing is right for you (e.g., for paying off high-interest student loans).
- ❑ Determine whether a balance transfer is right for you (e.g., for paying off high-interest credit card debt).

Student Loan Template

Use this template when reviewing your student loans.

STUDENT LOAN OVERVIEW

Student Loan	Un/ subsidized	Servicer/ Company	Balance	Payment	Interest Rate
Student loan "A"	*Subsidized*	*Nelnet*	*$30,000*	*$300*	*3.4%*

Debt Overview Template

Use this template to create your debt overview.

DEBT OVERVIEW

Debt Type	Debt Balance	Interest Rate	Minimum Payment
Car loan	*$10,000*	*4%*	*$400*

Debt Payoff Strategy Template

Use this template to compare your repayment options with (i) no additional payment, (ii) an additional payment and the snowball method, and (iii) an additional payment and the avalanche method.

Use a debt repayment calculator (see NerdWallet.com's debt calculator) and refer to the examples in Chapter 8 for more.

Debt Payoff Strategy	Strategy 1: with No Additional Payment	Strategy 2: Debt Snowball (with additional payment)	Strategy 3: Debt Avalanche (with additional payment)
Debt payoff order	N/A	1. 2.	1. 2.

Debt Payoff Strategy	Strategy 1: with No Additional Payment	Strategy 2: Debt Snowball (with additional payment)	Strategy 3: Debt Avalanche (with additional payment)
		3. 4. 5.	3. 4. 5.
Additional payment amount	$0	$0	$0
Time frame			
Estimated total principal			
Estimated total interest			
Estimated total debt to be paid			

Refinancing and/or Balance Transfer Template

Use this template if you are considering refinancing your debt or taking on a balance transfer. Remember that the key to using this strategy is to have a clear plan—with a deadline—by which to pay off your debt.

REFINANCING AND/OR BALANCE TRANSFER PLAN

Old Debt	New Debt and Interest Rate	Monthly Payment	Repayment Deadline
Credit Card 1 (20% APR) with a $2,200 balance and Credit Card 2 (15% APR) with a $5,000 balance	*Credit Card 3 (0% APR for 18 months) with a $7,200 transferred balance*	*$400*	*18 months from today*

Pillar 6: Master Your Credit and Your Credit Cards

- ❑ Pull your credit report from the three bureaus (Experian, Equifax, and Transunion).
- ❑ Review your credit reports.
- ❑ Address any inaccuracies in your credit reports.
- ❑ Review your credit score.
- ❑ Review your credit card statement(s).
- ❑ Review credit card options with rewards.
- ❑ Consider whether being or making someone an authorized user is right for you.
- ❑ Review secured credit card options (if applicable).

Credit Report Tracker

Use this template when reviewing your credit report.

CREDIT REPORT REVIEW

Source	Date Reviewed	Notes
Equifax	*August 2*	*All information is correct.*

Credit Score Tracker

Use this template when reviewing your credit score.

CREDIT SCORE REVIEW

Source	Date Reviewed	Score	Range	Notes
Experian	*August 2*	*720*	*Good*	*Goal by the end of the year is to raise score by 30 points.*

Overcoming Debt, Achieving Financial Freedom

Credit Improvement Template

Use this template when strategizing how to maximize the five factors that make up your credit score.

CREDIT IMPROVEMENT STRATEGY

Category	Percentage	**Strategy** *(specify the action that you will take for each category)*
Payment history	35%	
Amounts owed	30%	
Length of credit history	15%	
New credit	10%	
Credit mix	10%	

Pillar 7: Invest for Future You

- ❏ Review your employer-sponsored retirement account options (e.g., 401[k], 403[b]).
- ❏ Determine whether your employer offers a match.
  - ▪ If they do, ask whether they have a vesting schedule.
- ❏ Review your individual retirement account options (e.g., IRA, Roth IRA).
- ❏ Run a projection to determine how much you should invest for retirement.
  - ▪ Step 1: Review your current numbers.
  - ▪ Step 2: Calculate your retirement number.
  - ▪ Step 3: Run a projection and adjust your budget as needed.
- ❏ Review your nonretirement investment options, including with robo-advisors.
- ❏ Review investment options for the children in your life (e.g., 529, IRA, UTMA/UGMA).

Compound Interest Template

Use this template to organize your numbers for your compound interest projections. You can use this template to project how much your investments will grow for both retirement and nonretirement accounts. I recommend using the Compound Interest Calculator at Investor.gov.

COMPOUND INTEREST TEMPLATE

Initial investment	
Monthly contribution	
Length of time in years	
Estimated interest rate (rate of return)	
TOTAL PROJECTED AMOUNT	

Retirement Accounts Template

Use this template to organize information on your retirement investment accounts.

RETIREMENT ACCOUNTS

Account type	
Brokerage firm	
Balance	
Match (Y/N)	
Vesting schedule details	

How Much to Invest for Retirement Template

Use this template to help you determine how much you should invest for retirement.

HOW MUCH TO INVEST FOR RETIREMENT

Step 1: Review your current numbers	How many years do you have until retirement? How much do you currently have invested for retirement?
Step 2: Calculate your retirement number	What are your annual expenses? Multiply your annual expenses by 25 to get your retirement number.
Step 3: Run a projection and adjust your budget as needed	Use a compound interest or retirement calculator to run your projection. Your projection will tell you how close or far you are to your target. Consult your budget and make any notes here if you need to adjust.

Pillar 8: Increase Your Income

- ❑ Assess your current pay and ask yourself when the last time was that you received a raise.
- ❑ Create a negotiation plan (for your current or prospective employer).
- ❑ Create an accomplishments document.
  - ■ Add a monthly calendar reminder to update your accomplishments document.
- ❑ Update your resume at least once a year.
- ❑ Update your LinkedIn profile including with a customized URL.
- ❑ Brainstorm whether a side hustle or starting your own business is right for you.
- ❑ Create a plan for your side hustle or small business.
- ❑ Include any additional income in your budget.

Accomplishments Document Template

Use this template to record your workplace accomplishments. Refer to this when preparing for a pay increase request, during employee evaluation season, or when updating your resume. Remember to update it at least once a month.

ACCOMPLISHMENTS DOCUMENT

Project or task name	
Date(s)	
Supervisor or manager	
Description of work performed, including any quantifiable metrics	
Results (highlight the value you added to your company's success or growth)	
Feedback received	

Side Hustle or Small Business Brainstorm Template

Use this template to brainstorm whether a side hustle or starting your own business is right for you.

BRAIN DUMP

Goal	
Time commitment	
Passion	
Upfront costs	
Skills	
Accessibility	
Notes	

Business Plan Template

Use this template to help structure your business plan. Remember that your business plan can be as detailed or as broad as you like.

BUSINESS PLAN

Purpose, mission statement, brand values	
Business overview, including product and/or service	
Industry and competitor analysis	

BUSINESS PLAN

Customer	
Team structure	
Marketing	
Revenue sources	
Pricing	
Business budget	

■ ■ ■

Financial freedom looks different for everyone. It depends on our circumstances, goals, time, resources, and more. Pursuing it often involves balancing multiple goals and becoming comfortable with the new habits, strategies, language, and objectives that you will develop along the way.

I hope that my story, the stories that others have graciously shared, and the information in this book inspire you and give you the resources to create a plan to become financially free.

Notes

Chapter 1

1. "Mitch Termed Central America's Disaster of the Century," CNN, November 6, 1998, available at http://www.cnn.com/WEATHER/9811/06/mitch.02/.

Chapter 2

1. "Text of President Obama's School Speech," ABC News (September 7, 2009), https://abcnews.go.com/Politics/president-obamas-back-school-message-students/story?id=8509426.
2. See "Third Way Names 10 CUNY Senior Colleges Among Nation's Best in Promoting Economic Mobility for Students from Low- and Moderate-Income Families," CUNY (February 3, 2022), https://www1.cuny.edu/mu/forum/2022/02/03/third-way-names-10-cuny-senior-colleges-among-nations-best-in-promoting-economic-mobility-for-students-from-low-and-moderate-income-families; Hans Johnson, Marisol Cuellar Mejia, and Sarah Bohn, "Higher Education as a Driver of Economic Mobility," Public Policy Institute of California (December 2018), https://www.ppic.org/publication/higher-education-as-a-driver-of-economic-mobility/#:~:text=College%20graduates%20have%20better%20labor,only%20a%20high%20school%20diploma; Ron Haskins, "Education and Economic Mobility," The Brookings Institution (July 2, 2016), https://www.brookings.edu/wp-content/uploads/2016/07/02_economic_mobility_sawhill_ch8.pdf.
3. See Andre M. Perry, Marshall Steinbaum, and Carl Romer, "Student Loans, The Racial Wealth Divide, and Why We Need Full Student Debt Cancellation," The Brookings Institution (June 23, 2021), https://www.brookings.edu/research/student-loans-the-racial-wealth-divide-and-why-we-need-full-student-debt-cancellation.
4. "What Is My Expected Family Contribution (EFC)?" U.S. Department of Education, Federal Student Aid, https://studentaid.gov/help-center/answers/article/what-is-efc (last accessed April 27, 2022).
5. As of this writing, the cost of an eight-week stay in a single bedroom in a shared apartment is $3,862.32 ("Summer Student & Intern Housing," Georgetown University Residential Living, https://residentialliving.georgetown.edu/summer/individual [last accessed May 2, 2022]).

6. "The price of law school is on the rise, with the average total tuition increasing by $1,065 per year." "Average Cost of Law School," Education Data Initiative, updated November 30, 2021, https://educationdata.org/average-cost-of-law-school#:~:text=The%20price%20of%20law%20school,%2468%2C211%2C%20or%20%2422%2C737%20per%20year.

7. William D. Henderson and Rachel M. Zahorsky, "The Pedigree Problem: Are Law School Ties Choking the Profession?" *ABA Journal* (July 1, 2012), https://www.abajournal.com/magazine/article/the_pedigree_problem_are_law_school_ties_choking_the_profession.

8. Most schools' admissions or financial aid offices offer a tuition and expense breakdown that accounts for living expenses and estimated fees and costs.

9. In 2017, Senator Catherine Cortez Masto became the first Latina U.S. Senator. See Dave Philipps, "Catherine Cortez Masto Wins Nevada to Become First Latina Senator," *New York Times* (November 9, 2016), https://www.nytimes.com/2016/11/09/us/politics/nevada-senate-catherine-cortez-masto.html.

10. "The 2021 Am Law 100," *The American Lawyer* (April 20, 2021), https://www.law.com/americanlawyer/rankings/the-2021-am-law-100.

11. For the current Big Law salary scale, and how it has changed over the years, see "Biglaw Salary Scale," Biglaw Investor, https://www.biglawinvestor.com/biglaw-salary-scale (last accessed May 2, 2022).

Chapter 3

1. Those who make federal student loan payments may be eligible to deduct a portion of the interest paid on their federal tax return (1098-E Tax Form, U.S. Department of Education, https://www.ed.gov/1098-e?src=rn [last accessed January 10, 2022]).
   Note that this differs from the American Opportunity Tax Credit. "The American opportunity tax credit (AOTC) is a credit for qualified education expenses paid for an eligible student for the first four years of higher education" ("American Opportunity Tax Credit," IRS, https://www.irs.gov/credits-deductions/individuals/aotc [last accessed January 10, 2022]). Under the AOTC, the taxpayer (or a dependent) claims the credit using Form 1098-T, which they obtain from an eligible educational institution.

2. "According to the 2014 S&P Global Financial Literacy Survey, only 57% US adults are financially literate" (Oscar Contreras, PhD, and Joseph Bendix, "Financial Literacy in the United States," Milken Institute, August 2021, https://milkeninstitute.org/sites/default/files/2021-08/Financial%20Literacy%20in%20the%20United%20States.pdf).

3. We cover the zero-based budget, and other budgets, in detail in Chapter 5.

4. "The Big 3 Expenses and Financial Independence," *Time Value Millionaire*, May 3, 2021, https://www.timevaluemillionaire.com/big-3-expenses). In December 2021, the U.S. Bureau of Labor Statistics (BLS) issued a report that provided the average annual spending for American households in 2020 as $61,334. Big three spending was as follows: food (groceries and dining out): $7,316; housing

232

Notes

(rent/mortgage, utilities, and household supplies): $21,409; and transportation (vehicle, gas, public transportation): $9,826. See "Consumer Expenditures in 2020," U.S. Bureau of Labor Statistics Report 1096, December 2021, https://www.bls.gov/opub/reports/consumer-expenditures/2020/pdf/home.pdf.

Chapter 4

1. The source of this quote has been the subject of debate.
2. We cover retirement accounts in Chapter 10.
3. We cover credit in Chapter 9.
4. These are estimates of my debt amounts that include the total interest that I ultimately paid.
5. I refinanced all my student loans into one private loan, which I discuss in Chapter 8.
6. "Changes in U.S. Family Finances from 2016 to 2019: Evidence from the Survey of Consumer Finances," *Federal Reserve Bulletin* 106, no. 5 (September 2020), https://www.federalreserve.gov/publications/files/scf20.pdf. This data was collected in 2019—before the COVID-19 pandemic—and therefore does not account for changes to the economy and/or to familial or individual wealth resulting from the pandemic.
7. Ibid., 11.
8. Ibid.
9. "Other families—a diverse group that includes those identifying as Asian, American Indian, Alaska Native, Native Hawaiian, Pacific Islander, other race, and all respondents reporting more than one racial identification—have lower wealth than White families but higher wealth than Black and Hispanic families" (Butta et al., "Disparities in Wealth by Race and Ethnicity in the 2019 Survey of Consumer Finances," Board of Governors of the Federal Reserve System [September 28, 2020], https://www.federalreserve.gov/econres/notes/feds-notes/disparities-in-wealth-by-race-and-ethnicity-in-the-2019-survey-of-consumer-finances-20200928.htm).
10. See ibid.
11. Ibid. (citing Darrick Hamilton and William Darity, "Can 'Baby Bonds' Eliminate the Racial Wealth Gap in Putative Post-Racial America?" *The Review of Black Political Economy* 37 [2010]: 207–216).
12. Rocky Mengle and Sandra Block, "9 States with No Income Tax," Kiplinger (October 18, 2021), https://www.kiplinger.com/slideshow/taxes/t054-s001-states-without-income-tax/index.html.
13. "Questions and Answers for the Additional Medicare Tax," IRS, https://www.irs.gov/businesses/small-businesses-self-employed/questions-and-answers-for-the-additional-medicare-tax (last accessed January 20, 2022).
14. "New York Paid Family Leave Updates for 2022," New York State, https://paid-familyleave.ny.gov/2022 (last accessed May 11, 2022).
15. "Topic No. 751 Social Security and Medicare Withholding Rates," IRS, https://www.irs.gov/taxtopics/tc751 (last accessed February 10, 2022).

16. "Self-Employment Tax (Social Security and Medicare Taxes)," IRS, https://www.irs.gov/businesses/small-businesses-self-employed/self-employment-tax-social-security-and-medicare-taxes (last accessed February 10, 2022).

17. New York Paycheck Calculator, smartasset, https://smartasset.com/taxes/new-york-paycheck-calculator (last accessed May 11, 2022).

18. "The UBS financial services firm predicts that this 'subscription economy' will grow to $1.5 trillion by 2025, more than double the $650 billion it's estimated to be worth now" (Heather Long and Andrew Van Dam, "Everything's Becoming a Subscription, and the Pandemic Is Partly to Blame," *Washington Post* [June 1, 2021], https://www.washingtonpost.com/business/2021/06/01/subscription-boom-pandemic).

Chapter 5

1. Eric Whiteside, "What Is the 50/20/30 Budget Rule?" Investopedia (updated October 28, 2020), https://www.investopedia.com/ask/answers/022916/what-502030-budget-rule.asp; "Income + Financial Stability in America," http://fiftythirtytwenty.com/ (last accessed January 24, 2022).

2. The 50/30/20 budget labels cell phone and internet as "wants" (see http://fiftythirtytwenty.com). But, given our reliance on these as a means of communication with loved ones and even potential employers, I consider these a need. Categorize as you deem best.

3. In high-cost-of-living areas like New York City, many households are severely rent burdened and pay more than 50% of their income toward rent ("Nearly Half of NYC Households Are Rent Burdened," *Curbed New York* [October 12, 2018], https://ny.curbed.com/2018/10/12/17965416/nyc-rent-burden-households-affordable-housing).

4. Paula Pant, "How to Budget for Taxes as a Freelancer," *The Balance* (updated June 29, 2022), https://www.thebalance.com/how-much-do-i-budget-for-taxes-as-a-freelancer-453676#:~:text=You%20should%20plan%20to%20set,calculate%20your%20estimated%20tax%20payments.

Chapter 6

1. "The Rise of American Consumerism," PBS, https://www.pbs.org/wgbh/americanexperience/features/tupperware-consumer (last accessed February 15, 2022).

2. Ibid.

3. Emily Stewart, "Why Do We Buy What We Buy?" *Vox* (July 7, 2021), https://www.vox.com/the-goods/22547185/consumerism-competition-history-interview.

4. Erin Blakemore, "How the GI Bill's Promise Was Denied to a Million Black WWII Veterans," History (updated April 20, 2021), https://www.history.com/news/gi-bill-black-wwii-veterans-benefits. ("Though the bill helped white Americans prosper and accumulate wealth in the postwar years, it didn't deliver on that promise for veterans of color. In fact, the wide disparity in the bill's

implementation ended up helping drive growing gaps in wealth, education, and civil rights between white and Black Americans.")

5. See ibid.
6. Consumer buying power refers to total income after taxes. See "Minority Markets Have $3.9 Trillion Buying Power," University of Georgia (March 21, 2019), https://www.newswise.com/articles/minority-markets-have-3-9-trillion-buying-power.
7. See J. Merritt Melancon, "Consumer Buying Power Is More Diverse Than Ever," *UGA Today* (August 11, 2021), https://news.uga.edu/selig-multicultural-economy-report-2021 ("The combined buying power of U.S. consumers grew from $11.3 trillion to $17.5 trillion between 2010 and 2020, or by 55%. Over the same time period, Asian American buying power grew by 111%; the buying power for those of Hispanic ethnicity grew by 87%; Native American buying power grew by 67%; and African American buying power grew by 61%.")
8. See ibid.
9. Stewart, "Why Do We Buy What We Buy?"
10. Merriam-Webster defines the phrase "keep up with the Joneses" as "to show that one is as good as other people by getting what they have and doing what they do." For example, "people trying to *keep up with the Joneses* by buying expensive cars and clothes that they can't afford." Merriam-Webster.com Dictionary, s.v. "keep up with the Joneses," accessed February 2, 2022, https://www.merriam-webster.com/dictionary/keep%20up%20with%20the%20Joneses.
11. "Why Americans Buy So Much Stuff: A Short History," NPR (December 1, 2021), https://www.npr.org/2021/11/29/1059861668/why-americans-buy-so-much-stuff.
12. "What Is Minimalism?" The Minimalists, https://www.theminimalists.com/minimalism (last accessed February 3, 2022).
13. Nancy L. Anderson, "How Not to Waste Money: Use the Cost per Use Formula," *Forbes* (May 31, 2019), https://www.forbes.com/sites/nancyanderson/2019/05/31/how-not-to-waste-money-use-the-cost-per-use-formula/?sh=3904b8134cb9.
14. Christine Ro, "Can Fashion Ever Be Sustainable?" BBC (March 10, 2020), https://www.bbc.com/future/article/20200310-sustainable-fashion-how-to-buy-clothes-good-for-the-climate.
15. See ibid.
16. "How Much Do Our Wardrobes Cost to the Environment?" The World Bank (September 23, 2019), https://www.worldbank.org/en/news/feature/2019/09/23/costo-moda-medio-ambiente.
17. For more on the impact that social media has had on fashion trends, see Eliza Rudalevige, "How TikTok Makes Fast Fashion Faster," *Lithium Magazine* (June 15, 2021). ("The reason that microtrends are so short-lived is due to the acceleration of something called the trend cycle. [T]he typical trend cycle consists of five stages: introduction, rise, acceptance, decline, and obsolescence. According to conventional fashion industry knowledge, this cycle used to last twenty years; however, with the rise of social media, its algorithmic segmentation of taste, and its uncanny ability to saturate every nook of your internet niche with the newest essential item, the duration of the trend cycle has drastically diminished.")

18. "How Much Do Our Wardrobes Cost to the Environment?"
19. Ibid.
20. Ro, "Can Fashion Ever Be Sustainable?"

Chapter 7

1. Karen Bennett, "Survey: Less Than Half of Americans Have Savings to Cover a $1,000 Surprise Expense," Bankrate (January 19, 2022), https://www.bankrate.com/banking/savings/financial-security-january-2022.
2. See ibid. 20% participants responded "charge to credit card and pay over time," 15% responded "pay it but cut spending on other expenses," 10% responded "borrow from family or friends," and 4% responded "take a personal loan."
3. If you have federal student loans, it is up to you whether to include your minimum payment in your emergency fund calculation. In the event of a job loss or rematriculating in school, deferment and forbearance may be available. These options allow borrowers to temporarily postpone or reduce federal student loan payments. See "What Is the Difference Between a Deferment and a Forbearance?" Federal Student Aid, U.S. Department of Education, https://studentaid.gov/help-center/answers/article/difference-between-deferment-and-forbearance (last accessed February 7, 2022).
4. Because I had refinanced my student loans (more in Chapter 8), my student loans were all private. This meant that if I lost my job, I could not defer my student loans the way I could if I had federal loans. Therefore, I included my student loan payment in my emergency fund calculation.
5. As of this writing in February 2022.
6. "About the FDIC," Federal Deposit Insurance Corporation, https://www.fdic.gov (last accessed February 8, 2022).
7. "Deposit Insurance," Federal Deposit Insurance Corporation, https://www.fdic.gov/resources/deposit-insurance (last accessed February 8, 2022).
8. Federal Deposit Insurance Corporation, "How America Banks: Household Use of Banking and Financial Services," 2019 FDIC Survey (October 2020), https://www.fdic.gov/analysis/household-survey/2019report.pdf.
9. Kristen Broady, Mac McComas, and Amine Ouazad, "An Analysis of Financial Institutions in Black-Majority Communities: Black Borrowers and Depositors Face Considerable Challenges in Accessing Banking Services," The Brookings Institution (November 2, 2021), https://www.brookings.edu/research/an-analysis-of-financial-institutions-in-black-majority-communities-black-borrowers-and-depositors-face-considerable-challenges-in-accessing-banking-services.
10. Ron Sanders, "The History of Women and Money in the United States in Honor of Women's History Month," One Advisory Partners (March 7, 2022), https://www.oneadvisorypartners.com/blog/the-history-of-women-and-money-in-the-united-states-in-honor-of-womens-history-month.
11. I still have the traditional savings account that I opened with my dad when I was in high school. Because that bank has ATMs all around my city, I keep a small amount in my traditional savings account.
12. Think traditional brick-and-mortar banks.

13. For simplicity, the example reflects a simple interest calculation.
14. For the most up-to-date list on best savings accounts, including those offering the highest APY, I recommend NerdWallet's list of the best high-interest savings accounts. See "Best High-Yield Online Savings Accounts," NerdWallet, https://www.nerdwallet.com/best/banking/high-yield-online-savings-accounts (last accessed May 16, 2022).
15. "Of the approximately 7.1 million American households that are unbanked, 34% said high fees were one reason for not having a bank account." Rebecca Lake and Daphne Foreman, "10 Ways to Bank Smarter in the New Year," *Forbes* (January 11, 2021), https://www.forbes.com/advisor/banking/ways-to-bank-smarter-in-the-new-year.
16. Other ways that HYSAs allow customers to withdraw funds are outgoing wire transfer, telephone transfer, and check request. Many online banks reimburse ATM fees that their customers incur. Review your bank's terms and conditions.
17. "Individual Taxpayer Identification Number," IRS, https://www.irs.gov/individuals/individual-taxpayer-identification-number (last accessed February 8, 2022). For more on applying for an ITIN, see "How Do I Apply for an ITIN?" IRS, https://www.irs.gov/individuals/how-do-i-apply-for-an-itin (last accessed February 8, 2022).
18. See the bank's website or visit a local branch for complete details.

Chapter 8

1. See "Debt," Investopedia (updated January 13, 2022), https://www.investopedia.com/terms/d/debt.asp (last accessed February 21, 2022).
2. Some loans also impose a loan origination fee or similar fees. Review the terms of your debt to ensure you understand what you are being charged.
3. Cecilia Clark, "Are Student Loans Simple or Compound Interest?" NerdWallet (April 13, 2021), https://www.nerdwallet.com/article/loans/student-loans/student-loans-simple-compound-interest.
4. For purposes of these examples, assume that Danielle does not make any payments to her loan during Years 1 and 2 (which would decrease the balance) and affect our calculations.
5. "What Is Interest Capitalization on a Student Loan?" Federal Student Aid, https://studentaid.gov/help-center/answers/article/what-is-loan-capitalized-interest (last accessed February 21, 2022).
6. "Interest Rates and Fees for Federal Student Loans," Federal Student Aid, https://studentaid.gov/understand-aid/types/loans/interest-rates (last accessed July 22, 2022).
7. James Chen, "Variable Interest Rate," Investopedia (updated March 31, 2021), https://www.investopedia.com/terms/v/variableinterestrate.asp.
8. More on this in Chapter 9.
9. Melanie Hanson, "Student Loan Debt Statistics," Education Data Initiative (updated May 30, 2022), https://educationdata.org/student-loan-debt-statistics (last accessed July 22, 2022).

10. "Loans made since July 1, 2006 have fixed interest rates that do not change, but the specific fixed interest rate that applies to an individual loan depends on when the loan was first disbursed (paid out)" ("Why Are the Interest Rates on My Federal Student Loans Changing?" Federal Student Aid, https://studentaid .gov/help-center/answers/article/why-are-federal-loans-interest-rates-changing [last accessed February 22, 2022]).

11. "Master Promissory Note (MPN)," Federal Student Aid, https://studentaid.gov/ mpn (last accessed February 22, 2022).

12. "What's the Difference between Direct Subsidized Loans and Direct Unsubsidized Loans?" Federal Student Aid, https://studentaid.gov/understand-aid/types/ loans/subsidized-unsubsidized (last accessed February 22, 2022).

13. "Choose the Federal Student Loan Repayment Plan That's Best for You," Federal Student Aid, https://studentaid.gov/manage-loans/repayment/plans (last accessed February 22, 2022).

14. "According to the Internal Revenue Service (IRS), student loan amounts forgiven under PSLF aren't considered income for tax purposes. For more information, check with the IRS or a tax advisor" ("Public Service Loan Forgiveness FAQ," Federal Student Aid, https://studentaid.gov/manage-loans/forgiveness-cancellation/public-service/questions [last accessed February 22, 2022]).

15. I also had a private student loan with a balance of approximately $25,000.

16. "Public Service Loan Forgiveness (PSLF)—Qualifying for PSLF," Federal Student Aid, https://studentaid.gov/manage-loans/forgiveness-cancellation/public-service (last accessed February 22, 2022).

17. Ward Williams, "Student Loan Forgiveness by State," Investopedia (updated June 26, 2022), https://www.investopedia.com/student-loan-debt-by-state-5198562.

18. For a list of student loan forgiveness programs grouped by federal options and occupation, see Andrew Pentis, "Student Loan Forgiveness: Programs for Relief, Plus the Latest on Mass Forgiveness," Student Loan Hero (updated February 25, 2022), https://studentloanhero.com/featured/the-complete-list-of-student-loan-forgiveness-programs.

19. Melanie Hanson, "Student Loan Debt Statistics," Education Data Initiative (updated May 30, 2022), https://educationdata.org/student-loan-debt-statistics (last accessed July 22, 2022).

20. Anna Helhoski and Ryan Lane, "Student Loan Debt Statistics: 2022," NerdWallet (May 25, 2022), https://www.nerdwallet.com/article/loans/student-loans/student-loan-debt.

21. Melanie Hanson, "Student Loan Debt by Race," Education Data Initiative (updated June 13, 2022), https://educationdata.org/student-loan-debt-by-race; see also Judith Scott-Clayton and Jing Li, "Black-White Disparity in Student Loan Debt More Than Triples After Graduation," The Brookings Institution (October 20,2016),https://www.brookings.edu/research/black-white-disparity-in-student-loan-debt-more-than-triples-after-graduation.

22. Board of Governors of the Federal Reserve System (US), "Student Loans Owned and Securitized [SLOAS]," retrieved from FRED, Federal Reserve Bank of St. Louis; https://fred.stlouisfed.org/series/SLOAS (last accessed February 22, 2022).

Notes

23. Anthony P. Carnevale, Artem Gulish, and Kathryn Peltier Campbell, "If Not Now, When? The Urgent Need for an All-One-System Approach to Youth Policy," Washington, DC: Georgetown University Center on Education and the Workforce, 2021, https://cew.georgetown.edu/allonesystem.
24. Robert Hildreth, "Student Debt: It's the Interest, Stupid," *The Hill* (Op-Ed) (January 23, 2022), https://thehill.com/opinion/education/590970-student-debt-its-the-interest-stupid?fbclid=IwAR0YLSMBMta7BYodJnnhoaH9JEaW_LR-F5ibzwTQcjqnI68GGS1jr7e_phA&rl=1.
25. Kathy has multiple federal student loans, but because she only makes one payment to her lender, she simplifies by grouping them and using her loans' average interest rate.
26. If your budget is tight and does not allow for additional debt payments, reread "When You Are in the Red" in Chapter 5 and Chapter 11.
27. "Debt Repayment Calculator," Credit Karma, https://www.creditkarma.com/calculators/credit-cards/debt-repayment (last accessed February 24, 2022).
28. Sean Pyles, "Debt Snowball Calculator," NerdWallet (August 5, 2021), https://www.nerdwallet.com/article/finance/debt-snowball-calculator.
29. Alexandra Twin, "Refinance," Investopedia (December 17, 2021), https://www.investopedia.com/terms/r/refinance.asp#:~:text=A%20refinance%2C%20or%20%22refi%22,to%20a%20loan%20or%20mortgage.&text=If%20approved%2C%20the%20borrower%20gets,place%20of%20the%20original%20agreement.
30. Reviewing your own credit is considered a "soft inquiry" and will not impact your credit score. But if someone else reviews your credit information to determine your eligibility for new credit, that is generally a "hard inquiry" and *may* impact your credit score. More in Chapter 9.
31. Since paying off my student loans, I have been fortunate to partner with SoFi.
32. See "Get Your Money Right," SoFi, https://www.sofi.com/products (last accessed May 17, 2022).

Chapter 9

1. "The Credit Card Accountability Responsibility and Disclosure Act of 2009 is a consumer protection law that was enacted to protect consumers from unfair practices by credit card issuers by requiring more transparency in credit card terms and conditions and adding limits to charges and interest rates associated with credit card use" ("Credit Card Accountability Responsibility and Disclosure Act of 2009," Cornell Law School Legal Information Institute (last updated June 2021), https://www.law.cornell.edu/wex/credit_card_accountability_responsibility_and_disclosure_act_of_2009); see also Melanie Hicken, "Credit Card Issuers Still Cashing in on College Students, Alums," *CNN Money* (December 17, 2013), https://money.cnn.com/2013/12/17/pf/college-credit-cards/index.html ("The CARD Act includes a number of protections for college students, such as banning the use of gifts to entice them to apply for credit cards and barring the marketing of pre-approved offers to those under 21 years old without their consent. It also prevents issuers from extending credit to someone under the age of 21, unless they have either proven their ability to make payments or have secured an adult cosigner.")

2. Jean Folger, "What Credit Score Should You Have?" Investopedia (updated April 30, 2022), https://www.investopedia.com/financial-edge/1111/what-credit-score-should-you-have.aspx.

3. "Why Employers Check Credit—and What They See," NerdWallet (February 3, 2022), https://www.nerdwallet.com/article/finance/credit-score-employer-checking.

4. "Using Consumer Reports: What Employers Needs to Know," Federal Trade Commission (October 2016), https://www.ftc.gov/tips-advice/business-center/guidance/using-consumer-reports-what-employers-need-know. States and local governments may impose additional limitations and restrictions, so consult your state's labor department for more.

5. Nicole Dieker, "Why Are There Different Types of Credit Scores?" Bankrate (January 22, 2021), https://www.bankrate.com/finance/credit-cards/different-types-of-credit-scores.

6. Some FICO scores, including the Auto Score Range and Bankcard Score Range, use a scale of 250–900. See Jim Akin, "What Are the Different Credit Scoring Ranges?" Experian (June 23, 2020), https://www.experian.com/blogs/ask-experian/infographic-what-are-the-different-scoring-ranges.

7. "Credit Scores," Federal Trade Commission Consumer Advice (May 2021), https://www.consumer.ftc.gov/articles/credit-scores#find (last accessed March 2, 2022); Jean Folder, "What Credit Score Should You Have?" Investopedia (updated April 30, 2022), https://www.investopedia.com/financial-edge/1111/what-credit-score-should-you-have.aspx (last accessed July 25, 2022).

8. "Free Credit Reports," Federal Trade Commission Consumer Advice (May 2021), https://www.consumer.ftc.gov/articles/free-credit-reports (last accessed March 2, 2022) ("Only one website—AnnualCreditReport.com—is authorized to fill orders for the free annual credit report you are entitled to under law."). You can also order your free credit reports by (i) calling 1-877-322-8228 or (ii) completing the Annual Credit Report Request Form (via the FTC's website) and mailing it to: Annual Credit Report Request Service, P.O. Box 105281, Atlanta, GA 30348-5281.

9. "Disputing Errors On Your Credit Reports," Federal Trade Commission Consumer Advice (May 2021), https://www.consumer.ftc.gov/articles/disputing-errors-your-credit-reports.

10. "Report Identity Theft and Get a Recovery Plan," Federal Trade Commission Identity Theft, https://www.identitytheft.gov (last accessed March 2, 2022).

11. "Free Credit Reports," FTC Consumer Advice.

12. As of March 2, 2022.

13. Elizabeth Gravier, "Does a $0 Balance on Your Credit Card Make Your Score Go Up?" CNBC Select (updated June 22, 2022), https://www.cnbc.com/select/what-is-a-good-credit-utilization-ratio.

14. Ibid.

15. Alexandria White, "The 3 Kinds of Credit Card Rewards Programs and How They Work," *CNBC Select* (updated October 29, 2021), https://www.cnbc.com/select/how-credit-card-rewards-programs-work.

16. Review the credit card issuer's authorized user minimum age requirements.
17. Julia Kagan, "Collateral," Investopedia (updated March 15, 2022), https://www.investopedia.com/terms/c/collateral.asp.

Chapter 10

1. James Royal, PhD, and Arielle O'Shea, "What Is the Average Stock Market Return?" NerdWallet (March 2, 2022), https://www.nerdwallet.com/article/investing/average-stock-market-return; see also J.B. Maverick, "What Is the Average Annual Return for the S&P 500?" Investopedia (updated January 13, 2022), https://www.investopedia.com/ask/answers/042415/what-average-annual-return-sp-500.asp. ("While it assumed its present size (and name) in 1957, the S&P actually dates back to the 1920s, becoming a composite index tracking 90 stocks in 1926.")
2. Royal and O'Shea, "What Is the Average Stock Market Return?"
3. Maverick, "What Is the Average Annual Return for the S&P 500?"
4. Jason Fernando, "Compound Interest: Definition, Formula, and Calculation," Investopedia (updated July 19, 2022), https://www.investopedia.com/terms/c/compoundinterest.asp.
5. "U.S. Inflation Rate 1960–2022," Macrotrends, https://www.macrotrends.net/countries/USA/united-states/inflation-rate-cpi (last accessed March 8, 2022); "FAQs: Why Does the Federal Reserve Aim for Inflation of 2% over the Longer Run?" Board of Governors of the Federal Reserve System (last updated August 27, 2020), https://www.federalreserve.gov/faqs/economy_14400.htm.
6. "Other families—a diverse group that includes those identifying as Asian, American Indian, Alaska Native, Native Hawaiian, Pacific Islander, other race, and all respondents reporting more than one racial identification—have lower wealth than White families but higher wealth than Black and Hispanic families" (Butta et al., "Disparities in Wealth by Race and Ethnicity in the 2019 Survey of Consumer Finances," Board of Governors of the Federal Reserve System (September 28, 2020), https://www.federalreserve.gov/econres/notes/feds-notes/disparities-in-wealth-by-race-and-ethnicity-in-the-2019-survey-of-consumer-finances-20200928.htm).
7. Janice Traflet and Robert E. Wright, "America Doesn't Just Have a Gender Pay Gap. It Has a Gender Wealth Gap," *Washington Post* (April 2, 2019), https://www.washingtonpost.com/outlook/2019/04/02/america-doesnt-just-have-gender-pay-gap-it-has-gender-wealth-gap.
8. Ana Lucia Murillo, "Forget Something? Americans Have Left More Than $1 Trillion Sitting in Old 401(k)s, a New Study Finds," *Money* (June 2, 2021), https://money.com/money-left-in-old-401k.
9. As of this writing, I am an affiliate of Capitalize. Before becoming an affiliate, I personally used their service. They seamlessly rolled the money from my previous employer's 401(k) into an individual retirement account.

10. "Amount of Roth IRA Contributions That You Can Make for 2022," IRS.gov, https://www.irs.gov/retirement-plans/plan-participant-employee/amount-of-roth-ira-contributions-that-you-can-make-for-2022 (last accessed March 10, 2022).

11. This calculation is based on the 4% rule, which is often used for retirement planning. It calculates the number that you need to have invested to last you through retirement. Note that this is a general guideline only. Your precise number depends on many factors. Consult a retirement planning professional for more. See Dana Anspach, "How the 4% Rule Works in Retirement," *The Balance* (updated November 26, 2021), https://www.thebalance.com/what-is-the-4percent-rule-in-retirement-2388273.

12. Ann Carrns, "New Law Expands Uses for 529 College Savings Accounts," *New York Times* (October 11, 2021), https://www.nytimes.com/2020/01/10/your-money/529-college-savings-accounts.html.

Chapter 11

1. Elise Gould, Jessica Schieder, and Kathleen Geier, "What Is the Gender Pay Gap and Is It Real?" Economic Policy Institute (October 20, 2016), https://www.epi.org/publication/what-is-the-gender-pay-gap-and-is-it-real.

2. Amanda Barroso and Anna Brown, "Gender Pay Gap in U.S. Held Steady in 2020," Pew Research Center (May 25, 2021), https://www.pewresearch.org/fact-tank/2021/05/25/gender-pay-gap-facts.

3. "Equal Pay Day 2022," Equal Pay Today, http://www.equalpaytoday.org/overview-2022 (last accessed April 4, 2022).

4. "Women Are Paid Less Than Men—and the Gap Is Closing Too Slowly," Lean In, https://leanin.org/equal-pay-data-about-the-gender-pay-gap (last accessed April 4, 2022).

5. "AANHPI Equal Pay Day 2022," Equal Pay Today, http://www.equalpaytoday.org/aanhpi-womens-equal-pay-day-2022 (last accessed April 4, 2022). ("For certain [Asian American / Native Hawaiian / Pacific Islander] communities, the wage gap is far greater.")

6. "Latina Equal Pay Day 2022," Equal Pay Today, http://www.equalpaytoday.org/latina-equal-pay-day-2022 (last accessed July 25, 2022).

7. Vanessa Romo, "On Equal Pay Day, Women Are Trying to Make a Dollar Out of 83 Cents," NPR (March 16, 2022), https://www.npr.org/2022/03/16/1086732450/on-equal-pay-day-women-are-trying-to-make-a-dollar-out-of-83-cents. ("Over their lifetimes, Latinas working full-time, year-round stand to lose more than $1.1 million, and Black women will miss out on close to $1 million.")

8. "Women Are Paid Less Than Men."

9. Carmen Reinicke, "Switching Jobs Is Often an Effective Way to Boost Income. When to Put Yourself On the Market," CNBC (November 9, 2021), https://www.cnbc.com/2021/11/09/switching-jobs-can-lead-to-higher-pay-heres-what-to-know.html.

10. Ibid. ("[A]ccording to the Atlanta Federal Reserve Bank's wage growth tracker, which uses data from the U.S. Bureau of Labor Statistics).

11. Paula Pant, "How to Budget for Taxes as a Freelancer," *The Balance* (updated June 29, 2022), https://www.thebalance.com/how-much-do-i-budget-for-taxes-as-a-freelancer-453676#:~:text=You%20should%20plan%20to%20set,calculate%20your%20estimated%20tax%20payments.

12. "Sole Proprietorships," IRS, https://www.irs.gov/businesses/small-businesses-self-employed/sole-proprietorships (last accessed April 4, 2022).

13. "Tax Information For Partnerships," IRS, https://www.irs.gov/businesses/part-nerships (last accessed April 4, 2022).

14. "Limited Liability Company (LLC)," IRS, https://www.irs.gov/businesses/small-businesses-self-employed/limited-liability-company-llc (last accessed April 4, 2022).

15. "What Is a Trademark?" United States Patent and Trademark Office, https://www.uspto.gov/trademarks/basics/what-trademark (last accessed July 25, 2022).

Index

249

Index